U.S. Army Uniforms of the Vietnam War

U.S. Army Uniforms of the Vietnam War

Shelby Stanton

Stackpole Books

Copyright © 1989 by Shelby Stanton

Published by
STACKPOLE BOOKS
Cameron and Kelker Streets
P.O. Box 1831
Harrisburg, PA 17105

Printed in the United States of America

10 9 8 7 6 5 4 3 2 1

Library of Congress Cataloging-in-Publication Data

Stanton, Shelby L., 1948–
    U.S. Army uniforms of the Vietnam War / Shelby Stanton.
       p.   cm.
    ISBN 0-8117-1852-2
    1. United States. Army—Uniforms—History—20th century.
  2. Vietnamese Conflict, 1961-1975—Equipment and supplies.
  I. Title. II. Title: US Army uniforms of the Vietnam War.
  III. Title: United States Army uniforms of the Vietnam War.
UC483.S62   1988
355.1′4′0973—dc19   88-19161
                                           CIP

Contents

Preface

This volume is designed to accurately record the development and utilization of U.S. Army clothing and individual equipment, as well as common organizational equipment carried by soldiers, during the Vietnam conflict (Second Indochina War). The insignia chapter in this book has been deliberately limited to an overview of placement and a few historical facts about Vietnam-related items, since a much larger work would be required to adequately cover that field.

This book is the product of extensive original research into the official documents regarding uniform and equipment testing, supply, and battlefield usage. The bulk of material for this work was obtained from the wartime records of the Defense Supply Agency, Army Materiel Command, Natick Laboratories, the Advanced Research Projects Agency, the Army Concept Team in Vietnam, MACV and USARV regulations, and unit historical reports. These sources are fully cited in the Notes at the end of each chapter. All photographs in the book are from Vietnam unless otherwise noted.

In general, the Army terminology for specific items has been adjusted in the book to conform with common parlance. Thus, the official title *Glove, Leather: Heavy Leather, Steel Sewed* has been altered to a more readable form, *steel sewed heavy leather glove*. Italics are used for an item's name where it is mentioned in the text for the first time.

Additionally, the final Army designation of an item during the Vietnam conflict has been used for consistency. Several identical items were labelled with different names during the course of the protracted Vietnam conflict. Most important, the term *tropical combat uniform* has been used throughout the text, although it was initially designated the *hot weather uniform* (and the latter term was used, in some manuals and regulations, throughout the war's length). The use of tropical combat uniform also avoids confusion with the female *hot weather field uniform*. For this book, the actual Military or Federal Specifications of the item were used to select the most appropriate title when designations in official publications overlapped or contradicted each other.

The author would like to thank the following individuals who helped with this project. John C. Andrews gave advice on U.S. and Vietnamese insignia; Carter Rila assisted on individual equipment; Danny M. Johnson researched Special Forces flash development; Gordon Rottman helped on the diver and dog-handler sections; Daniel Priest III rendered insights on fabric evolution in military attire; and Melissa Priest provided photographic support. At Stackpole Books, Peggy Senko and Mary Suggs gave the necessary editorial assistance. Finally, some of the most valuable help was given by those Vietnam veterans who kindly shared photographs of themselves.

Vietnam-related photographs showing uniforms, weapons, or equipment that might be appropriate for future reference books are always welcome. Anyone interested in contributing photographs should contact the author in care of the publisher at P.O. Box 1831, Harrisburg, PA 17105. Any photographs published will receive full credit as the owner desires.

Shelby L. Stanton
Bethesda, Maryland
1 February 1988

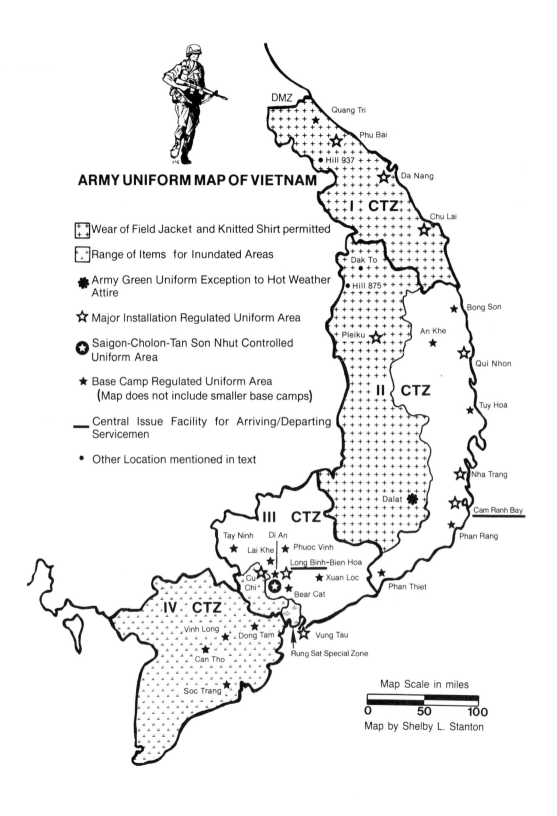

ARMY UNIFORM MAP OF VIETNAM

Legend:

⊞ Wear of Field Jacket and Knitted Shirt permitted

⊡ Range of Items for Inundated Areas

❁ Army Green Uniform Exception to Hot Weather Attire

☆ Major Installation Regulated Uniform Area

★ Saigon-Cholon-Tan Son Nhut Controlled Uniform Area

★ Base Camp Regulated Uniform Area
(Map does not include smaller base camps)

— Central Issue Facility for Arriving/Departing Servicemen

• Other Location mentioned in text

Map labels:

DMZ
Quang Tri
Phu Bai
Hill 937
Da Nang
I CTZ
Chu Lai
Dak To
Hill 875
Bong Son
An Khe
Pleiku
Qui Nhon
II CTZ
Tuy Hoa
Nha Trang
Dalat
Cam Ranh Bay
III CTZ
Phan Rang
Tay Ninh
Di An
Lai Khe
Phuoc Vinh
Long Binh-Bien Hoa
Cu Chi
Xuan Loc
Bear Cat
Phan Thiet
IV CTZ
Vinh Long
Dong Tam
Vung Tau
Can Tho
Rung Sat Special Zone
Soc Trang

Map Scale in miles
0   50   100

Map by Shelby L. Stanton

1

Army Uniform Requirements in Vietnam

1.1 Wartime Clothing Considerations

Army uniform requirements are based primarily on considerations of climatic and combat protection, as well as military appearance. In Southeast Asia, Army uniforms consisted of personal clothing and equipment issued for mission accomplishment within a tropical environment. These uniforms combined lightweight components, designed for hot weather use, with standard field items used throughout the Army on a global basis.

The Second Indochina War was a prolonged conflict waged against a jungle-proficient adversary whose guerrilla tactics and elusive mobility forced American soldiers to undertake extended search-and-destroy operations. Army troops pushed through dense rain forests or swampy marshlands, crossed muddy rice paddies, and climbed jungle-covered mountains to find and engage the enemy. Battles were fought in torrid heat or monsoon rain. These conditions mandated the use of multi-functional, lightweight individual clothing and equipment, or LINCLOE items, as abbreviated by Army development specialists.

The Army also relied on sophisticated weapons and airmobile tactics that demanded high levels of materiel, fuel, transport, and maintenance. Since existing Vietnamese facilities were insufficient, the United States created an immense network of logistical bases and lines of communication to support Army formations in the field. (*See* Army Uniform Map of Vietnam.) Most military machinery and many airfields, ports, supply depots, ammunition points, and mechanical shops were built, maintained, or supervised in Vietnam by Army personnel. Their construction and support demanded a wide range of specialized clothing and gear.

Most of the Army's clothing and equipment was developed by the Army Quartermaster Research and Engineering Command headquartered at Natick, Massachusetts. On 20 June 1963, this command was reorganized as U.S. Army Natick Laboratories, an activity reporting directly to the Headquarters of Army Materiel Command. The mission of Natick Laboratories was to accomplish assigned re-

Typical battle dress in Vietnam *(left to right)*: armor, aviation, infantry, military police, scout dog, and long range reconnaissance patrol members pose at Bong Son, 1969. *Author's collection.*

U.S. Army Natick Laboratories of the Army Materiel Command at Natick, Massachusetts, 1963. *Natick Laboratories.*

search and development in the physical, biological, and earth sciences, and in engineering fields to meet military requirements in textiles, clothing, body armor, footwear, organic materials, insecticides and fungicides, subsistence equipment, containers, food service equipment, field support equipment, tents and equipage, and air delivery equipment.[1]

The Vietnam conflict was the first war in which the U.S. Army made widespread use of nylon, other advanced synthetic fabrics, and plastic in clothing and equipment. These synthetics resulted in lightweight apparel and gear of improved quality, strength, and utility that did not deteriorate as rapidly as natural-fiber materials. Although synthetic chemicals produced textiles with many good characteristics, the textiles also had limitations. Synthetic fabrics, for example, retained larger charges of static electricity than did cotton. In the wet climate of Vietnam, however, synthetic fibers were particularly valuable because they did not absorb water very readily. Natural materials, such as cotton and leather, absorbed moisture, which added to their weight and caused mildew.

Synthetic fibers provided greater protection against explosive and chemical hazards. Soldiers in many service support specialties required industrial chemical and fuel handling protection. Dacron, Dynel, and Orlon cloth offered good resistance to moderate concentrations of acids and caustics, but they were intended to protect against only small splashes or drops of corrosive liquids. When hazards became more severe, chemical-spill-resistant rubber or plastic hoods, aprons, and gloves were worn.

Fire resistance was a great Army concern during the Vietnam conflict. Cotton clothing burned easily, and available fire-resistant treatments for cotton cloth were imperfect. The treatments either added stiffness to the fabric, weakened it, caused dermatitis, or had toxic effects. Laundering often reduced or removed flame-resistant properties. Synthetic fibers, such as rayon, acetate, nylon, Orlon, and Dacron, offered about the same fire resistance as cotton but tended to melt at certain temperatures and severely burn the wearer. The military services pressed industry to develop improved flame-resistant textiles, but progress was slow during the war years.

Before and during the Vietnam conflict, Army clothing and equipment development was sporadic, even though considerable financial support was allocated. Some items, like tropical combat uniforms and boots, were superb products of great combat utility. Development of other items was less successful. Personal body armor, for instance, never provided desired levels of protection because of technological limitations and failure to fully exploit available materials. Finally, some important military-product developments, such as the im-

Army combat attire (left to right): World War I wool service coat and britches with M1917 helmet; World War II wool field jacket and trousers with M1 helmet; Korean conflict wool field shirt and trousers with M1951 pile field cap; Vietnam-era tropical combat uniform with M1 helmet. *U.S. Army.*

Newly arrived replacements are welcomed to Vietnam by a 90th Replacement Battalion liaison team at the Tan Son Nhut airport in Saigon, May 1967. *U.S. Army.*

3

The functional comfort of the tropical combat uniform in Vietnam is demonstrated by a 25th Inf Div battalion commander, cradling his M16 rifle, and a OH13S Sioux pilot relaxing after an aerial reconnaissance mission north of Cu Chi. *Author's collection.*

The 1941 suit, parachute jumpers, modification no. 1, was the original garment design that eventually evolved into the Vietnam-era tropical combat uniform. *U.S. Army.*

The tropical rain forest of Vietnam, here in the A Shau Valley, mandated a lightweight uniform design that permitted maximum combat efficiency under hot-wet climatic conditions. *101st Abn Div PIO.*

A formation of Company C, 54th Inf (Separate), wear tropical combat uniforms with their individual equipment, fully loaded lightweight rucksacks, and weapons ready for inspection at Pleiku, 12 February 1970. *Author's collection.*

provement of infantry helmets, failed to benefit soldiers fighting in Vietnam.

1.2 Tropical Combat Uniform Development

Tropical combat clothing was developed to sustain a certain degree of comfort for soldiers operating in regions of high temperature and humidity. Military comfort meant that soldiers were clothed so as to maintain a high rate of activity for several hours before suffering heat exhaustion. The goal was not comfort in the ordinary sense but the avoidance of acute discomfort that impaired combat efficiency, created critical physiological heat stress, and limited performance.

The Army conducted developmental work on hot-wet and hot-dry uniforms from 1952 to 1955 when several tropical and desert clothing variations were evaluated. On 11 October 1962, DA (Department of the Army) requested the

Quartermaster Research and Engineering Command to develop a functional hot weather uniform for Special Forces personnel in Southeast Asia. On 22 October, Maj. Gen. William "Bill" Rosson, assistant chief of staff for Special Warfare, reviewed a tropical combat uniform prototype, which he immediately accepted.[2]

The *tropical combat uniform* was based on a "bush style" design patterned after the *coat, parachute jumper* ("M1942 parachutist jacket") of World War II and represented a compromise among several competing requirements. The uniform needed to be as lightweight as possible but required additional material for several cargo pockets. If it were loose fitting, it would permit reasonable air ventilation, avoid movement constriction, and minimize chafing. Conversely, if it fit more tightly, it would cool more efficiently when "soaked to the skin" because the fabric would touch the body and cause perspiration to be

Troops of the 2d Bn, 327th Inf (101st Abn Div), wear the tropical combat uniform. The uniform's bellows cargo leg pockets permitted many items to be carried in a readily accessible fashion. Also note "claymore mine bag" being used to carry spare batteries just below antenna on PRC-77 radio set (left). Near FSB Rendezvous, 26 March 1971. *John Del Vecchio.*

transferred to the garment's outer surface to evaporate.

Thin material was chosen to minimize heat stress. Moisture and heat escaped rapidly through thin fabric with little insulating effect, allowing body heat to be quickly dissipated by evaporation. World War II Pacific experiences also demonstrated that front-line soldiers preferred tighter woven but thinner poplin over thicker fatigue fabric, even though the latter was more porous. Cotton was selected because it was more comfortable than other materials when in contact with the skin. Fabrics with high nylon content tended to be scratchy, and continuous filament fabrics often felt clammy.[3]

The tropical combat uniform was type-classified on 20 June 1963, which meant it could be procured for immediate operational use, prior to completion of testing. The uniform consisted of a loose-fitting 5.5-ounce cotton poplin coat and trousers with large pockets. Some characteristics desired in military clothing—such as thermal and chemical protection, camouflage coloration, fungus and insect proofing, and residual radioactive-contamination reduction—were not initially provided by the tropical combat uniform. These shortcomings were waived because they could "not be met within current state of the art."[4]

Design criteria were continuously reviewed. For instance, on 26 August 1964, the Army Materiel Command approved coat pocket flaps over pocket buttons to prevent snagging. At the same meeting, the Command rejected the 6-ounce nylon/cotton tropical combat clothing that was proposed.

Since the tropical combat uniform was not as mosquito-resistant as hoped, in March 1968, USARV (U.S. Army, Vietnam) requested a uniform with improved mosquito protection, without the heat exchange problem of a tighter weave. Natick Laboratories' evaluation of several fabrics included tests at Gainesville, Florida, for mosquito protection. The final fabric selected was a 6.5 ounce per square yard oxford weave, nylon/cotton material. Though air flow through this fabric was inhibited, the material provided nearly 98 percent protection from mosquito bites, compared to about 92 percent for the standard tropical combat uniform fabric.

The Army airlifted 4,500 *uniforms, combat tropical, improved mosquito protection,* to Vietnam, where testing within divisions commenced 2 June 1969. Unfortunately, most of the experimental clothing was too large for the average soldier. The uniforms also became mixed with standard uniforms during distribution to evaluating units or were lost in centralized laundries, thus preventing later attempts to locate or identify thousands of test uniform sets. In September 1969, USARV responded that the experimental uniform was uncomfortable and "no good" but admitted that the test was poorly controlled. As a result, this uniform variant was not adopted.[5]

6

Many Army officers felt that the thick natural foliage of Vietnam offered sufficient camouflage for soldiers wearing olive green tropical combat uniforms, such as this rifleman firing near Bao Loc on Operation Klamath Falls. *101st Abn Div.*

1.3 Coloration and Camouflage of Tropical Combat Clothing

The most common Army color used in Vietnam was Olive Green army shade 107. First used extensively in the Korean war, it was adopted to provide a deeper green than the olive drab of World War II. The dyestuff formula depended on the fabric; cotton required a combination of two vat greens and black, while nylon consisted of acid green, acid brown, acid yellow, and acid orange.

The Vietnam-era Olive Green army shade 107 tropical weave uniform used a rip-stop poplin fabric with cotton rip-stop yarns, col-ored in accordance with the vat dye formula. The uniform proved durable and comfortable and had reasonably good camouflage properties for vegetated areas. The clothing met the visual range, binocular with filter, and photographic requirements. The near-infrared sniper-scope range control treatment was not applied to the standard uniform, however, primarily to minimize the material's solar heat load. Very late in the war, special warfare units were issued nonstandard Olive Green army shade 107 tropical combat uniforms with infrared control treatment as a response to the increased sophistication of the Vietnam battlefield.

7

Camouflage clothing was introduced to the Army during World War II, and postwar studies of the spectral characteristics of commercial dyes made it possible to formulate both visual and infrared camouflage. The Army's standard camouflage cotton cloth in Vietnam was of two types: printed; and printed and water-repellent, treated with Quarpel. The camouflage pattern was first introduced by the U.S. Army Engineer Research and Development Laboratory (USAERDL) in 1948, and was known as ERDL camouflage. The irregular free form, four-color pattern consisted of Yel-

The tropical sunlight and dark shadows of the jungle floor contrasted starkly with Vietnam's open marshes and rice paddies and initially confused attempts to reach one satisfactory camouflage pattern for the tropical combat uniform. *Richard McLaughlin.*

low Green army shade 354, Dark Green army shade 355, Brown army shade 356, and Black army shade 357. The cloth was usually dyed to a ground shade matching the yellow green area of the pattern and subsequently roller overprinted using the other three colors. The pattern could also be achieved with a four-roller printing on dyed and undyed cloth, or printed by automatic flat or rotary screen processes.[6]

The Army Engineer Research and Development Laboratories conducted extensive camouflage tests and experiments at Fort Benning in May 1962. These were known as the "Users' Review of Camouflage for the Individual Combat Soldier in the Field." The researchers compared various camouflage patterns to the Olive Green army shade 107 uniform.

The 1962 review demonstrated that personnel wearing the standard Olive Green army shade 107 uniform were easily detected and identified by new surveillance systems such as long-wave infrared, passive, microwave, light amplification, and field television systems. On human visual levels, various experimental camouflage-patterned uniforms were advantageous at close ranges of 25 to 350 meters, but at distances over 500 meters all uniforms blended into a solid color. The review also concluded that movement and sound, not uniform color or particular pattern, were the primary means by which soldiers detected other individuals on the battleground.

A Tropical Combat Uniform Board was convened in Vietnam during November 1965 to

The 1948 ERDL four-pattern camouflage was standardized for the tropical combat uniform in 1967 and proved remarkably effective in a variety of Southeast Asian tropical terrains. Here 173d Abn Bde long-range patrol members rehearse a parachute jump. *Army News Features.*

survey the tropical combat uniform's suitability. This panel resisted pressure to either adopt various South Vietnamese camouflage patterns or develop U.S. equivalents. The board ruled against camouflage uniforms for two stated reasons: (1) movement by camouflaged soldiers caused easier detection because of noticeable pattern changes; and (2) solid olive green or drab uniforms enabled rapid, essential identification of fellow Army soldiers. For example, the board cited quick friendly troop recognition by low-flying helicopters as overriding any requirement for camouflage against enemy observation.[7]

USARV recommended retention of the current solid olive green uniform in preference to camouflage patterns, but, on 10 December 1965, requested 300 camouflage tropical combat uniforms for further evaluation. Natick Laboratories possessed a few hundred tropical combat uniforms already roller-printed with the ERDL pattern, and they airmailed 300 sets to Vietnam on 23 December. Meanwhile, in the field, combat soldiers were encouraged to apply paint, mud, or local foliage to their plain tropical combat uniforms if camouflage was needed. Special Forces recon teams of MACV-SOG sometimes resorted to spraying uniforms with dull black paint splotches.

While the camouflage tropical combat uniforms were being tested in Vietnam throughout 1966, Natick Laboratories continued research. Many difficult decisions needed to be made. Four different patterns were being considered for Southeast Asian terrain. A large problem involved dye stability. Washing, continuous perspiration, and sunlight exposure could cause fading to unacceptable colors. The four-color Army 1948 ERDL pattern was finally chosen as the best overall, partially as a result of favorable experiences with the ARPA reversible uniforms of 1964. (*See section 4.2,* Indigenous Combat Clothing.)

The ERDL camouflage was produced with full infrared control treatment. The dyestuffs possessed the following reflectivity measured at 1 micron: yellow green, 48 percent; dark green, 28 percent; brown, 16 percent; and black, 8 percent. Although not specifically designed for Vietnam, its camouflage properties were so effective that helicopter observers often could not locate patrols dressed in the material. The

first ERDL camouflage tropical combat uniforms were brown dominant for highland areas, and green dominant for lowlands. Such allocation was logistically impractical, however, and was soon discarded.[8]

USARV urgently requested 18,373 sets of camouflage tropical combat uniforms for "pathfinders, long range reconnaissance patrol members, and scout/recon personnel" on 6 February 1967. Although there was no specific mention of Special Forces, their personnel in Vietnam were considered "for purposes of the camouflaged tropical combat uniform to be in a scouting and reconnaissance activity," even though this was not technically true for every Vietnam-based Special Forces member.

The Department of the Army approved the USARV request on 9 March 1967 and directed the Army Materiel Command to expedite procurement under ENSURE (expedited non-standard, urgent requirement for equipment) priorities. The Army reclassified ERDL camouflage tropical combat uniforms as standard issue for selected units on 20 June 1967, but the first deliveries were not made until December. For instance, the 9th Infantry Division ordered 500 sets for its long range patrol detachment but only received 199 coats and 112 trousers by the end of the year.[9]

The ERDL camouflage tropical combat uniform was technically restricted, being distributed first to pathfinder and other reconnaissance combat units during 1968. The only MACV advisors authorized this camouflage clothing were "MACV airborne advisory and ranger advisory personnel when assisting or advising similar Vietnamese combat units." Incoming U.S. advisors assigned to MACV-SOG, the ARVN Ranger Command, and the Airborne Division received five sets under this authority. By mid-1969, however, enough camouflage tropical combat uniforms were available to begin outfitting selected line infantry companies.[10]

A few units familiar with Vietnamese camouflage clothing complained initially that the thin cotton ERDL camouflage material was not durable enough. During the spring of 1968, Company F (Long Range Patrol) of the 51st Infantry charged that the "material was too thin to withstand the thick vegetation in which long range patrols operate. Especially when

A mortar squad of the 173d Abn Bde trudges through a battlefield in Phuoc Tuy Province, burdened by the weight of individual and organizational equipment and weapons required for Vietnam warfare. *Army News Features.*

wet, these uniforms rip easily . . . recommend that a jungle uniform be made with a thickness comparable to that of the Vietnamese jungle uniform, the so-called tiger fatigue, for use in long range patrol operations."[11]

The Army ERDL camouflage tropical combat uniform quickly gained very high field acceptability, despite its tendency to tear while traversing dense jungle. The lighter material was more comfortable and better crafted than indigenous camouflage attire. (*See section 4.2,* Indigenous Combat Clothing.) The American camouflage was also vastly superior in resisting infrared and other thermal-imaging detection that NVA snipers increasingly employed.

1.4 Combat Load of the Infantryman

Soldiers in Vietnam carried enormous burdens in order to accomplish their mission. Even though often landed by helicopters, the soldiers searched for NVA/VC caches and base areas on foot. Sometimes these operations extended for weeks through rugged jungle and steaming rice fields. The soldiers "humped" the equipment necessary to sustain themselves in the field. They also packed large quantities of munitions since the Vietnam battlefield was dominated by rockets, grenades, and automatic weapons.

Basic ammunition loads were amounts required to be on hand within units. USARV Regulation 735-28 specified requirements in Vietnam, and the 1 May 70 edition reflected several years' combat experience in weapon/ rounds per weapon: shotgun/50, automatic pistol/21, M16 rifle/360, M14 sniper rifle/120, M60 machine gun/880, M79 grenadier launcher/36, and 90mm recoilless rifle/12 rounds. In addition, each infantry company was authorized 60 claymore mines and 50 light anti-tank weapons, distributed among the troops.

Troops in Vietnam carried varying amounts of ammunition. Rifle companies of the 23d Infantry Division (American) carried 9,000 M60 machine gun rounds, 900 M79 grenade rounds, 72 smoke grenades, 200 flares, 70 pounds of demolitions, and a minimum of 18 claymore mines. This general load had to be distributed throughout the company. In addition, each rifleman carried 360 rounds of M16 ammunition and 4 fragmentation grenades. All company personnel also carried their individual weapon; bayonet; load-carrying equipment, including rucksacks; poncho and poncho liner; pneumatic mattress; intrenching tool; weapon cleaning kit; extra socks and toilet articles; a change of clothing; and 9 individual combat meals.[12]

From 1967 to 1969, the 1st Infantry Division's 1st Battalion, 18th Infantry, required the following individual loads on all operations: riflemen carried 14 rifle magazines, 2 smoke grenades, 2 fragmentation grenades, a protective mask, weapon cleaning equipment, and 2 canteens, in addition to personal gear. Each platoon was also required to have 6 light anti-tank weapons for "bunker busting," 20 pounds of demolitions, and 2,000 spare rounds of machine gun ammunition. On overnight movements, every soldier also carried 3 individual combat meals, a claymore mine, trip flares, an intrenching tool, 20 sandbag covers, and a poncho and poncho liner. Battalion officers admitted that "the individual troop load is still too great, but the position of all commanders has been that combat-essential loads must be high in order to sustain an element in a long fire fight."[13]

Warfare in Vietnam swamps, like the Rung Sat Special Zone, called for special considerations. The 3d Battalion, 22d Infantry,

conducted Operation Bremerton in the zone's mangrove forests during November 1966. Each platoon carried 3 nylon ropes, 150 meters in length; 3 pneumatic mattresses; 2 compasses; and 6 flashlights. Every second soldier carried a machete. In addition to 5 canteens, each man carried personal gear that included a carabiner ("snap-link") used for securing nonswimmers and sliding equipment on ropes across the water. Combat field packs were used instead of rucksacks because they were more compact and easier to carry through dense undergrowth or to float across waterways. The need to save weight and rely on ambush tactics was reflected in the ammunition loads of 200 rounds per

An infantryman of the 5th Bn, 46th Inf (198th Inf Bde), clad in body armor, swelters in the tropical heat west of Chu Lai, 5 April 1970. Even this late in the war, his lightweight rucksack is overloaded with a full pack, intrenching tool, machete, poncho roll, combat meal cans in sock containers, and other articles. *U.S. Army.*

Individual combat loads carried by Army infantrymen in Vietnam averaged 50–60 pounds and could reach greater weights, as demonstrated by this soldier of the 1st Bn, 11th Inf (5th Inf Div), at FSB Eagle, 30 October 1970. *U.S. Army.*

M16 rifle, 18 rounds per M79 grenade launcher, and 600 rounds per M60 machine gun.[14]

Combat loads were modified by tactical maneuvers like night-ambush patrols. The 9th Infantry Division's Company A of the 2d Battalion, 60th Infantry, conducted a typical Mekong Delta night ambush on 22 November 1967. On this 22-man mission the two M60 machine gunners carried 400 rounds each; they were assisted by two riflemen who doubled as ammo bearers and carried 600 more rounds of M60 ammunition. All riflemen carried 300–400 rounds of M16 ammunition, and the M79 grenadier carried 30 high-explosive rounds. Radios, light anti-tank weapons, starlight scopes, claymore mines, and numerous

smoke and incendiary grenades were also carried.[15]

Ordinary Vietnam combat conditions brought the average weight of equipment and ammunition loads to between 50 and 60 pounds. During the hard-fought Dak To campaign of 1967, waged in the mountain jungles near the Cambodian border, soldiers fought from hill to hill against the usual pattern of NVA resistance: rear guard ambush parties, companies entrenched in bunkers and interconnecting tunnels, and snipers. The parachutist riflemen of the 173d Airborne Brigade toiled under 50-pound rucksacks crammed with three days' rations and other gear, along with 500 rounds of M16 ammunition, 4 fragmentation and 2 smoke grenades, 200 machine gun rounds, and 3 canteens of water. Parachutist grenadiers carried the same amount of gear and water, but their ammunition load consisted of 50 high-explosive rounds and 50 shotgun rounds with adapters.[16]

At the end of January 1967, after a series of strenuous expeditions into the western highland mountain ranges, the 4th Infantry Division at Pleiku recommended, "Units should reduce weight loads of individual soldiers by maintaining no more than 300 rounds of ammunition per man. Experience has proven that more than 300 rounds per man is excessive weight and reduces his efficiency in movement over rough terrain."[17]

The 23d Infantry Division (American) commented in May 1968, "During the hot weather season, the weight of the equipment greatly reduces the maneuverability of the individual soldier, and is one of the major contributing factors causing heat casualties. . . . His combat load must be reduced to a maximum of forty pounds."

Recommendations that "the use of the LRP (Long Range Patrol) dehydrated-type rations would reduce the three days' ration weight by 13 pounds and further lessen the volume of the C-rations" were perennial. But the slow delivery of lightweight items prevented the easing of this burden for much of the war.[18]

Notes

1. Natick Laboratories, *Historical Report FY 70,* 1; DA General Order 27, 20 Jun 63.
2. Army Materiel Command, *Clothing & Equipment Support to U.S. Army in Vietnam,* Feb 67, 13.
3. Dr. S. J. Kennedy, *Clothing & Equipment Support to Our Troops in Vietnam,* Natick Laboratories, 24 Jun 69, 25–27.
4. Army Materiel Command, *In-Process Review of Integrated Field Combat Clothing,* 14 Oct 64.
5. DA CRDCM Fact Sheet, Subj: uniform, combat tropical, improved mosquito protection, 1 Dec 69; 1st Cavalry Division, *Operational Report,* 15 Nov 69, Tab E.
6. Military Specification MIL-C-43468B, 11 Mar 68; MIL-C-43468C, 12 Jun 72.
7. Infantry School Engineer Committee, "No Camouflage Uniform," in *Infantry,* Jan–Feb 67, 47–48.
8. Frank Rizzo, *Textiles Save Lives in Vietnam,* Natick Laboratories, 24 Jun 69, 17–27.
9. Defense Supply Agency, ACSFOR DS Status Report, 31 Aug 67; 9th Infantry Division, *Operational Report,* 25 Dec 67, 41.
10. MACV Directive 735-2, 25 Sep 70 and 12 Mar 72.
11. II Field Force, Vietnam, *Operational Report,* 15 Aug 68, 68.
12. American Division, *Operational Report,* 7 May 68, 84.
13. 1st Battalion, 18th Infantry, *Unit Historical Report,* 1 Mar 68, 24, and 31 Mar 69, 16.
14. 3d Brigade, 4th Infantry Division, *Operational Report,* 23 Feb 67, 44.
15. 19th Military History Detachment, *Combat After Action Interview 11-67.*
16. 173d Airborne Brigade, *Combat After Action Interview,* 7 Dec 67, 4.
17. 4th Infantry Division, *Operational Report,* 1 Feb 67, 37.
18. American Division, *Operational Report,* 7 May 68, 85.

2

Clothing and Equipment Supply and Wear

2.1 Clothing Authorization and Supply

The cotton poplin tropical combat uniform was classified as standard issue, three sets per individual, in selected hot climate regions on 20 June 1963. Procurement of these uniforms and direct-molded-sole tropical boots was initiated in quantities sufficient to meet Special Forces operational requirements in Vietnam.[1] The massive deployment of numerous divisions and brigades to Vietnam throughout 1965 and 1966, however, rapidly depleted supplies of tropical uniforms and boots.

Tropical uniforms were considered essential for troop efficiency in Southeast Asia. Secretary of Defense Robert S. McNamara monitored shortages of such critical items through coded FLAGPOLE status reports. The Joint Chiefs of Staff at the Pentagon established a Joint Materiel Priorities Allocation Board to control FLAGPOLE item procurement and distribution. The board mandated aerial delivery overseas, direct from clothing factories.[2]

In September 1965, the Army directed Vietnam-bound soldiers to deploy with four utility uniforms and two pairs of regular leather boots, since tropical uniform stocks were nonexistent within the United States. Once in Vietnam, individuals received the tropical items based on their unit's priority: (1) Special Forces, (2) advisors, (3) infantry, armor, and cavalry, (4) artillery and combat support personnel, and (5) service support. For example, most engineer, military police, and signal units were not authorized tropical combat boots until November 1966, when the expedited arrival of 206,773 pairs permitted distribution to Priority 4 combat support personnel.[3]

During that same month, increased uniform stocks allowed USARV to begin requisitioning them on a routine shipment basis. During this transition phase of November–December 1966, normal sea transportation supplemented the use of air cargo. Within this period, 326,020 coats and 433,641 trousers were sent by ship, and 819,300 coats and 839,359 trousers were dispatched by air. USARV's actual receipts during the same

The 41st Signal Battalion arrives at Qui Nhon in July 1965, wearing utility uniforms and leather combat boots. Within two years, all support units would be completely outfitted with tropical combat uniforms and boots. *Author's collection.*

period totalled only 728,693 coats and 452,543 trousers because of deliveries that did not reach Vietnam until January.[4]

Some front-line infantry still lacked tropical clothing. The 173d Airborne Brigade's 4th Battalion of the 503d Infantry (Airborne), which arrived in Vietnam in June 1966 with standard leather combat boots, made repeated requests for tropical combat boots. As late as Operation Winchester, fought 8 October–4 De-

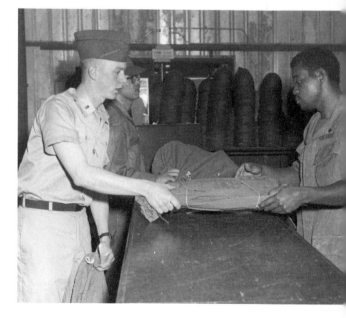

A new lieutenant receives his initial set of five tropical combat uniforms at the Central Issue Facility of the 266th Supply & Service Bn, located with the 90th Replacement Bn at Long Binh. *U.S. Army.*

Supply Sgt. Franklin Callines of the I CTZ Signal Group shows stocks of supplies and individual equipment to senior officers at Phu Bai, 3 December 1968. *221st Signal Company.*

cember 1966 in monsoon weather, the parachutists sloshed through flooded rice fields west of Da Nang in their original boots. Their mismatched uniforms consisted mostly of tropical coats worn with utility trousers and regular combat boots.[5]

By the end of December, tropical boot inventories reached the point that partial shipment by sea was recommended for January 1967. Outfitting of line units was completed, and a month later, the footwear was authorized for Priority 5 service and support personnel. On 13 February, USARV announced that the supply of tropical boots was no longer critical. Supplies of other tropical clothing also improved, and combat support troop allotments were increased from two to five tropical combat uniform sets per man on 21 March 1967. In April, USARV extended tropical uniform issuance to service support personnel, two sets per individual.[6]

By summer the clothing supply crisis was over. Tropical combat uniform and boot production forecasts enabled USARV to switch from air to regular shipping schedules. Commencing on 30 June 1967, all Army personnel

in Vietnam were authorized five sets of tropical combat uniforms and two pairs of boots. This allowance continued for most of the war, although shortages in smaller sizes persisted because of South Vietnamese Army demands for some of the clothing.[7]

The situation was further eased after 1 August 1967 when Army replacements for Vietnam were issued four tropical combat uniforms and one pair of tropical combat boots in United States processing centers before they went overseas. Field-grade officers, sergeants major, and warrant officers were exempt from this policy, since they travelled directly to Vietnam by airline, without stopping at processing centers, and were issued their tropical clothing there. The total five-set tropical combat uniform allowance was not reduced until 12 March 1972 when khaki became normal duty attire in Vietnam and authorizations for tropical clothing dropped to three sets.

Other uniforms worn in Vietnam included utility, service, and dress uniforms. For travel, soldiers were outfitted with one complete, "properly fitted" uniform, without unauthorized alterations. Khaki uniforms served as standard travel attire upon departure from Vietnam until 1967 when tropical combat uniforms were permitted. Commencing 1 October 1970, however, khaki attire was again mandated for exiting Vietnam. Field coats were authorized because summer service uniforms were unsuitable for arrival during cold weather in the United States and many other locations. Army green uniforms were not issued because of the waste of refitting involved, but officers and career enlisted personnel were permitted to wear their Army green uniforms if desired. Civilian clothing was not worn unless specified by the individual's travel orders.[8]

The 1st Logistical Command established a joint clothing sales store in Saigon, next to the Cholon PX at 100 Hung Vuong Avenue, in March 1966. The store stocked Army and Navy uniform and insignia items, and common clothing items for all services. This store was the sole source for retail issue of female military clothing in Vietnam until October 1967 when women's articles were discontinued. Thereafter, women's items had to be ordered by mail from military clothing sales stores located in Japan or Okinawa.[9]

2.2 Individual Equipment Authorization and Supply

Natick Laboratories formally began supporting Special Forces Asian operational clothing and equipage during 1962. This task led to a number of equipment items—including jungle hammocks, poncho liners, multi-purpose nets, lightweight rucksacks, collapsible two-quart canteens, and nylon canteen covers—being "type-classified limited production" for special warfare purposes by June of the same year.

Natick Laboratories developed another set of items by June 1963: jungle hats with head nets, combat tropical uniforms, spike-resistant insoles for the tropical boots, survival kit covers, mosquito gloves and head nets for the survival kits, and machete sheaths. All of the above items were procured as quickly as

Processing center—issue field gear for Vietnam-bound replacements at Fort Lewis on 12 January 1968: body armor, lightweight rucksack, mosquito net and bar, sunglasses with case, general purpose carrying strap, four mosquito poles, and poncho liner. *U.S. Army.*

Newly arrived troops receive individual equipment from the 266th Supply & Service Bn Central Issue Facility as they process through the 90th Replacement Bn at Long Binh. *U.S. Army.*

possible for Special Forces operational requirements in Vietnam.[10]

After larger Army formations reached Southeast Asia, MACV and USARV issued guidelines on basic combat attire in Vietnam. "Personnel traveling outside of a secure area within RVN regardless of mode of travel will be attired and equipped for operations under field or combat conditions. Items of clothing and equipment will include *as a minimum*: (a) appropriate field clothing to include boots, (b) web belt, (c) canteen with fresh water, (d) first aid kit, (e) individual weapon and ammunition."[11]

The actual combat attire of soldiers on field operations included the minimal USARV requirements and a lot more. Individual load-carrying equipment was loaded down by a wide range of special lightweight gear, ponchos, collapsible canteens, and other apparatus to cope with the tropical conditions. USARV needed large amounts of such gear, and the Joint Materiel Priorities Allocation Board sped these items from the factories to Vietnam using "Push Package" air deliveries. By May 1967,

A 1st Supply & Transport Bn (1st Inf Div) Petroleum Reaction Team pose with their M131 5,000-gallon fuel semi-trailer and organizational equipment, Di An, 1968. Although most of this gear would be transported by vehicle, a lot of organizational equipment was man-packed in Vietnam. *Author's collection.*

sufficient quantities of tropical supplies enabled USARV to use normal logistical channels.[12]

Major combat operations always cut deep into accumulated supplies. During Operation Attleboro of November 1966, the first large-scale search-and-destroy operation of the war, a single battalion (the 2d Battalion, 27th Infantry) received the following resupplies in just three weeks: 2,000 bottles of mosquito repellent, 1,000 cans of foot powder, 180 pneumatic mattresses, 140 ponchos, 105 flashlights, 75 shovels, 100 machetes, and 70 packboards.[13]

A 57th Medical Detachment helicopter crew's individual gear: 4 body armor vests, 4 APH5 helmets, 4 M16 rifles, 1 map case, 1 flashlight, and 4 smoke grenades. Long Binh, 28 November 1964. *Author's collection.*

Local shortages of specific, high-use items were common. Poncho liners were usually difficult to obtain anywhere in the country. The separate 1st Brigade of the 101st Airborne Division at Phan Rang exhausted its rucksack supply in mid-October 1967. The brigade did not receive more rucksacks until it moved north to Phu Bai and joined the rest of the division in late February 1968.[14]

Supplies of individual and general wet-weather equipment were almost always insufficient during Vietnam's monsoon season. This miserable period of rainy weather was punctuated by violent thunderstorms that unleashed torrential downpours and occasional hail. The northwest monsoon was dominated by low misting clouds and "crachin," an ugly mix of cold drizzle and dense fog. Unit preparation for the monsoon season was usually highlighted by a mad scramble for wet-weather suits, ponchos, field jackets, blankets, poncho liners, nylon rope, carabiners, and extra footwear.

Many fire support bases and other outposts depended on aerial resupply and were cut off during severe monsoon weather. The habit of filling these remote locations with extra equipment rapidly diminished stock levels. Years of experience never completely diminished the adverse impact of such heightened logistical activity. As late as October 1970, the 23d Infantry Division (Americal) at Chu Lai was completely unprepared for the heavy materiel losses incurred by typhoons Kate and Joan.[15]

Any operations within extremely difficult terrain, such as the saltwater swamps of the Rung Sat Special Zone, took a heavy toll on equipment. Materials for weapon-cleaning and preservation were quickly depleted; ropes were lost in stream crossing; pneumatic mattresses were easily punctured; and clothing and ponchos were torn by thorny vegetation.

The United States produced an overwhelming abundance of materiel throughout the conflict. Operational supply stocks were hampered, however, by tropical weather, terrain, Vietnam combat levels, and the Army's own morass of paperwork. During the crucial Tet Counteroffensive of 1968, the 1st Cavalry Division lacked essential JP4 aviation fuel because a written requisition form was missing.

Administrative errors could also block the arrival or replacement of combat gear, and soldiers constantly complained about the absence of mosquito nets, poncho liners, radios, and other jungle warfare essentials.[16]

2.3 Uniform Appearance and Disposition

Tropical clothing rapidly became unserviceable in the harsh climate, razor-sharp elephant grass, and dense jungles of Vietnam. The 1st Infantry Division, based at Di An and Lai Khe, was critically short of tropical combat

Troop appearance varied with duty positions, but by 1969, reflected the grime and strain of constant combat. Left to right: armored vehicle crewman, helicopter crew chief, infantryman, military policeman, scout dog handler, ranger. *Author's collection.*

uniforms, underwear, and socks throughout 1966 and most of 1967. The need for resupply of tropical combat boots was particularly acute. One urgent appeal for higher allocations added this understatement in October 1967: "Common sizes of boots and clothing are being worn out rapidly in the conditions under which the division has been operating."[17]

The 4th Infantry Division's war in the western mountains ripped tropical clothing to shreds. One battalion reported in 1967 that "a critical shortage of combat fatigues developed.

Truck drivers of the 572d Transportation Company with one of their M52 5-ton trucks and 12-ton semi-trailers loaded with barbed wire. They wear typical attire of service and support troops working in tropical heat. March 1968. *U.S. Army.*

The lightweight material of the jungle fatigues, though making movement in hot, humid jungle more comfortable, proved vulnerable to the many thorns and branches of vegetation."[18] Fire and movement was usually accomplished while crawling across the ground. Sleeves could be rolled up and shirts even discarded, but pants sustained constant wear. The division reported wear-out rates of trousers and coats as six to one.[19]

Another problem that caused an individual soldier's supply of clothing to dwindle was

Front-line troops of the 3d Bde, 82d Abn Div, often fought stripped to the waist in torrid heat conditions. The absence of his tropical coat has caused at least one parachutist (backrow, fifth from left) to wear his metal parachutist badge on his camouflage helmet band. 1968. *Author's collection.*

The 1st Logistical Command laundry point at Qui Nhon processed 20,000 pounds of dirty clothes daily during 1967. Here WO Donald Groner turns in a bag of soiled clothing to Sp4 James Wright, 14 October 1967. *Larry Grant.*

the difficulty of receiving laundered clothing in the field. Sp4 Michael Belis of the 1st Battalion, 22d Infantry, 4th Infantry Division, stated, "While with the 4th Division we *stayed* out in the boonies, living out of rucksacks, and being resupplied every four days or so by helicopter. Every third or fourth resupply, we would get a change of uniforms which were dumped out in a heap, and you tried to find a set of jungle fatigues to fit. I usually ended up with a set too large, and cut the legs off the trousers to fit."[20]

Laundry mix-ups were common, and many Vietnamese laundry contractors were suspected of being Viet Cong. The uniforms of SSgt. Kenneth B. Sowands, of the 3d Squadron, 4th Cavalry, were cleaned by a laundry just outside the 25th Infantry Division's base camp at Cu Chi. Early in May, he discovered a tropical uniform coat missing from his laundry bundle. His unit found the missing coat late in June while searching a captured Viet Cong bunker on the eastern edge of the Iron Triangle. Sergeant Sowands commented, "The last time I saw my coat, it was on the way to the laundry. I'm surprised I didn't get a pair of black pajamas in its place.[21]

Replacement rates for clothing always es-

calated with the tempo of combat. The punishing pace of prolonged field maneuver was typified by the replacement-clothing needs of one 25th Infantry Division battalion during Operation Attleboro, 4–25 November 1966. During these three weeks, the 500-man 2d Battalion, 27th Infantry, was resupplied with 150 sets of tropical uniforms, 1,360 pairs of socks, and 750 sets of underwear.[22]

Combat clothing was also hard to obtain in stable field environments with only sporadic combat episodes because it was difficult to convoy or fly supplies to widespread locations. For example, the 1967–69 historical summaries of the 1st Battalion, 18th Infantry, reveal its men were fortunate to receive more than two sets of clothing. Supply priorities were reserved for ammunition and gasoline, forcing clothing and equipment requisitions to be filled (according to the 3d Battalion of the 22d Infantry) on a "fill or kill" basis from the nearest depot.[23]

Command emphasis on approved military appearance inevitably slackened under field conditions. Haphazard wear, unauthorized clothing modifications, and individual styling became noticeable during 1967. Disobeying regulations was widespread by late 1968. Some commanders were more stern than others. The

Soldier *(left)* of the 3d Bn, 187th Inf (101st Abn Div) wears extremely modified tropical shirt with poncho lining and added bandoleer pockets. Medical specialist *(right)* wears cap made from lightweight knitted shirt, a tight neck wrap, and green undershirt. I CTZ, 26 June 1970. *Ivan Pinnell.*

Sp4 Richard Champion, a squad leader in 4th Bn, 21st Inf (23d Inf Div) wears cut-down tropical shirt, beads on tropical hat, and swastika and peace medallions during the battle for Hill 56, 19 January 1971. *U.S. Army.*

commander of the 11th Armored Cavalry (Regiment), Col. George S. Patton, would not tolerate disregard of uniform regulations any more than would his famous father during the Second World War. On 6 October 1968, Colonel Patton issued his directive on standards of appearance.

Recently it has come to my attention that the standards of appearance, maintenance, and military courtesy throughout this organization have fallen below the acceptable level. Each of these items individually is a significant indicator of the quality of leadership within a unit and collectively they form a yardstick by which the overall capability of the unit is measured. . . . Within this area of personal appearance, the following specific items have been noted:

(1) Personnel wearing the jungle hat with the tie-down string either at the back of the head or looped over the crown. There are only two places that the tie-down string is authorized for wear—either inside the crown of the hat or under the chin.

(2) Lack of haircuts. Hair will be kept cut short and neatly trimmed.

(3) Identification tags missing or improperly worn.

(4) Shirt sleeve rolled up improperly. Shirt sleeves will be rolled above the elbow or will be all the way down and buttoned.

(5) Sagging pistol belts.

(6) Trousers not bloused.

(7) Boots dirty and/or unserviceable.

(8) Generally dirty uniforms, to include headgear. The policy and regulations covering these items should be clear to all concerned. Enforcement should start at the lowest command level, i.e., vehicle commanders, section leaders, and work up to platoon and troop/company/battalion level.

All of the above items apply to units at Blackhorse Base Camp [at Xuan Loc]. Units in field locations will have greater difficulty maintaining comparable standards, but there is no reason, no matter in what conditions a unit finds itself, to condone (items) 1–8 above. I will, however, allow the senior officer on the ground to prescribe the uniform while in a field location. For example, troops engaged in strenuous physical labor may be allowed to remove their fatigue shirts. Nevertheless, during mounted operations outside the assembly or night defensive area, I expect all vehicle commanders to be equipped with weapons and appropriate webbing and to be wearing steel helmets and body armor. The same uniform is prescribed for

Undershirts with bandoleers or M79 grenade carrier vests are worn in front-line uniformity within the 4th Bn, 31st Inf (23d Inf Div) near Chu Lai, 3 December 1970. *U.S. Army.*

dismounted operations with the exception that body armor is optional.[24]

In the 1960s, when civilian male hairstyles became fashionably longer in the United States, soldiers tried to circumvent strict military haircut policy. One regulation of the 9th Infantry Division's 3d Brigade stated, "Military personnel will be cleanly shaven. Facial hair is limited to short sideburns extending no lower than mid-ear level; and to short, neat, conservative mustaches. Specifically prohibited are beards, goatees, bushy handlebar, freak, cavalry, hussar, or cossack mustaches and strictly forbidden mutton-chop sideburns."[25]

Visible jewelry was limited by regulation to wedding rings, fraternal or academic rings, ornamental rings in good taste without dangerous surfaces or edges, watches, identification bracelets, and friendship bracelets. These Army mandates were increasingly disregarded as the years passed and nonconformity became fashionable. By 1969, a typical mix of platoon

Soldiers of the 173d Abn Bde, several wearing slave bracelets on their right wrists, give the Black Power salute at Bong Son. *Author's collection.*

23

The appearance of Army troops during the Cambodian incursion of June 1970 varied considerably from the standard tropical combat uniforms of earlier years. These troops bring rations to the front line using an M274 mechanical mule. They wear tiger stripe camouflage and tropical trousers. *USARV PIO.*

riflemen would probably be wearing such ornaments as neck jewelry, peace medallions, war crosses, earrings, bangles, slave bracelets, swastika pendants, and silver combs wedged in Afro-style haircuts.

Aviation personnel had special zeal for stylish outfits, as the following excerpt from the *1st Aviation Brigade Commander's Notes* (a command bulletin distributed to brigade aviation units in Vietnam) of 10 February 1969 reveals.

The standard of appearance and dress of many of our soldiers has deteriorated to an alarming level. Some of the most notable violations of established standards are: (a) Pegged

A rifle squad of the 173d Abn Bde wears typical mix of military and civilian clothing while resting between operations. Note ERDL camouflage tropical coats being worn with plain trousers, wet-weather parka over ordinary clothes, and leather belt with utility uniform. *Author's collection.*

trousers, (b) Zippers in boots, (c) Pegged trousers cut off just below the top of the boot, (d) Wearing of several types of crests all round the side of the baseball caps, (e) Wearing of beads, (the men) excuse it as part of their religion, (f) Hair only being trimmed around ears and growing very long back of neck, (g) Moustaches curling on end and not trimmed along lip, (h) Excessively long sideburns."[26]

2.4 Area Uniform Policies

Off-duty soldiers were encouraged to wear civilian clothing downtown. When the communist Tet-68 offensive struck Saigon and other urban locations, however, the widespread confusion and misidentification of persons in civilian clothing caused many adverse incidents. Because of this experience, MACV changed its policy on 16 September 1968. After that date,

Army personnel throughout Vietnam could wear civilian clothing only in their billets, military installations, Vietnam rest & recuperation (R & R) areas such as China Beach or Vung Tau, and "at Camp Alpha (at Long Binh) and aboard aircraft for personnel traveling to out-of-country R & R and leave sites."[27]

Soldiers were restricted to wearing Army khaki, tan, and green uniforms when off-duty in the Saigon-Cholon-Tan Son Nhut metropolitan area (*See* Army Uniform Map of Vietnam.) Field or work uniforms were prohibited in Vietnamese bars, restaurants, or other "places of public entertainment." Personnel who wore field or work clothing as part of their duty uniform were required to proceed directly to their residence, unless stopping for a meal at a U.S. armed forces mess facility.[28]

Notes

1. Natick Laboratories, *Annual Historical Summary FY 63,* 82.
2. Lt. Gen. Joseph M. Heiser, Jr., *Vietnam Studies: Logistic Support,* Dept. of the Army, 1974, 46.
3. USARV, *Logistical Summary #33-66,* 16 Dec 66, 6.
4. USARV, *Logistical Summary #34-66,* 12 Jan 67, 7.
5. 173d Airborne Brigade, *Combat After Action Report,* 4 Jan 67, 55.
6. USARV, *Logistical Summary #1-67,* 13 Feb 67, 7.
7. 1st Logistical Command, *Operational Report,* 15 Aug 67, 174; USARV Reg 735-1; MACV Directive 735-2.
8. MACV Directive 735-2, 25 Sep 70 and 12 Mar 70; USARV Reg 670-5, 26 Feb 68, Appendix I.
9. USARV Circular 700-2, 6 May 67; MACV *Observer,* Vol. V. No. 39, 30 Jan 67, 9.
10. Natick Laboratories, *Annual Historical Summary FY 63,* 81–82.
11. MACV Directive 670-1, 2 Jul 65; USARV Reg 670-5, 26 Feb 68.
12. Heiser, 47.
13. 2d Battalion, 27th Infantry, *Operational Report,* 28 Apr 67, 12–13.
14. 1st Brigade, 101st Airborne Division, *Operational Report,* 12 Feb 68, 12.
15. Americal Division, *Operational Report,* 15 Nov 70, 33–62.
16. Shelby L. Stanton, *Anatomy of a Division,* Presidio Press, 1987, 114.
17. 1st Infantry Division, *Operational Report,* 15 Aug 66, 7-2, and 31 Oct 67, 70.
18. 1st Battalion, 8th Infantry, *Annual Historical Summary: 1967,* 1 Mar 68, 31.
19. 4th Infantry Division, *Operational Report,* 1 Feb 67, 44.
20. Letter from Michael Belis, 22 Dec 86.
21. MACV *Observer,* Vol. 6, No. 10, 12 Jul 67, 1.
22. 2d Battalion, 27th Infantry, *Operational Report,* 28 Apr 67, 12.
23. 3d Battalion, 22d Infantry, *1966 Historical Summary,* 44.
24. 11th Armored Cavalry Regiment, *Operational Report,* 10 Nov 68, Incl 9.
25. 3d Brigade, 9th Infantry Division Draft Reg 670-5, 7 Feb 70.
26. *1st Aviation Brigade Commander's Notes #2,* 10 Feb 69, 3.
27. MACV Directive 670-1, 16 Sep 68, 5, and 12 Apr 72, 2.
28. USARV Reg 670-5, 26 Feb 68.

3

Headgear

3.1 Steel Helmet and Helmet Liner

The Army's standard combat helmet of the Vietnam conflict was the *M1 steel helmet,* which rendered protection against flying shrapnel and ricocheting bullets. The metal helmet shell fitted over a nylon liner with adjustable headband, giving the assembly a combined weight of 3.44 pounds. In 1965, the laminated nylon *helmet liner* had replaced the old resin-impregnated, cotton duck model, which had less ballistic protection.[1] An adjustable suspension band and nape strap stabilized the liner on the head but proved unsatisfactory. Better-fitting suspension systems having leather-foam pad inserts or Velcro-taped nylon straps were developed too late to be used in Vietnam.

Helmet liners, often worn without the metal helmets, became distinctive uniform items. For example, the 22d Replacement Battalion at Cam Ranh Bay wore white helmet liners with decals of the battalion distinguishing insignia on the right and USARV organizational shoulder sleeve insignia on the left. Enlarged insignia of rank decals were placed on the liner front. The 90th Replacement Battalion at Long Binh wore both white and blue helmet liners. Blue helmet liners commonly designated cadre of division and independent brigade-replacement training centers. As part of their uniform, security and military police troops used black helmet liners. (*See section 10.10,* Military Police.)

Despite considerable technological progress, helmet capability was not upgraded in Vietnam. A secret wartime-product-improvement test of infantry helmets was conducted at Aberdeen Proving Grounds in Maryland from 12 June to 15 December 1968. The protective levels of three developmental helmet types — nylon LINCLOE, titanium LINCLOE, and titanium Type III — were compared to the M1 steel helmet. Although each helmet stopped a significant percentage of fragments from nearby 82mm and Chinese 120mm mortar explosions, the titanium Type III helmet afforded the best protection, followed by the titanium and nylon LINCLOE models. The M1 steel helmet used by combatants in Vietnam gave the poorest performance.[2]

The typical M1 steel helmet worn in the Rung Sat Special Zone by Sergeant Henry of the 2d Bn, 3d Inf (199th Inf Bde), 8 March 1967. *Author's collection.*

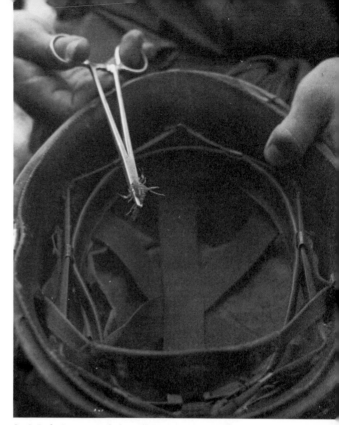

Sp4 Bob Rosane of the 4th Bn, 3d Inf (198th Inf Bde), removes a scorpion from his helmet liner. The suspension band and nape strap can be seen. West of Chu Lai, 27 May 1971. *U.S. Army.*

Major Huntsinger and First Sergeant Jacobs wear the distinctive white helmet liners of the 90th Replacement Bn at Long Binh, 2 December 1968. Note battalion pocket patch. *Author's collection.*

Left to right, Sp4 Steven Bacon, Sp4 John Rhoades, and Sp4 Jerry Badeaux, Company C, 54th Inf, wear the PG (Patrol Guard) black helmet liners with white over red color bands, as part of the 94th MP Bn at Phu Hiep, May 1969. *Author's collection.*

Security Guard (SG) troops, wearing white helmet liners with USARV decals and SG brassards, undergo weapons inspection prior to assuming defensive positions at Da Nang, June 1971. *Author's collection.*

Security Patrol (SP) troops of the 1st Logistical Command in formation at the U.S. Army Depot, Da Nang, February 1970. Note the highly polished individual equipment belt. *Author's collection.*

The helmet's regular shape and characteristic surface sheen made it a very conspicuous part of the combat ensemble. The cloth *helmet cover,* designed to modify these shortcomings, was printed with a disruptive camouflage pattern using selected organic dyes and resin-bonded pigments. This was a duotone reversible cover with leaf patterns in green colors for spring and summer wear and brown colors for fall or winter operations. Unfortunately, the helmet cover camouflage was better suited for temperate than tropical zones and did not match ERDL coloration.

For additional camouflage, the helmet cover contained small slots for inserting natural foliage. The elastic cotton webbing *camouflage helmet band* was also designed to hold

SSgt. Henry Randle, 199th Inf Bde, wears the blue helmet liner of an instructor at the brigade's "Redcatcher's Joint Forces School," 26 June 1967. *W. J. DuPuis.*

Soldiers of the 2d Bn, 27th Inf (25th Inf Div), wear helmet liners while cleaning M16 rifles after assault on Tram Canal, 12 August 1968. Note helmet on ground with cover still affixed and cover flaps tucked inside *(lower left)*. Note identity marking on liner *(right)*. *Author's collection.*

foliage in order to blend the helmet shape and color into the surrounding terrain. In Vietnam, however, the helmet band more commonly held cigarettes, insect repellent or an extra rifle magazine—whatever needed to be high and dry and within easy reach.

Early in 1967, as troops sought to individualize their uniforms, creative writing on helmet covers began to proliferate. Most commonly seen were nicknames, names of girl friends, and names of home states or towns. The latter served to attract the attention of other people from the same geographic area. Various versions of "short" calendars, peace and flower power symbols, and slogans were also popular. Typical slogans included "Think Ice," "Peace in Our Time," "Don't Follow Me— I'm Lost Too," and "God Is My Point Man."

3.2 Sun Helmet

The *sun helmet,* or "pith helmet," was authorized early in the war as part of the utility

Sp4 Billy Meyers of the 1st Bn, 502d Inf (101st Abn Div), was saved from NVA machine gun fire by his M1 steel helmet during the Tet-68 Counteroffensive. *Author's collection.*

Center parachutist of the 1st Bde, 101st Abn Div, has his helmet chin strap laced through the parachutist's chin strap preparatory to a training jump at Dong Ba Thin, 28 July 1965. *U.S. Army.*

Pfc. Charles Crawford of the 4th Bn, 9th Inf (25th Inf Div), was saved by his M1 helmet from an AK47 round during a fire fight southwest of Tay Ninh, 5 June 1969. *Author's collection.*

Lt. Col. Burton Walrath points out enemy positions to Capt. Dwain Bailey, 2d Bn, 12th Inf (25th Inf Div), west of FSB Pershing, 16 September 1969. Note camouflage helmet bands and positioning of helmet chin strap. *Army News Features.*

On his helmet camouflage cover, Lt. Col. Joseph Perlow, commander of the 4th Bn, 42d Artillery, from 26 February to 6 August 1969, has embroidered ''Highlanders,'' from the unit's Vietnam nickname, ''Highland Redlegs.'' *Author's collection.*

Sp5 Ogden Boullard II of the 2d Bn, 7th Cav (1st Cav Div), with rifle magazine in camouflage helmet band and sock carrier for individual combat meal cans. Note burlap camouflage strips and netting on helmet covers. *U.S. Army.*

Sp4 Keith Miller uses a PRC-77 radio to call in a fire mission. He wears an unauthorized decorative band around his helmet, typical of individualization by 1970. *U.S. Army.*

The sun helmet or "pith helmet" worn with the utility uniform was in limited use by support personnel in Vietnam before 1967. *E. Tarr.*

The AFH1 flying helmet worn by a OH13 scout pilot of the 199th Inf Bde, 16 March 1967. Note padded helmet retention strap. *Richard Peoples.*

Major Shedden, the commander of the 73d Aviation Company, wears white APH5 flying helmet in his OV1 Mohawk aircraft at Vung Tau, 27 June 1967. *U.S. Army.*

uniform. The helmet consisted of a rigid, one-piece fiber shell with a cotton twill covering and a percale lining. It featured an ornamental design with a rolled-edge brim. The sun helmet came in three colors: white, khaki, and olive green. This helmet was issued primarily to engineer and support troops in 1964 and 1965.

The sun helmet's demise followed a request by the Vietnam-based 22d and 90th Replacement Battalions seeking permission to wear specially decorated sun helmets on 31 October 1966. The cadre of both battalions processed arriving and departing Army personnel and were directed to adopt conspicuous uniform apparel for easy recognition by transient soldiers who needed processing assistance. Lt. Col. V. R. Teigland's 22d Replacement Battalion, located on the hot sands of Cam Ranh Bay, wanted the sun helmet instead of the helmet liner for coolness and comfort. However, Col. Stuart A. MacKenzie, the USARV Adjutant General, decided that "con-

Crew chief wears the APH5 flying helmet and M1952 fragmentation protective body armor as he loads Vietnamese wounded aboard his UH1B helicopter in 1962. *U.S. Army.*

tinuity of supply, serviceability, military appearance, and acceptability by military personnel favor the helmet liner."[3]

The request triggered a review of the sun helmet, and its fate was effectively sealed by USARV Regulation 670-5 of November 1966, directing "commanders to judiciously authorize wear of the sun helmet (pith)." The ease of supplying and servicing the less expensive helmet liners was the stated reason for the sun helmet's rapid disappearance. Actually, the reasons included military sentiment against mixing different helmet types that interfered with standard uniform appearance; senior officer convictions that the sun helmet symbolized former colonial occupation attire; and troop feelings that it resembled NVA pith helmets.[4]

3.3 Aviator and Combat Vehicle Crewman Helmets

The *APH5 crash-type flying helmet,* or "brain bucket," was the Army's standard aviation headgear at the beginning of the Vietnam conflict. In response to battlefield experiences, a program to upgrade the helmet's ballistic-protection capability was initiated during 1962. Design shortcomings detected in the May–June 1964 testing at Fort Rucker, Alabama, however, were not satisfactorily corrected until 21 October 1965. The modified helmet was similar to the older version, except that its shell was fabricated of ballistic-resistant nylon fabric, laminated with 40 percent modified phenolic resin. Unfortunately, depending on its size, the helmet's weight increased up to 1.5 pounds. The helmet also included a new retractable glare visor and an expanded plastic liner with sizing pads for better fit.[5]

The modified helmet, officially known as the *crash ballistic protective flying helmet, nylon outer shell,* or more commonly as the *AFH1* helmet, was classified as standard Vietnam issue on 16 November 1965. The Army announced that APH5 helmets were being relegated to stateside use. Production testing requirements were waived, and priority purchasing was approved to expedite overseas delivery. Although 14,500 AFH1 helmets were ordered, only 1,878 were in Vietnam by the end of January 1967.

The slow delivery of the projected 12,475

helmets alloted to the 1st Aviation Brigade prompted its commander, Brig. Gen. George P. Seneff, to alert his officers, "This will be all that will be available for some time, and delivery at this time is only being made in RVN. Until firm word is received, all ballistic helmets will stay in-country. Your guys should keep their APH5 helmets and take them home with them. Don't let any [AFH1] ballistic helmets get away from the units when your people rotate to CONUS (Continental United States)." Critical shortages persisted, and the brigade received only 4,779 helmets by May 1967. There was also a shortage of tinted glare visors, and the visor screw heads kept breaking off. Production continued to slip, and the brigade ran out of AFH1 helmets during July 1968.[6]

The Army awarded a new contract for

Sp5 Daniel Bauer prepares his camera for a photo mission in an AH1G Cobra helicopter of the 334th Aviation Company, 23 September 1969. He wears the SPH4 flyer's helmet. *U.S. Army.*

Battered and split flying helmet of a crew chief who died of cerebral edema and contusion with uncal herniation when Major General Ramsey's command UH1H helicopter crashed 7 miles west of Chu Lai, 17 March 1970. The helmet sometimes failed to provide the levels of protection desired by the Army. Other personnel, including Ramsey, survived this crash. *Author's collection.*

AFH1 helmets in March 1968, and these 7,000 helmets finally started arriving in Vietnam in early 1969. They were issued within the 1st Aviation Brigade according to the following crew priorities: (1) light-observation helicopters in air cavalry squadrons, (2) armed helicopters, (3) UH-series troop helicopters and remaining light-observation helicopters, (4) reconnaissance fixed-wing aircraft, (5) CH47 and then CH54 cargo helicopters, (6) utility fixed-wing aircraft.[7]

In the meantime, the Army's next-generation flight helmet was being developed and procured for Vietnam utilization. This helmet was

Sp4 Terry Wray, an M48 tank loader of the 2d Bn, 34th Armor (1st Inf Div), wears the combat vehicle crewman helmet with sun, wind, and dust goggles, near Lai Khe, 1 January 1968. *U.S. Army.*

Sp4 William Conklin, 1st Bn, 5th Inf (25th Inf Div), an armored personnel carrier crewman, was saved by his combat vehicle crewman helmet from an AK47 round to the head, 4 August 1969. *25th Inf Div PIO.*

copied from the Navy SPH3 helmet, and the Army version was tentatively called the SPH3B modified helmet. Using Epoxy One resin, the primary shell was increased in thickness from 0.065 inches to 0.10 inches, and the ear cups were redesigned. The helmet offered significantly higher crash and acoustic protection but weighed less than either the APH5 or the AFH1 models. An improved *M87 microphone* eliminated the hollow boom of the old *M33 microphone*, which indiscriminately picked up and amplified any sound. An easily adjustable helmet suspension made of fire-resistant synthetic webbing was added.[8]

This design was adopted as the *SPH4 flyer's helmet,* and the first 900 helmets were delivered to the Army on 18 July 1969. In December, the new helmet was reclassified as standard issue throughout the Army, but low production rates forced its issue to be on an

established-priority basis, even in Vietnam. Spare parts for the helmets did not reach Vietnam until March 1970. The first 20,000 SPH4 helmets had acrylic visors, since the polycarbonate visors had optical distortion problems. It was not until the fall of 1972 that these visors were brought up to acceptable standards. By September 1972, enough helmets were available to meet all Army requirements, and the APH5 and AFH1 helmets were declared obsolete.[9]

Many aviators were saved by their helmets in Vietnam. The monthly USARV Aviation Pamphlet often featured such "helmet saves." One January 1968 item recounted how a UH-34D helicopter gunner ran behind his aircraft to retrieve the port window that had fallen out during a landing approach. He stepped in a puddle of water, lost his balance, and fell into the arc of the spinning tail rotor blade. The

General Westmoreland and Vietnamese commanders inspect front lines at Vam Long, 1 May 1964. Major Park (*extreme right*) and others wear the stiffened M1951 cotton field cap. *U.S. Army.*

rotor struck his helmet six times, demolishing the back side with a series of slashing gouges that penetrated to a depth of one and a half inches. The gunner, who suffered only a few minor cuts to his scalp in the incident, got up, picked up the window, and finished the job.[10]

The *combat vehicle crewman helmet* was constructed of laminated ballistic nylon with a roll-back, over-the-brow design, which allowed access to vehicular sighting equipment. It came in two sizes with adjustable headbands and energy-absorbing pads, which gave a certain degree of bump protection. The helmet's quick-disconnect plug and communication equipment were designed specifically for com-

patibility with tank equipment, and, therefore, the helmet was easily used for internal vehicular communications.

3.4 Utility and Service Caps

The privately purchased blocked utility Spring-up cap was initially worn in Vietnam, along with the M1951 *cotton field cap* stiffened with cardboard or plastic inserts. The preferred blocked caps, with metal spring reinforced rims and stiffened sides, were made by the Louisville Cap Company and could be purchased at post exchanges.

Although the stiffened cap could not be

laundered, and special care was required to avoid crushing it, senior commanders approved of its military smartness. Gen. Maxwell D. Taylor, the Army Chief of Staff from 1955 to 1959, had favored the Korean war blocked version of the field cap, but the stiff Spring-up cap proved especially troublesome in hot weather and was unsuited for Vietnam. Its use was terminated there on 1 July 1964.[11]

The *utility cap* was a visored, baseball-style cap made of polyester and rayon gabardine cloth, dyed Olive Green army shade 106. This cap was adopted in 1962 for wear with field uniforms, following an extensive, seven-year development program to replace the Army's field headgear of the World War II and Korean war periods. Expensive polyester and rayon fabric was selected because DA insisted that the cap maintain a satisfactory military appearance, without ironing or shaping after being machine washed and tumble dried.[12]

The utility cap was standardized in November 1963 and became available in Army clothing sales stores during the summer of 1964. As the Vietnam conflict intensified, soldiers increasingly grew to dislike the cap's "beanie" or "pinhead cap" form. And there were other reasons for dissatisfaction. The intense heat of Vietnam caused individuals to perspire profusely. Permanent sweat stains appeared around the caps. These absorbed dust, became discolored, and were usually delineated by pronounced squiggly salt lines. The soldiers also disliked the cap's association with noncombat stateside duty, where it was also issued. Nevertheless, the utility cap remained a staple of Vietnam field and work uniforms.

A utility cap variant with a shortened brim became available at post exchange facilities during 1967. This cap was favored by officers and NCOs because it was more stylish and could be peaked forward, with the addition of cardboard stiffening to the front, to give a rakish baseball-cap effect. The Vietnamese-made versions had a higher peaked top and could be shaped better. These caps came in different colors, but their wear was restricted by USARV regulations: "Solid color baseball caps may be worn with the field and work uniform by members of aerial equipment and supply, aviation, and aviation maintenance units while in working areas. However, the wear of

Pfc. Craig Walters, 2d Squadron, 17th Cav (101st Abn Div), wears M1951 cotton poplin field cap while using a PRC-77 radio to adjust artillery fire. Note lightweight knitted shirt under tropical coat. 25 December 1970. *101st Abn Div PIO.*

these solid color caps will be on an optional basis. These caps are for safety and a means of identification." In 1972, this authority was extended to the staff of the in-country R & R Center at Vung Tau.[13]

Black baseball caps were worn by pathfinders and some division replacement training

Sfc. Cecil Bruton, Jr., a mine and demolitions advisor to the Vietnamese Engineer School at Phu Cuong, wears a Navy issue cotton utility cap, sateen Olive Green shade 107. Note subdued pin-on insignia of rank. April 1969. *Author's collection.*

Troops of the 864th Engineer Bn land at Qui Nhon. They wear standard utility caps and utility caps purchased from stateside post exchange facilities *(left and right foreground)*. 9 June 1965. *U.S. Army.*

The rigger commander and a warrant officer of the 109th Quartermaster Company (Air Delivery) receive decorations at Cam Ranh Bay, 22 March 1968. They wear the better-appearing Vietnamese-produced red baseball caps. *Author's collection.*

Col. Theodore Mataxis *(right)* wears private purchase utility cap with shorter brim, decorated with rank and master parachutist's badge on background trimming, as he confers with Maj. Gen. Stanley Larsen at Phan Rang, 1966. Note first-pattern tropical coat. *Author's collection.*

Sp5 Barnett, 815th Engineer Bn, repairs a generator on a large rock-crushing machine at Pleiku. He wears the tropical hat. The utility cap is worn at right. *Author's collection.*

center cadre. Some aviation personnel, especially medical evacuation air crewmen, wore blue or maroon caps. Red caps were worn by riggers and aircraft maintenance personnel. Within the 1st Cavalry Division, various colored baseball caps were worn by technical supply, direct support, and shop personnel of the 15th Transportation Battalion (Aircraft Maintenance). Although colored baseball caps sported a variety of cloth and pin-on insignia in Vietnam, USARV Regulation 670-5 specified that only officer rank or unit distinctive insignia for enlisted personnel could be worn. After 19 April 1968, only subdued insignia of grade could be placed on colored baseball caps. Many formations issued local regulations, however, which allowed special skill badges to also be worn.[14]

3.5 Military Hats

An almost infinite variety of military hats, ranging from cowboy stetsons to tropical tricornes, were worn by Army personnel in Vietnam. Many hats had only local authorization at best. For instance, numerous locally made "bush hats" or "cowboy hats" proliferated within advisory detachments and other training elements. Some of the cowboy-style hats became a hallmark of Vietnam advisory duty

SSgt. George Carter, 101st Abn Div combat leadership school instructor at Phan Rang, wears black baseball cap with sewn-on organizational shoulder sleeve insignia. He looks at F100 Supersabre fighter 20mm cannon shells. 23 January 1968. *U.S. Air Force.*

from 1962 to 1966, but interest in them began to wane once the eminently practical and individualistic tropical hat became widely available.

Several air cavalry units wore dark blue or black pseudo–cavalry frontier campaign hats sporting gold-colored metallic cords with gold-colored acorns procured from police officer or

Sfc. Philip Griggs, an instructor at the Combat Indoctrination Course of the 1st Inf Div, wears a locally authorized Australian-style "bush hat" at Lai Khe, 1 January 1968. *U.S. Army.*

Tunnel rat of the 1st Engineer Bn (1st Inf Div) wears locally purchased tab on his Vietnamese-produced "bush hat." He poses in a VC tunnel west of Lai Khe, 3 January 1969. *U.S. Army.*

highway patrol supply outlets. These were privately purchased at the direction of senior officers wishing to promote unit morale, and their reception by the aviators was mixed. The cavalry hats were worn by the 1st Cavalry Division at Phuoc Vinh and Bien Hoa, and by several separate air cavalry units, such as the 7th Squadron of the 1st Cavalry (Regiment) at Vinh Long.

Another attempt to instill organizational pride led to the tropical tricorne "distinctive regimental combat parade hat" of the 2d Battalion, 3d Infantry. This unit, assigned to the 199th Infantry Brigade in Vietnam, was part of the Army's "Old Guard" regiment, and the hat was deliberately designed as a link to the regiment's colonial tradition.

Some Army commands, like MACV-SOG, discarded special headgear that might draw undue attention to their personnel. Since there was an abundance of locally procured black hats in I CTZ (I Corps Tactical Zone),

Recon team of 1st Bn, 28th Inf (1st Inf Div) wear Vietnamese-produced camouflage "bush hats" during Operations Billings in Phuoc Long Province, 21 June 1967. *U.S. Army.*

40

Long range patrol of the 101st Abn Div confer about enemy target during a 1970 recon mission. They wear Vietnamese-produced tiger-stripe camouflage ''bush hats.'' *Author's collection.*

Lt. Col. Jack J. Isler of Command & Control North, MACV-SOG, ordered wear of the "black flop type hat, brim modified to conform to neat standards of appearance" at Da Nang and other sites commencing 31 March 1969. The hats were worn in lieu of the conspicuous green beret, which he deemed "unacceptable headgear."[15]

The hat that eventually epitomized the Army's headgear in Vietnam was the immensely popular *tropical hat*. The tropical hat was variously termed the *hot weather hat,* or *hat and insect net,* but it was commonly known and cherished by the troops as the "boonie hat." This hat was first proposed by Army Materiel Command on 7 April 1966, after USARV noted that a full-brim field hat was needed in Vietnam to protect the face and neck from rain and sun. Natick Laboratories had already completed much of the basic research during its 1962 special-warfare program. A total of 309 test hats in three different styles were sent to ACTIV (Army Concept Team in Vietnam) during August 1966.

The reconnaissance platoon of the 2d Bn, 327th Inf (101st Abn Div) wear a variety of Vietnamese-produced camouflage ''bush hats'' at Camp Eagle. *Author's collection.*

Combat tracker team of the 61st Inf Platoon prepares for a mission near Lai Khe wearing a mixture of tropical hats and Vietnamese-produced "bush hats." 19 October 1969. *U.S. Army.*

All of the prototype hats shared the same basic design: a full-brimmed, round hat with a band for holding local foliage for camouflage. A mosquito head net slipped over the hat and extended over the neck where it was fastened with an elastic closure. Style *T66-3* was a multiple-stitched hat with full brim and felt lining. Style *T66-4* was a round-domed, full-brimmed hat similar to the Army's fatigue hat of the 1930s. *T66-5* was a flat-topped, full-brimmed model made of material similar to T66-3. Most of these hats were issued to the 1st Battalion, 7th Cavalry, and were tested from September to October 1966. All prototype designs were fa-

Maj. Gen. George Putnam, Jr., 1st Cav Div commander, wears the pseudo-cavalry frontier campaign hat while decorating combat engineers wearing tropical hats at Phuoc Vinh, 11 February 1971. *Author's collection.*

vored over the utility cap by the evaluating troops.[16]

ACTIV completed its report on 6 December 1966, but the Army did not expedite procurement until 29 April 1967, at a cost of $3.50 per hat. The final design contained an adjustable chin strap, screened eyelets on each side of the crown, and a headband with slots for insertion of camouflage materials. The total weight of the hat, with its detachable head net, was about 4 ounces. The tropical hat was functional in the field; offered good protection from sun, weather, and insects; and was stylish. The hat's low-slope crown and semi-rigid brim could be reshaped, cut, or altered to meet individual desires.

The Army Materiel Command air expressed the tropical hats to USARV under the ENSURE program beginning 16 August 1967. The tropical hat was reclassified as a standard

Sp5 James Maye wears the tropical tricorne of the 2d Bn, 3d Inf (199th Inf Bde), at Nha Be, 1967. *Author's collection.*

Color Guard of the 2d Bn, 3d Inf (199th Inf Bde), wearing tropical tricornes at Nha Be, 21 September 1967. Note Vietnamese Ranger pocket patches. *Richard Peoples.*

A mixture of tropical hats (one decorated with the peace symbol), utility caps, and Vietnamese-produced ''bush hats'' is worn by the 66th Engineer Company at Long Binh. *Author's collection.*

Sfc. Earnest Brannum, who led the counter-attack against NVA sappers entering his engineer compound after the platoon leader was killed, wears the tropical hat in the prescribed manner. *Author's collection.*

Army item on 20 December 1967 and became available through normal supply channels. On 8 April 1968, it was ordered by Army Materiel Command in the standard ERDL camouflage pattern. Unfortunately, this camouflage tropical hat was never widely worn in Vietnam. After considerable development and procurement delays, it was finally shipped to Vietnam just as Gen. Creighton W. Abrams was taking steps to limit the wear of all tropical hats.[17]

General Abrams became the MACV commander on 2 July 1968. He strongly disapproved of the tropical hat, which he called the jungle field hat. He disliked its "unmilitary appearance" and was especially upset over its widespread, nonconformist wear. His strong dissatisfaction reached a boil on 15 September 1971 when he personally ordered his MACV staff to "frustrate all incoming jungle hats; stop the shipments if we can!" The commander of the Inventory Control Center, Vietnam, was directed to prevent further shipments of the hats at once, and other staff officers began coordinating the substitution of utility caps.[18]

Tighter restrictions on tropical hat pro-

This soldier of the 4th Bn, 21st Inf (11th Inf Bde), has pinned up the brim of his tropical hat with a metal Combat Infantryman's Badge during a mission south of FSB Debbie, 10 December 1970. *U.S. Army.*

Soldier of the 2d Bn, 14th Inf (25th Inf Div), scans the bank of the Song Sai Gon as he wears the ERDL camouflage tropical hat, 10 October 1970. *Author's collection.*

Exhausted soldiers of the 4th Bn, 9th Inf (25th Inf Div), wearing tropical hats in typical field style, rest during a mission near FSB St. Barbara, 9 September 1969. *25th Inf Div PIO.*

This trooper of the 1st Bn, 327th Inf (101st Abn Div), uses a towel to form a protective head wrap as he hacks out a fire lane with his machete at FSB Nuts. *Author's collection.*

1Lt. Wilbert Crockett *(left)* wears a construction worker's helmet and Capt. Thomas Weaver *(right)* wears the maintenance personnel protective hat as these 92d Engineer Bn officers confer at the Phu Cuong bridge site, 21 March 1969. *Author's collection.*

curement were implemented just two days later. USARV dispatched a message on 17 September 1971: "Effective immediately, only specified combat units will be authorized to draw jungle hats from US Army depots and DSU's [Direct Supply Units]. Units must be designated Armor, Infantry, Field Artillery, Air Defense, or Combat Engineers at battalion level or lower, working strictly from base camps or fire bases in order to Rqn [requisition] jungle hats, with the exception of WAC's and Nurses."[19]

Units throughout Vietnam vehemently protested the stringent policy. On 25 September, General Abrams responded: "Subject Hat was designed to be worn by all personnel on field operations for protection against climatic conditions (rain and hot sun), bugs, and mosquitoes. The hat was not intended as a carrier of grenade rings, colorful headbands, peace symbols, patches, and other unauthorized

Two boxers of the 2d Bn, 501st Inf (101st Abn Div) wear boxing head protectors during a match at Phu Bai. *Author's collection.*

items. Commanders may authorize the wear of the jungle field hat by personnel in combat and combat support units on field operations *only*. Henceforth, issues will be made to only these units until supply is exhausted. Commanders will take action to insure proper wear of the jungle headgear by personnel concerned."[20]

The 1st Cavalry Division's separate 3d Brigade was scattered in defensive positions around several critical facilities. The combat troops were stunned when rear area commanders began insisting on the removal of their tropical hats. On 28 October 1971, brigade commander Brig. Gen. Jonathan R. Burton formally requested that either all personnel of his formation be allowed to wear the tropical hat, or that Bien Hoa, Bear Cat, Long Binh, Phu Loi, and Vung Tau also be classified as field fire bases for his command. As backup for his position, Burton claimed stocks of utility caps were limited.

General Abrams denounced the request as an attempt to either liberalize or negate his decision. The MACV Deputy Chief of Staff for Personnel, Maj. Gen. James J. Ursano, briefed Abrams on the hat situation. Ursano reported 85,000 utility caps were in Vietnam, and more could be purchased at the Long Binh clothing sales store. His briefing concluded, "The progression of actions as outlined above has resulted in the frustration of incoming stocks of the tropical hat, the ultimate goal being that once on-hand stocks are depleted, the hat will no longer be authorized for wear by U.S. personnel in Vietnam, To submit a request to MACV for an exception to policy on the scale envisioned by BG Burton, could only be interpreted as an attempt to reverse the accomplished fact, which from a practical viewpoint is irreversible."[21]

Shortly thereafter, Abrams' deputy, Lt. Gen. William J. McCaffrey, wrote a brisk reply to General Burton. He conceded that "it is recognized that the constraints placed on the wear of the tropical combat hat pose some problems for commanders. However, these constraints are necessary to establish a policy that promulgates the spirit and intent of General Abrams' desires in this area. . . . I am fully confident that with your continued support, adherence to the spirit and intent of current policy can be accomplished with minimum adverse effects on

Sp4 Steven Horton of the 2d Bn, 77th Artillery, uses the towel as a head and neck protective wrap as he prepares a ditch for the trails of a howitzer at FSB Chamberlain, 1969. *25th Inf Div PIO.*

the morale and efficiency of your command." The letter sealed the fate of the beloved tropical hat. But it also underscored the insensitivity of the high command to the common soldier's welfare, and it struck a final blow at already diminished morale in a rapidly retreating army.[22]

3.6 Protective Headgear

Certain Army personnel wore civilian protective hats or helmets with the utility or field uniform during construction work in Vietnam. The *protective aluminum hat* was a natural an-

Sp4 Richard Guth, a sniper of Company F (Ranger), 75th Inf (25th Inf Div) wears muslin field dressing as a bandanna. He holds his M14 rifle prior to an airmobile raid into VC territory near Hieu Thien, 2 April 1970. *Author's collection.*

odized color with a rolled-edge brim and was used by military engineers and other workers requiring lightweight protection from falling objects. It could not be worn, however, around electrical equipment, overhead transmission lines, energized cables, or in places where exposure to electrical contact was possible.

The *worker's construction helmet* was used for greater protection. This was a rigid helmet, usually white or yellow, with full-floating, adjustable suspension. The helmet protected against falling objects and contact with electrical current up to 10,000 volts. The *line-*

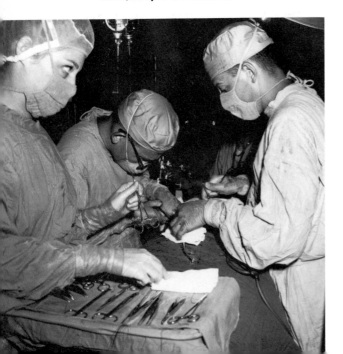

Surgeons and nurses wear protective operating caps and masks during an operation on a wounded soldier in Vietnam. *Army News Features.*

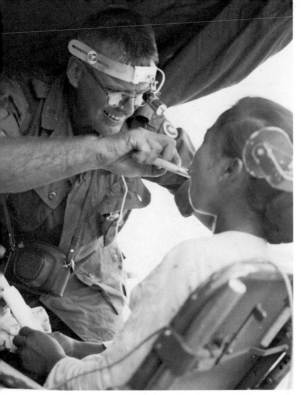

Maj. Raymond Morrow, a dentist of the 257th Medical Detachment, wears a field dental headband (with light) in Binh Duong Province, 7 October 1966. *U.S. Army.*

The rifle green wool beret worn by the 5th Special Forces Group commander, Col. Jonathan Ladd, and members of Project RAPID FIRE, Detachment B-36 (Provisional), at Long Hai. *Author's collection.*

man's safety hat, with full-floating suspension and 10,000-volt electrical resistance, was worn by signal troops near electrical lines.

3.7 Berets

The only beret officially sanctioned for wear by Army male personnel during the Vietnam conflict was the *wool beret, Rifle Green army shade 297,* authorized for members of Army Special Forces. The beret consisted of a knitted, wool outer shell, a lining of silesia fabric, and a leather binding around the bottom edge. It came with a rayon braid threaded through the binding and tied in a bow at the back; but the ends of this adjusting ribbon were normally cut off, and the ribbon knot was secured inside the edge binding. The beret was equipped with a badge stay on the left front and two eyelets with an eyelet protector on the right side. The regulation manner of wear was with the headband or edge binding straight across the forehead, one inch above the eye-

brows. The top of the beret was draped over the right ear, with the stiffener for affixing insignia positioned over the left eye.

The green beret's official adoption followed a long, difficult fight by Special Forces. During the summer of 1955, Col. Edson D. Raff, the commander of the Army's Psychological Warfare Center, prescribed, without DA sanction, the wearing of green berets by Special Forces personnel. These berets were procured by Special Forces individuals, at a cost of $1.80 each, from the Dorothea Knitting Mills, Ltd., of Toronto, Canada. This local authorization touched off the "green beret controversy," although bright green, floppy, French-manufactured berets had been worn by Special Forces troops in Europe. On 2 April 1956, DA disapproved any Special Forces beret, but it was barraged with protests following its decision.[23]

The Army finally relented in September 1961, after President John F. Kennedy remarked that the "Army should look into adop-

The *Biệt-Động-Quân* garnet beret with the ranger beret badge worn by Maj. Bill Thompson at the Duc My Ranger Training Center, 13 September 1965. *U.S. Army.*

The green beret worn at a typical slant by Sp4 Michael Hand of 5th Special Forces Group during presentation of the Distinguished Service Cross in recognition of his heroic actions of 22 November 1965. Tan Son Nhut, 10 February 1966. *Author's collection.*

The green beret as typically worn in Vietnam during a parade of the sergeant major and other sergeants of Detachment B-42, 5th Special Forces Group, at Chau Doc, 15 March 1966. *Author's collection.*

Col. William Roop *(left)*, senior advisor to ARVN Airborne Division with fellow advisor Lt. Col. John Nicholson *(right)*, who wears ranger tab above divisional shoulder sleeve insignia on his Vietnamese airborne camouflage tunic. Both wear rose-red *Nhảy-Dù* berets with *Sú-Đoàn Nhảy-Dù* beret badge, 28 July 1969. *MACV PIO.*

Lieutenant Colonel Fairfield wears the *Thiết Giáp Binh* armored corps black beret as he congratulates a South Vietnamese tank commander. June 1966. *Author's collection.*

MSgt. Guy Stockton wears the *Biệt-Động-Quân* garnet beret in the stylish cock's comb fashion at Duc My Ranger Training Center, 15 September 1965. *U.S. Army.*

tion of berets, such as is worn by strategic air command air police." DA Message 570488, dated 23 September 1961, permitted Maj. Gen. William P. Yarborough's Special Forces troops to wear the beret during the 12 October special warfare demonstration for President Kennedy at Fort Bragg, North Carolina. President Kennedy was very impressed with Special Forces capabilities and with their beret, which he described as a symbol of excellence, a mark of distinction, and a badge of courage. DA moved quickly to procure Canadian airborne rifle green berets for all Special Forces, and it was officially designated as their headgear on 10 December 1961.[24]

The *Biệt-Động-Quân* (Special Mobile Corps, or ranger) beret, which was garnet in color, was worn by Army advisors to the Duc My Ranger Training Center at Nha Trang commencing in 1965. The berets were also worn by advisors attached to ARVN ranger command groups and battalions in the field. This semistiff beret was often procured a size and a half too large, soaked in beer or water, and deliber-

Capt. Jerry Hyatt, an advisor with 1st ARVN Div, wears the *Hắc-Báo* black beret in the shrunk down, crushed style of ARVN division recon companies, northeast of An Khe, 9 June 1967. *U.S. Army.*

Major Shippey, commander of Company N (Ranger), 75th Inf (173d Abn Bde), wears the black ranger beret with company tab above the background trimming, through which his insignia of rank is pinned, at Ranger Hill, LZ English, April 1971. *Author's collection.*

Sgt. Michael Frazier of Company F (Long Range Patrol) 51st Inf, wears Vietnamese-produced tiger stripe camouflage beret during a recon mission, 31 January 1968. *U.S. Army.*

ately shaped into a style resembling a cock's comb. The Vietnamese considered this style of beret to represent masculine power.

The *Sú-Đoàn Nhãy-Dù* (Division Airborne, or paratrooper) beret, which was rose in color, was worn by Army advisors to the ARVN airborne division and its battalions. The Vietnamese general service olive drab beret was also worn occasionally by Army advisors to other South Vietnamese units or facilities.

The black *Thiết Giáp Binh* (Armored Branch) beret was worn by advisors to ARVN tank and mechanized units. Black berets were also worn by advisors to the *Cảnh-Sát Quốc-Gia* (National Police Field Forces). Advisors with the *Hắc-Báo* (Black Panther) divisional ranger or strike companies wore their black berets shrunk down to fit snugly over the head.

1Lt. James Southerland of Mobile Advisory Team 80 wears the black ''MAT beret'' at Chau Xuan hamlet, 8 November 1970. *U.S. Army.*

On 12 February 1968, the USARV Advisor School was opened at Di An for the primary purpose of training Mobile Advisory Teams (MAT) for province and district service with Vietnamese regional and popular forces. The school cadre and MAT advisors adopted berets that could be either black or ultramarine. An idea of the extent of this beret's wear can be ascertained from the fact that 7,988 Army MAT personnel were fielded before the school ceased operations on 29 September 1971.[25]

In 1967, black berets began to gain acceptance among many Army scout-dog and combat-tracker teams, as well as among some long-range reconnaissance units. For example, Company F of the 52d Infantry, 1st Infantry Division, was completely outfitted with black berets when organized on 20 December 1967. Some units, however, like Company F of the 51st Infantry (Long Range Patrol), 199th Infantry Brigade, wore locally manufactured tiger-stripe camouflage berets instead. The black beret became accepted as ranger headgear after the Army's long range patrol units were redesignated as ranger companies of the 75th Infantry on 1 February 1969.

USARV authorization usually lagged far behind local procurement. For example, the 1st Cavalry Division authorized members of Company H (Ranger), 75th Infantry, to wear black berets on 16 August 1970. Brig. Gen. Jack MacFarlane, commanding the 173d Airborne Brigade, formally presented black berets to Company N (Ranger), 75th Infantry, during a ceremony with guidons in April 1971.

3.8 Protective Masks

Anti-riot gas was widely used in Vietnam to flush bunkers and tunnels of NVA/VC occupants. Wind, close combat, and even enemy employment often exposed U.S. infantry to the gas as well. The *ABC M17 chemical-biological field mask* gave routine protection against anti-

Lieutenant Grange of Company L (Ranger), 75th Inf (101st Abn Div), wears the black ranger beret with ranger tab above his insignia of rank. He has just been awarded the Silver Star at Camp Eagle near Phu Bai. *Author's collection.*

Sergeant Rothwell of Company L (Ranger), 75th Inf (101st Abn Div), wears the black ranger beret with parachutist badge and regimental distinctive insignia. He has just been awarded the Silver Star with Oak Leaf Cluster at Camp Eagle near Phu Bai. *Author's collection.*

riot gases and was not required to protect against stronger chemical and biological agents since they were not used in Vietnam.

In 1967, the Israeli government received the M17 masks and complained that the component filter elements did not provide promised levels of protection against chemical blood and nerve agents. In early 1971, testing at Edgewood Arsenal confirmed the Israeli findings about the mask filter deficiency. The problem was caused by migration of the plastisol edge-sealing material into the activated-charcoal filter's aerosol paper. Thus, the serviceability of the filters stored in the mask was about two years, while filters kept separate

Brig. Gen. Jack MacFarlane, commanding the 173d Abn Bde, formally presents black ranger berets to Company N (Ranger), 75th Inf, at Ranger Hill on LZ English, April 1971. *Author's collection.*

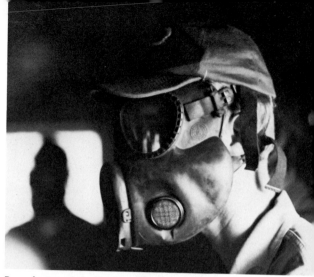

Parachutist of the 3d Bn, 503d Inf (173d Abn Bde), wears his M17 protective mask under his utility cap with the parachutist badge on background trimming, during training at Tuy Hoa. *Author's collection.*

Military police of the 97th MP Bn receive training with the M17 protective mask at Cam Ranh Bay, July 1968. Note the mask carrier strapped around hip. *Author's collection.*

from the masks might last four years. A June 1971 survey disclosed a deficiency of over 4,400,000 filter elements, with only 1,200,000 serviceable worldwide.[26]

The 9th Infantry Division discovered that its M17 protective masks became ineffective once the cheek filters got wet. No air could be drawn through the filters, and gas leaked in through the face piece. The masks constantly became wet in the division's sector of the Mekong Delta, despite troop care in keeping the carriers as high as possible and wrapping them in plastic bags. Rainstorms soaked mask carriers worn over the shoulder, and swamp thickets tore the plastic bags.[27]

The M17 mask was also heavy and bulky, and USARV requested smaller, less bulky, lightweight gas masks for field use during 1966. In response, the Army Munitions Command investigated hasty troop protection against

Soldiers of the 2d Bn, 27th Inf (25th Inf Div), wear M17 protective masks while battling Viet Cong troops in Binh Duong Province, 28 February 1968. *U.S. Army.*

Armored vehicle crewmen of the 4th Bn, 23d Inf (25th Inf Div), wearing the XM28 lightweight protective mask *(left)* and the M17 protective mask *(right)* during action near Nui Ba Den mountain, 1969. *25th Inf Div PIO.*

The improved XM28 lightweight protective mask. *U.S. Army.*

riot-control chemical agents, or "tear gas." Development of low-resistance mask filters and transparent silicone rubber led to a silicone-version M17 protective mask called the *XM27*. The command also produced the *XM28 lightweight protective mask* by vulcanizing flat sheets of silicone rubber into a face-blank, which then received polycarbonate plastic lenses and laminated filter elements. This 13-ounce mask had a vinyl, waterproof carrier, which fitted into the tropical combat uniform's trouser cargo pocket.[28]

Pfc. Don Adams of the 191st Ordnance Bn renovates an M15 land mine using the chemical cartridge respirator, a half-mask face piece equipped with activated charcoal cartridges for protection against vapors. Cam Ranh Bay. *Author's collection.*

A special DA team brought 300 XM27 and XM28 masks to the 1st Cavalry Division at An Khe and the 1st Infantry Division at Di An on 6 May 1967. Field tests were also conducted by the 5th Special Forces Group at Nha Trang, and USARV evaluation was completed on 4 October. The XM28 was preferred, but exhaled air escaped from the top of the mask, and troops breathing heavily in combat were unable to intake enough air.[29]

The quality of the XM28 mask was upgraded, and an improved model was produced on 22 November 1967. USARV requested 117,283 XM28 masks for Army forces on 7 December 1967, and Special Forces ordered 112,243 additional masks for its native Civilian Irregular Defense Group. Each mask cost $13.90. Production problems, however, prevented the initial batch of 40,080 masks from reaching Vietnam until a year later, on 31 December 1968.[30]

3.9 Face Shields and Ear Protection

Several types of face shields were used in Vietnam for face protection. Normally, these shields were mounted on a lightweight head frame to provide a full range of vision while offering protection against chemical splashes, sparks, and flying chips. The *industrial face shield* was equipped with either a hinged or unhinged, clear or tinted plastic face shield, which varied in thickness. The black fiber *welder's helmet* featured a fixed lens retainer and adjustable head suspension.

Although noise hazards in Vietnam were particularly intense, ear protection was almost nonexistent for the average soldier. Devices that muffled battlefield or helicopter noise interfered with the need to receive verbal information. For soldiers conducting tasks away from the actual battlefield and exposed to constant noise levels about 85 decibels, the *aural protector, sound* ("ear muff") was available. The rubber or plastic *plug, ear, hearing protective, universal* ("ear plug"), fitted into the outer ear canal. *Ear-canal caps* were composed of two plugs mounted on a metal, adjustable headband that was enclosed in a plastic tube. Finally, many soldiers substituted plain cotton for ear plugs, although this was officially discouraged.

A 69th Engineer Bn welder uses the fiber welder's helmet with fixed lens retainer while emplacing pierced steel planking (PSP) at the Can Tho Army Airfield, July 1968. *Author's collection.*

Sp5 Melvin Nance welds down attaching points for securing helicopters on the USNS Corpus Christie Bay, the floating base of the 1st Transportation Bn off Vietnam. He wears the welder's helmet. *Author's collection.*

Sp4 George Lardner, 557th Maintenance Company, prepares sheet metal for truck repair at Nha Trang. He uses eyecup goggles designed for chipper and grinder protection. 17 July 1970. *U.S. Army.*

A 1st Supply & Transport Bn (1st Inf Div) driver with Army sun, wind, and dust goggles. Brig. Gen. James Hollingsworth *(right)* wears highly irregular and unauthorized short sleeve alterations to the tropical coat. *Author's collection.*

Communications Team of the 1st Bn, 321st Artillery (101st Abn Div), wear industrial plastic ventilated dust goggles south of Hue, 23 April 1971. *101st Abn Div PIO.*

Corp. Larry Whitt of the 4th Bn, 9th Inf (25th Inf Div), wears military issue spectacles outside FSB St. Barbara, 1969. *25th Inf Div PIO.*

3.10. Protective Eye Wear

The Army utilized a wide assortment of eye wear in Vietnam, since 37 percent of all American troops in Vietnam wore some form of corrective lenses.[31] In many cases, eye wear had to provide protection from external hazards, as well as improve vision. Toughened glass lenses inserted in the eye cups of goggles or spectacles were designed to protect against flying particles or heavy impact, such as might be encountered in grinding, drilling, or in operating machinery. Filter lenses were employed where stray light, with ultraviolet and infrared rays, was encountered in welding or cutting.

Spectacle type safety glasses were used where heavy industrial-type goggles were not required. Close-fitting *protective eyecup goggles* were issued to chippers, grinders, and welders. These were essential for welders because of the intense infrared and ultraviolet light they encountered. The goggles had an adjustable nose bridge and circular lenses mounted on each cup by a screw-on retaining ring.

The Army's *sun, wind, and dust goggles* were used in great quantities by wiremen, vehicle crewmen, engineers, and aircraft mechanics in Vietnam. Troops regularly employed them for protection against ground debris and flying stones spewed by whirling helicopter blades. The goggles were the close-fitting, plastic, single-aperture type with elastic headband.

Spectacle type sun glasses, or "aviator sunglasses," were employed to counter sunlight glare. The sunglasses were extremely hard to

1 Lt. Ronald Houck of the 1st Squadron, 10th Cav (4th Inf Div), wears spectacle-type sunglasses during a mechanized patrol along Highway QL-19 west of An Khe. *Lonnie Voyles.*

A combat engineer wears civilian "grannie" wire rim spectacles and the tropical hat during construction tasks in Vietnam. *Author's collection.*

The head-mounted SU50 night vision goggles with AN/PAS-8 aiming light on the M16 rifle, as used during MACV-SOG and 46th Special Forces Company missions from 1971 to 1972. *Author's collection.*

secure in Vietnam and remained on the command controlled list of the 1st Aviation Brigade until 22 November 1968, when 12,000 pairs were ordered. This large quantity was shipped in unmarked Sea-Land containers for security, since theft had lowered stock levels in Vietnam to only 1,150 pairs in Qui Nhon and 2,500 pairs as back-up storage at Da Nang. Consequently, most aviators relied on privately purchased sunglasses.[32]

The wearing of sunglasses was discouraged on patrol because they hindered spotting of booby traps, such as concealed trip wires, tilt sticks, and punji stakes. During September 1967, SSgt. Edwin Beck trained arriving troops in Vietnam for the 196th Infantry Brigade at Chu Lai. As his first group of 120 men traversed the ambush course, "the 12 men with the shades all hit just about every device I had planted out there. I had one of the men with prescription (shaded) lenses remove his glasses and put on his clear glasses. He walked the course again and saw every device but one."[33]

3.11 Head-Mounted Night-Vision Devices

Head-mounted night-vision devices were among a range of high-priority night-vision equipment developed by the Army in response to the tendency of NVA/VC forces to move at night. During the Vietnam conflict, research conducted by several firms under Army contract enabled the military to field several new weapon night sights and night scopes using far-infrared technology. The Army also needed a head-mounted device or night-vision goggles for soldiers performing detailed night missions.

The night-vision goggle program resulted in the head-mounted *SU50 electronic binocular* and its companion weapons-mounted, diode-emitting aiming light, *AN/PAS-8*. The assembly was developed under two sets of specifications: a high quality instrument for global Army adoption, and a less stringent standard for immediate procurement within Southeast Asia. The contract was awarded to International Telephone & Telegraph Corporation in July 1968, but technical difficulties in tube manufacturing delayed the program and prevented suitable intensifier tubes from being supplied to the Army.[34]

By August 1969, the Army became impatient for some type of head-mounted night-vision device that could be used where hand-held thermal viewers were not practical, such as by drivers or weapons handlers who needed free use of both hands. For this reason, DA negotiated for devices with capabilities below its specifications. Low-performance tubes with short life spans were supplied for testing of the

SU50 electronic binocular in October 1969. Not surprisingly, the results were disappointing.

The SU50 electronic binocular was fitted with expensive special-purpose tubes in time to be used for the Task Force Ivory Coast raid into Son Tay, North Vietnam, on 21 November 1970, and later by MACV-SOG and 46th Special Forces Company commandos operating in Laos. The head-mounted binoculars were employed successfully during these missions, but further procurement ceased because the night-vision goggle, *AN/PVS-5,* was being developed. The war ended, however, while the newer goggle was still undergoing preliminary testing.[35]

Notes

1. Army Materiel Command Pamphlet 385-63, Jan 65, 33.
2. Army Materiel Test Directorate, *Final Report on Product Improvement Tests of Infantry Helmets: Special ARRAY Test,* Mar 69.
3. USARV AVHAG-R Disposition Form, Subj: Distinctive Uniform Item for 22d & 90th Repl Bns, 29 Nov 66, with attached correspondence.
4. USARV AVHGA-SM letter, Subj: Request for Authority to Wear Distinctive Uniform Item, 8 Dec 66, with attached correspondence.
5. Army Materiel Command RD-DM-E Disposition Form, Subj: Helmet, Flying, Crash Type, 24 Nov 65.
6. *1st Aviation Brigade Commander's Notes #11,* 14 Mar 67, *#19,* 19 Feb 68, *#23,* 9 Jul 68; 1st Aviation Brigade, *Operational Report,* 15 May 67, 10.
7. *1st Aviation Brigade Commander's Notes #25.*
8. *Aviation Digest,* Sep 68, 59.
9. *Aviation Digest,* Dec 69, 63, and Sep 72, 56.
10. USARV Aviation Pamphlet 95-1, Jan 68, 11.
11. Quartermaster Research & Engineering Command, *Clothing and Equipment Development Branch Series Report No. 36,* Feb 63.
12. Defense Supply Agency Memorandum, Subj: GAO Draft Report, 6 Jan 64.
13. USARV Reg 670-5, 26 Feb 68; MACV Directive 670-1, Suppl 1, 23 Sep 72.
14. USARV Reg 670-5, 26 Feb 68 and Change 2, 19 Apr 68; 1st Cavalry Division Reg 670-5, 16 Aug 70.
15. Special Operations Augmentation CCN, 5th Special Forces Group, Drawer 22 letter, 31 Mar 69.
16. Army Concept Team in Vietnam, *Final Report of Tropical Hats,* Proj ACL-84/67, 6 Dec 66.
17. Defense Supply Agency, ACSFOR DS Status Report, 8 Apr 68.
18. Maj. Jon L. Sampson, per Staff Officer to DCS P & A, letter, Subj: Verbal query of DCS concerning MACV guidance on wear or issue of the boonie hat, 17 Sep 71.
19. USARV Message 170735Z, Sep 71.
20. MACV Message R250941Z, Sep 71.
21. MACV AVHDP-MMW Disposition Form, Subj: Wear of the tropical combat hat Decision Paper, 21 Nov 71.
22. MACV AVHDP-MMW letter, Subj: Wear of the tropical combat hat, Record file copy of 1st Cavalry Division.
23. DA Deputy Chief of Staff for Personnel letter, Subj: Berets for Special Forces units, 21 May 56.
24. DA DCSPER Memorandum for Record, Subj: Berets for Special Forces, 24 Oct 61, and attached papers.
25. USARV Army Advisor School, *After Action Report,* 12 Oct 71.
26. DA Deputy Chief of Staff for Logistics DPD letter, Subj: M17 series protective mask, 28 Jun 71.
27. 9th Infantry Division, *Operational Report,* 12 May 68, 70.
28. U.S. Army Munitions Command, *Annual Summary FY 67,* 63.
29. 5th Special Forces Group, *Combat Development Report,* 8 Aug 67, Incl 8-2.
30. Defense Supply Agency, ACSFOR DS Status Report, 30 Jun 69.
31. *Army Reporter,* Vol. 5, No. 1., 6 Jan 69, 10.
32. *1st Aviation Brigade Commander's Notes #28,* 9 Dec 68, 6.
33. *The Army Reporter,* Vol. 3, No. 35, 9 Sep 67, 15.
34. Army Electronics Command Night Vision Laboratories, *Annual Historical Summary FY 70,* 9.
35. Army Electronics Command Night Vision Laboratories, *Annual Historical Summary FY 71,* 11–12.

4

Uniform Compositions

4.1 Tropical Combat and Hot Weather Uniforms

The tropical combat uniform, or "jungle fatigues," was the primary field uniform in Vietnam after 1963. Its use was expanded on 27 October 1967 when USARV announced that the tropical combat uniform was also the principal duty uniform for all Army personnel in Vietnam.[1]

The uniform was a rare example of Army clothing that combined functional practicality with comfort and attractive design. The quick-drying coat and trousers were made of a tightly woven, lightweight, rip-stop or twill cotton poplin fabric that offered good protection against solar radiation, insects, and other tropical hazards. The loosely fitting garment promoted body-heat ventilation and moisture dissipation. (*See section 1.2*, Tropical Combat Uniform Development; *section 2.1*, Clothing Authorization and Supply.)

The tropical combat uniform was worn with the coat outside the trousers, and the trousers bloused into boots. Often, because of the high temperatures in Vietnam, sleeves were rolled up or even cut off. On 17 November 1965, MACV declared, "Cutting sleeves off field clothing is specifically prohibited."[2] MACV insisted that sleeves be rolled down for mosquito protection in April 1965. As malaria fears faded because of medical advances, permission was granted to roll up sleeves, if mosquitos were not prevalent. Rolling the sleeves neatly above the elbow became mandatory in most Vietnam military installations by 1967, although, in the field, sleeves were usually worn rolled down.

The tropical coat was modified over the course of the war but retained its basic bush-style design. The coat had two slanted, chest bellows pockets and two lower bellows pockets. There were three basic patterns of the tropical coat worn in Vietnam, which were issued chronologically as follows: (1) all-cotton, wind-resistant poplin, dyed Olive Green army shade 107, with exposed buttons on the shoulder loops and side tabs, and an inner gas flap at the front closure; (2) all-cotton, wind-resistant poplin, dyed Olive Green army shade 107,

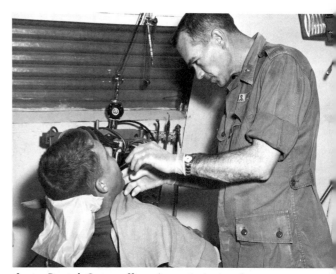

First-pattern tropical combat uniform, with exposed buttons on pockets, is worn by 21st Aviation Company Maj. George Prater *(right)*, while other officers wear second-pattern coat with concealed buttons. Leather combat boots are worn for flight safety. Chu Lai, 16 June 1968. *Author's collection.*

Army Dental Corps officer (note insignia of branch on collar) of the 85th Evacuation Hospital wears the first-pattern tropical coat with exposed buttons on pockets, shoulder loop, and side tab plainly visible. *Author's collection.*

Brig. Gen. Richard Allen, commander of the 173d Abn Bde, wears the second-pattern tropical coat with whistle chain and combat leader's identification ''green tab'' on the shoulder loop at Bong Son, 1968. *Author's collection.*

A mix of second- and third-pattern tropical coats with subdued and unsubdued insignia worn by headquarters section sergeants and specialists, 2d Bn, 502d Inf (101st Abn Div), 1969. *Author's collection.*

Tropical coat of the Army tropical combat uniform.

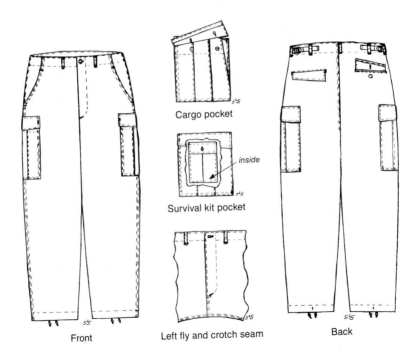

Cargo pocket

inside

Survival kit pocket

Front

Left fly and crotch seam

Back

Tropical trousers of the Army tropical combat uniform.

Rangers of Company C, 75th Inf (I Field Force, Vietnam), wear ERDL camouflage tropical combat uniforms as they inspect captured NVA weapons at An Khe, 11 June 1970. *U.S. Army.*

with buttons on the pockets concealed beneath a flap to prevent snagging; and (3) all-cotton poplin or rip-stop cotton poplin fabric, with concealed buttons and no shoulder loops, side tabs, or gas flap. With this third pattern a class system was introduced to distinguish between Olive Green army shade 107 (Class 1) and the Army ERDL camouflage pattern (Class 2). The latter were fabricated of cotton rip-stop poplin. (*See section 1.3*, Coloration and Camouflage of Tropical Combat Clothing.)

The trousers had two front pockets, two hip pockets, and two bellows cargo leg pockets. The latter pockets contained drain holes, and the buttons were later concealed to prevent snagging. A small pocket inside the left cargo pocket was designed to hold a special survival kit—which was never satisfactorily developed. The trousers had either a slide-fastener fly or a five-button fly. The tunneled draw cords at the bottom of the trouser legs were used to either tie or blouse the trousers over the boots. The cords could be untied to permit better air flow and to allow the lower trouser legs to dry, but when the trouser legs were untied, dousing with insecticide to ward off leeches and insects was recommended.

Black-dyed tropical combat uniforms were often worn by Army liaison and advisory personnel in MACV Civil Operations and Rural Development Support (CORDS), especially within the CORDS Revolutionary Development or Rural Development Cadre. Special Forces members of Detachment A-41 (Ranger),

Sgt. Maj. Ralph Pitcher of the 3d Bn, 6th Artillery, wears the third-pattern tropical combat uniform with concealed buttons on pockets but no shoulder loops. Note cloth insignia worn parallel to ground, and pin-on insignia of rank on collar. Pleiku, 1969. *Author's collection.*

Recon team of Company E, 3d Bn, 503d Inf (173d Abn Bde), wear typically battle-worn ERDL camouflage tropical combat uniforms after clashing with NVA 35 miles southwest of An Khe, March 1971. *Author's collection.*

Tropical combat uniform in typical field combat uniform mode. Pfc. James Fullerton of the 1st Bn, 8th Inf (4th Inf Div), prepares to move out on a patrol to search Hill 1049, southeast of Dak To, 17 December 1968. *U.S. Army.*

46th Special Forces Company wore Thai black combat fatigues. Some MACV-SOG teams dyed their tropical combat uniforms black because it quickly faded to a charcoal gray and so provided darker camouflage characteristics for night movement.

One typical MACV-SOG fashion was worn by Sgt. Jeffrey L. Junkins, reconnaissance team commander with Command & Control North (CCN). He dyed his tropical combat uniform charcoal gray and modified it

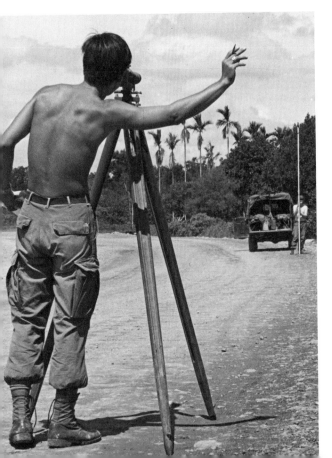

Surveyor of the 815th Engineer Bn works on Highway QL-20. The hip pockets and bellows cargo leg pockets of the tropical combat uniform trousers can be seen. 24 May 1971. *Alan E. Dodd.*

Tropical combat uniform in typical duty uniform mode. Note Vietnamese rank centered on coat and II CTZ pocket patches on these Second Regional Assistance Command officers at Pleiku, 23 February 1972. The commander, Mr. John Paul Vann (*center*), was killed on 9 June 1972. *Author's collection.*

to prevent bug and leech intrusion during 1968 missions into Laos. He buttoned up the tropical coat, rolled down the sleeves, and wore gray aviator sheepskin gloves. With the lower coat pockets removed, he tucked the coat into the trousers, which were cut off above the ankles to eliminate bulk within the boot. Long gray cotton socks, which were cut off just below the ankles, were pulled up over the pant legs in the style of knickers. He taped the tops of these just below the knees with blackened surgical cloth tape. The footless socks gave barefoot comfort within the tropical combat boots. No underwear was worn, just the lightweight, knitted shirt beneath the tropical coat.[3]

In addition to the standard cotton tropical combat uniform and modifications thereof, several variants were also issued in Vietnam.

Two experimental types of nylon/cotton, mosquito-resistant tropical combat uniforms were tested in 1964 and 1968–1969, respectively. (*See section 1.2,* Tropical Combat Uniform Development.) The prototype explosive ordnance disposal protective thermalibrium system utilized a specially treated and modified tropical combat uniform as its outer layer. (*See section 5.7,* Protective Suits). Another tropical combat uniform type was fabricated of experimental, fire-resistant cotton/Nomex material—Nomex was a new DuPont polyamide fiber. This uniform was worn by selected munitions handlers and explosive ordnance disposal specialists. Finally, infrared control treatment was applied to all ERDL camouflage and to some late-war Olive Green army shade 107 tropical combat uniforms in Southeast Asia. (*See section 1.3,*

Tropical combat uniform in typical work uniform mode. Some asphalt spreader crew members of the 46th Engineer Bn have removed the coat during road surfacing near Phu Loi, 24 March 1969. *Author's collection.*

Coloration and Camouflage of Tropical Combat Clothing.)

Beginning in 1960, prior to tropical combat uniform adoption, Natick Laboratories developed several prototype uniforms to provide Special Forces with jungle clothing. The *T61-3* and *T62-4 special warfare hot weather shirt and trousers* were fabricated of 6-ounce nylon/cotton poplin, Olive Green army shade 107, and both types resembled the utility uniform's design. These test uniforms were delivered to

Tropical combat uniform in typical ceremonial uniform mode. An honor guard of the 2d Bn, 28th Inf (1st Inf Div), wearing M1956 individual equipment belts, fire a memorial salute honoring fallen division commander Maj. Gen. Keith Ware at Lai Khe, 16 September 1968. *Robert Cooper.*

Third-pattern tropical combat uniforms (left and center) and second-pattern utility uniform (right), worn with shirt out. In front of the 437th Medical Detachment Dental Clinic, 1968. *Author's collection.*

Tropical combat uniform in typical specialized combat uniform mode. Sp4 Robert Roedocker of the 173d Engineer Company wears first-pattern uniform as he sweeps a trail with an AN/PRS-3 metallic mine detector during Operation Yorktown. *Army News Features.*

Southeast Asia in considerable quantity and were worn by some advisory personnel in Vietnam as late as 1965.[4]

The hip-length, box-type shirt had a six-button front closure with inside gas flap. The two-piece, set-in sleeves had gusset closures and adjustable cuffs, and there were button-down flaps on the two breast patch pockets. On some versions, there were buttons inside the neckline, fronts, and cuffs for attaching the chemical warfare/thermal liner underneath. This reflected early U.S. fears of gas attack from Chinese intervention in Southeast Asia. The shirt was normally worn outside the trousers, which had a five-button front fly with inside gas flap, seven belt loops, waistline-adjustment tabs on the sides, slant-opening front patch packets, hip back pockets with button-down flaps, draw-cord leg hems, and six buttonholes inside the waistline tabs.

4.2 Indigenous Combat Clothing

The Republic of Vietnam's *Quân-Nhu* (Quartermaster) Military Clothing Production Center was activated 1 December 1954. The center's task was manufacturing textiles and producing uniforms for the entire South Vietnamese armed forces. The center's responsibilities included receiving raw materials, cutting cloth in quantities required for mass production, fabricating garments in quantities sufficient for initial and replacement issue throughout the RVN armed forces, and baling and shipping finished apparel to the base depots. The center was located at Yen-The in

Special Forces Detachment A-331 Heavy Weapons Leader Sfc. James Brown, commander of the 482d CIDG Border Surveillance Company, in "duck hunting" dapple camouflage at Camp Dan Thang, 15 April 1965. *Author's collection.*

Saigon. During the Second Indochina War, it was assisted by MACV Advisory Team 118.

The Vietnamese Clothing Production Center produced approximately four million pieces of military clothing in 1965, but rapid expansion enabled it to reach annual manufacture of 7,890,000 items by 1969. The Defense Personnel Support Center in Philadelphia sent a technical assistance team to Vietnam from 28 July to 28 August 1969. The team noted that improper techniques were being used for mass production, and specialized equipment was lacking. In October 1970, 157 industrial sewing machines and allied devices were sent to Yen-The. These proved too complex for the Vietnamese to assemble, however, and a second U.S. Defense Support Center team arrived in Vietnam on 12 March 1971 to install the equipment and train the Vietnamese to operate and maintain it. Indigenous combat clothing did not reach American standards until this time.

Special Forces Sgt. Arthur Videen, the assistant medical specialist of Detachment A-9 wears the T61-3 hot weather special warfare uniform with truncated sleeves. Camp Minh Thanh, 1964. *Author's collection.*

Special Forces Detachment A-331, under Capt. Charles Mendoza (back row, third from right), pose in Vietnamese tiger stripe camouflage, with prototype Davis fasteners on some of their individual equipment belts, clearly visible in back row (second and fourth from right). Camp Dan Thang, 10 April 1965. Author's collection.

There were several sources of textiles at the Vietnamese Clothing Production Center. The United States supplied chambray, denim, cotton duck, gabardine, wool, linen, polyester, and nylon cloth, as well as cotton and nylon thread. Vietnam supplied its own sateen, calico, muslin, and poplin cloth; nylon netting; brass and plastic buttons; khaki; and *Nhảy-Dù* (Airborne) camouflage fabric. "Offshore" sources were relied upon for the *Thủy-Quận Lục-Chiến* (Marine Corps) tiger-stripe camouflage fabric. The center's production in 1969 was divided roughly as follows: 32.5 per-

Army Phoenix operations officer of the MACV Civil Operations and Rural Development Support Territorial Security Directorate (center) wears black-dyed tropical combat uniform and holds an M2 carbine. He stands next to the Army district advisor major at Van Lam in Ninh Thuan Province, 1968. Author's collection.

cent shirts, 30 percent trousers, 8.5 percent drawers, 8.5 percent ammunition bandoleers, 7 percent caps, 5 percent mosquito bars, 5 percent overcoats and jackets, and 3.5 percent duffel bags.[5]

Lt. Col. Nguyen Van Viec commanded the center from 3 January 1967 until the war's conclusion. The organization's strength was typically 300 percent above assigned authorization, and, on 25 September 1970, contained 20 officers, 43 NCOs, 109 enlisted men, 15 women Army personnel, 967 piece tailors, 186 civilian contract workers, 482 direct-hire laborers, and 169 contract laborers. Even at this size, its capacity was insufficient to fully support Vietnam's military requirements. The work of the center was assisted by 24 private charitable societies, selected families in dependent quarters, and clothing detachment shops established at Da Nang, Qui Nhon, and Nha Trang during November 1968.[6]

The Vietnamese Clothing Production Center developed, manufactured, and printed the "pinks" camouflage material. This camouflage was known as pinks because of the subdued stone-pink or mauve colors incorporated into it. It was modeled after the World War II–era British Special Air Service pattern used in lightweight parkas and trousers, and was first brought to Vietnam by the French in the First Indochina War. In the early 1960s, Army advisors to the *Sú-Đoàn Nhãy-Dù* (Division Airborne) wore either the French lizard-pattern camouflage uniforms, or the Vietnamese pinks camouflage. As American influence increased, however, the standard Vietnamese airborne camouflage was changed to poplin material printed in an ERDL variant fashion.[7]

Of the Vietnamese combat clothing utilized by American forces, the various green tiger-stripe camouflage garments were the most popular. These were produced using textiles originally procured from "offshore" sources, such as Japan, Hong Kong, Korea, or Taiwan, as introduced by early Marine and Special Forces advisors. Tiger-stripe clothing was developed as an alternative to early CIA-supplied duck-hunting or *Beo-Gấm* (leopard) fabric, which was purchased from ordinary American commercial distributors. The leopard pattern was not popular because a dapple-type ca-mouflage was not needed in Vietnam's rain forests where there was little sunlight.

The *Thũy-Quận Lục-Chiê'n* (Marine Corps) adopted tiger-stripe clothing as its uniform basis. The Special Forces also chose various tiger-stripe uniforms for use in its Civilian Irregular Defense Group (CIDG) program. And later, the wearing of tiger-stripe fatigues proliferated among allied reconnaissance troops. With the popularity of tiger-stripe apparel, new sources for the material or manufactured clothing were needed. These sources included Korean, Ryukyuan (Okinawa), Thai, and Taiwanese contracts secured by American officials.

The fact that *Thũy-Quận Lục-Chiê'n* camouflage clothing remained the only authorized Vietnamese tiger-stripe quartermaster clothing, and the source of this fabric was always "offshore," supports the theory that this material was introduced to Vietnam at American direction. The tiger-stripe clothing, except for limited Marine issue, was never officially endorsed by the Vietnamese military authorities. The Special Forces and its LLDB clone outfitted the other primary users of tiger-stripe clothing, the CIDG, with special counterinsurgency support funding outside of normal military channels.

The geographical extent of the wearing of tiger-stripe camouflage by Americans was determined by individual preferences relating to uniform style and color pattern, coupled with availability. While tiger-stripe fatigues were all cotton, they came in various weights depending on manufacturer. Heavier sateen prevailed initially, until fast-drying poplin was adopted in 1963. Some foreign producers reverted to heavier cotton fabric later in the war. The heavier cloth was sometimes preferred for highland operations, because of its warmth, or in dense jungle movement, because it was quieter and resisted damage from branches and thickets. (*See section 1.3,* Coloration and Camouflage of Tropical Combat Clothing.) The lighter cloth was commonly reserved for other operational areas, especially where its quicker-drying properties were important.

Indigenous uniforms were qualitatively inferior to standard tropical combat uniforms. Additionally, the pockets were too small to hold many combat-essential items, such as sig-

588th Engineer Bn command section officers wearing a mix of first- and second-pattern utility uniforms, the latter having clip-cornered pocket flaps. Note cuffless sleeve *at far left*. Phu Loi, November 1965. *Author's collection.*

Staff sergeant of the 588th Engineer Bn wears first-pattern pre-1964 utility shirt with straight pocket flaps and low top button. Note unsubdued insignia and standard utility cap. Phu Loi, November 1965. *Author's collection.*

First sergeant of Headquarters Company, 588th Engineer Bn, wears the 1964–66 second-pattern utility shirt with clip-cornered pocket flap and higher top button. Note distinctive insignia worn on stiffened utility cap. Phu Loi, November 1965. *Author's collection.*

4th Transportation Command sergeants major wear utility uniforms with a mix of subdued and unsubdued insignia. Cat Lai, 1968. *U.S. Army.*

nal mirrors, maps, notebooks, and spare ammunition, which could be carried in the bellows pockets of American uniforms. Local tailors replaced the thin buttons, which easily snagged or broke, with American-made buttons wherever available. The tiger-stripe fatigues, however, became the most common choice for Army units requiring camouflage clothing before ERDL camouflage tropical combat uniforms became available. Even afterwards, the association of elite status with tiger-stripe garments insured their preferred wear by many troops.

The Advanced Research Projects Agency Research and Development (ARPA) field unit, of DOD, developed a Vietnamese lightweight, reversible field uniform that provided a military camouflage pattern on one side and was black on the other. The black side approxi-

mated the habitual peasant dress of indigenous natives, and, therefore, could serve as a disguise. This uniform originated with the U.S. Combat Development Test Center, Vietnam, which was equipping the Vietnamese special battalions (ranger) with camouflage clothing in late 1962. The center proposed a uniform that might offer this dual advantage of combat visual camouflage and peasant farmer disguise to rangers infiltrating Viet Cong–dominated areas.

The reversible uniform, printed with a camouflage pattern on one side and black on the other, was then developed by Natick Laboratories. The 10th Ranger Battalion field tested 140 of these prototype uniforms from November 1962 to February 1963. The Combat Development Test Center, Vietnam, rendered an interim report in early 1963, which stated that the

Lieutenant Simmons and Captain Clark point to bullet holes their UH1B medical evacuation helicopter received while over Bac Lieu, 27 October 1964. The Utility uniforms have truncated sleeves. Additional pencil pocket on captain's uniform (right) was typical of shirts tailored in Korea and worn in Vietnam at the time. *U.S. Army.*

concept of a reversible uniform was valid, and the uniform was especially effective if viewed from a distance by VC trail watchers and the like, but that second-generation models should be made of lighter-weight material.[8]

Beginning in early 1964, materials and patterns for the second-generation reversible uniform were sent to Vietnam's *Quân-Nhu* (Quartermaster) Military Clothing Production Center. By March, 450 ARPA reversible combat uniforms were manufactured, and most were distributed in April 1964 for combat evaluation as follows: (1) 120 sets to the 3d Airborne Ranger Company, 77th LLDB Group, at Do Xa in I CTZ; (2) 20 sets to SOG at Gia Vuc; (3) 100 sets to the 8th Airborne Battalion in III CTZ; (4) 110 sets to the 1st Airborne Ranger Company of the 31st LLDB Group in II CTZ; (5) 35 sets to the 33d Ranger Battalion at Tay Ninh; and (6) 50 sets to the 1st and 3d Marine Battalions in IV CTZ. Two of the test units,

SOG and the 77th LLDB Group, had the opportunity to use the black side of the uniform as a deception device and were able to approach the Viet Cong, in daylight, to within 10 meters before being detected.[9]

The ARPA reversible jacket and trousers were fabricated of a 5-ounce poplin made from 2-ply, all-cotton yarns, almost identical to the tropical combat uniform material. The fabric was imprinted on one side with ERDL camouflage. Black, 3-ply cotton fabric was used on the other side. The sleeves of the jacket had button closures on the cuff. There were two simple, open pockets at the bottom of the jacket on the black side, and two breast pockets with buttoned flap closures on the camouflage side. The trousers had no pockets on the black side but contained two front slash pockets and two hip pockets with buttoned flap closures on the reverse side.

The final report, following combat evalua-

Utility uniform trousers worn typically by a gun section of Battery B, 2d Bn, 13th Artillery. The center artilleryman wears the tropical combat uniform; the soldier second from right wears tropical trousers. 1967. *Author's collection.*

tion, was rendered by the Advanced Research Projects Agency on 2 January 1965. One of the most important results was the finding that ERDL camouflage provided effective camouflage in the jungle, mountain, savanna, and rice paddy regions of Vietnam. The ARPA reversible camouflage uniforms were never adopted as standard, but more were produced, especially in late-war response to requests from Provincial Reconnaissance Unit advisors of Project Phoenix. Some of these advisors remembered the earlier use of the ARPA reversible uniforms.

The Republic of Vietnam's 92d Quartermaster Air Equipment Repair Depot at Camp Van Don in the Saigon area was responsible for providing and repairing individual aerial gear of the South Vietnamese armed forces. An example of depot products were Vietnamese-produced McGuire rigs for MACV-SOG and Special Forces. Technical support was rendered by subordinate units. For example, parachute

material support for the ARVN Airborne Division was rendered by the 91st Quartermaster Aerial Supply Company.[10]

4.3 Utility Uniforms

The Army's *utility uniform*, or "fatigues," functioned as authorized field and work uniforms in Vietnam (the only other uniforms authorized for both purposes were the tropical combat uniform and hot weather field uniform). This uniform consisted of cotton sateen shirt and trousers Olive Green army shade 107; utility cap, or helmet if combat conditions warranted; and black leather service boots or tropical combat boots.

The *utility shirt* was normally worn tucked inside the *utility trousers*, unless senior commanders determined that unusually hot weather conditions made this arrangement uncomfortable. USARV regulations stated, "Major subordinate commanders may judi-

First-pattern utility uniform with straight pocket flaps worn by Maj. Gen. Delk Oden, commander of Army Support Command, Vietnam. Uniform has unsubdued insignia and is worn with general officer's belt, May 1964. *Author's collection.*

109th Quartermaster Company (Air Delivery) rigger Specialist Fourth Class Essley *(right)* and General Gates *(left)* wear the post-1966 third-pattern utility uniform having V-cut pocket flaps. Cam Ranh Bay. *Author's collection.*

ciously authorize the shirt to be outside the trousers as appropriate."[11] In cases of colder weather in Vietnam, the *field coat* was sometimes worn if permitted in the area. *See* Army Uniform Map of Vietnam.

The utility shirt was initially single-breasted with a collar and had two patch pockets with buttoned flaps, a straight-cut bottom, and plain sleeves. The shirt was worn open to the first button, which was sewn level with the top of the pocket flaps, exposing an unacceptably large expanse of the white T-shirt beneath. In 1964, the upper button was raised to reduce undershirt visibility. Cuffed sleeves were later added and became common by 1966.

The utility trousers contained two front patch pockets, two hip patch pockets with but-

toned flaps, hemmed bottoms, and either button or slide fastener front closure. A lightweight utility uniform of the same design, but fabricated of poplin, was used in Vietnam from 1969 to 1972.

USARV restricted the wear of the utility uniform to "only when absolutely necessary," after the tropical combat uniform was declared the principal duty uniform on 27 October 1967. This change was implemented because the utility uniform was not specifically designed for tropical climate, and stocks of tropical combat

A lieutenant of the 926th Medical Detachment wearing the third-pattern utility uniform, stands beside his ¼ ton vehicle. Typically, his uniform has sagged and become rumpled in the tropical heat despite obvious ironing. *Author's collection.*

Specialist Fourth Class Franz, 109th Quartermaster Company (Air Delivery) rigger, wears waist belt with black buckle, second-pattern utility trousers with button fly, and third-pattern utility shirt with V-cut pocket flaps at Cam Ranh Bay, 1968. *Author's collection.*

uniforms reached levels that encouraged this transition.[12]

The durable press, polyester cotton utility uniform was not tested in the United States until 9 March 1973, the same month that the last American troops withdrew from Vietnam in accordance with the Paris peace accords. The field testing of this uniform was originally scheduled to begin in March 1972, but production problems delayed its manufacture. As early as 1970, however, some durable press utility uniforms were privately purchased through post exchanges.

4.4 Khaki and Tan Summer Service Uniforms

Khaki and tan uniforms constituted the Army-wide summer service uniform apparel throughout the Vietnam era. In 1956, Military Advisory and Assistance Group, Vietnam (MAAG-Vietnam) decided that these summer service uniforms would function well for year-round duty in the region's tropical climate. In 1960, Lt. Gen. Lionel C. McGarr, the commander of MAAG-Vietnam, designated the khaki and tan uniforms as the normal duty uniform in Vietnam, unless the soldier was in the field or on fatigue or security details. This ruling was affirmed by MACV upon its inception in 1962.

During mid-1967, because the level of combat in Vietnam had risen, USARV reviewed its duty uniform policy in Vietnam. As a result of this review, General Westmoreland declared that field or work uniforms (i.e., tropical combat and utility uniforms) were bet-ter suited for most Vietnam conditions, and he designated these as the principal duty attire. The wearing of khaki and tan uniforms declined drastically after October 1967, even for travel purposes. This situation did not change for three years.

The MACV policy on khaki and tan uniforms began to reverse itself under General Abrams' direction in late 1970. He desired to enhance U.S. public perceptions that the South Vietnamese were taking over more of the fighting. This meant favoring service uniform apparel over field clothing (which had combat connotations) wherever possible. On 1 October 1970, for instance, he ordered khaki and tan uniforms worn on flights returning from Vietnam to the United States. This transition was only a token substitution, however, because of the actual battlefield demands on Army troops still stationed in Vietnam. General Abrams ordered an extensive study of the duty uniform policy in the spring of 1972, but the sudden North Vietnamese *Nguyen Hue* (Easter) offen-

Special Forces troopers, wearing Army khaki uniforms with M1956 shirt patterns with pleated pockets, salute a fallen comrade killed in Vietnam as his coffin is flown from Tan Son Nhut, 9 May 1963. *Robert Cabral.*

The Army khaki uniform with second-pattern shirt being worn by Sp4 Stephen Murray. Nameplate, Sharpshooter Qualification Badge, and Combat Infantryman's Badge above service ribbons adorn uniform. *Author's collection.*

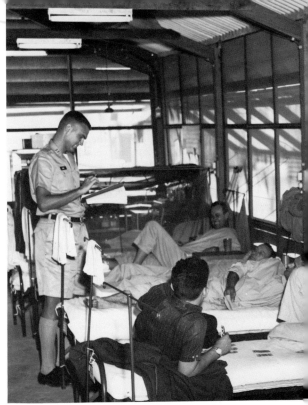

Abbreviated Army khaki uniform being worn by medical officer checking ward of the 3d Field Hospital in Saigon, 1965. *Author's collection.*

sive temporarily blocked plans to downgrade the field uniform status.

In June 1972, Gen. Frederick C. Weyand became the commander of MACV. He was presented the staff study favoring the return of khaki and tan uniforms as the normal duty uniform in Vietnam. The study cited lowered levels of combat activity, diminishing numbers of troops stationed in the country, and a need to improve soldier appearance as reasons for the change. On 1 July 1972, General Weyand ordered MACV to again designate khaki and tan uniforms as the standard duty attire for non-field situations, and this policy remained in effect until the end of the conflict in 1975.[13]

The Army *khaki uniform* consisted of cotton twill shirt and trousers, 8.2-ounce Khaki army shade 1. This cotton khaki cloth could not hold a crease and had to be starched to maintain a decent appearance. With the Vietnam "rice starching," which did not hold up well, the khaki uniforms looked very disheveled after only a short time in tropical heat. Garrison caps and black low-quarter shoes were normally worn with the khaki uniform, but certain elements, such as color guards, military police, or airborne units, were authorized to wear black leather boots instead.

The khaki uniform was issued in a long-sleeve shirt and conventional trouser combination and in an "abbreviated" version. The latter was adopted in 1955, consisting of short-sleeve shirt, knee-length shorts, and socks reaching just below the knee. During 1959, regulations were amended to allow the wearing of the short-sleeve shirt with conventional trousers, and this style became so popular that many long sleeves were truncated by 1965.

In Vietnam, the abbreviated uniform was discouraged because of its French colonial appearance; it was specifically banned past 20 December 1966. The short-sleeve shirt/long trouser uniform became the accepted khaki or tan uniform version, and MACV Directive 670-1 of 20 June 1966 stated, "Effective 1 July 1966, the Army Khaki and Army Tan short sleeve shirt is the only shirt authorized for wear. Shortening of the sleeves of the long sleeve shirt in accordance with DA Circular 670-1 is authorized."[14]

Below: Capt. Roger Harms (left) and 1Lt. Eugune Doll (right) wear the Army tan, or "tropical worsted (TW)," uniform with coat while attending a 11th Inf Bde party in Hawaii with their wives prior to the unit's departure for Vietnam. *Author's collection.*

Although long-sleeve shirts were eliminated from Vietnam service, an earlier MACV announcement of 17 November 1965, ordered that "garments with short sleeves will be worn only in areas where the malaria hazard does not exist." This decision was made after malaria devastated the fighting strength of the newly arrived 1st Cavalry Division at An Khe.[15] Although short-sleeve shirts were prohibited in

Above: First MACV commander Gen. Paul Harkins (center) wears the Army tan uniform with frame buckle at Tan Son Nhut, 10 September 1963. Aviation officer (right) wears PX-purchased utility uniform featuring shoulder loops and cargo pockets on trousers. The uniform was popular among parachutists at the time. *U.S. Army.*

certain malarial-prone regions, medical case-by-case decisions downgraded local hazard levels, and numerous exceptions eventually nullified the restriction.

The Army *tan uniform* was composed of shirt and trousers, shade M1 or army shade 445. It was made of one of the following fabrics: 9.5-ounce tropical wool, 11-ounce wool gabardine, a polyester/wool blend, or a polyester/rayon durable press fabric, which was the

latest to be used. The polyester/rayon fabric was preferred in Vietnam because of the breathability of the weave. The tan uniform remained private purchase throughout the war, however, because large quantities of khaki uniforms existed within the supply system. The tan uniform was normally worn with garrison cap and low-quarter shoes. Parachutists and military police wore black leather boots.

In February 1968, the Army Chief of Staff ordered the expeditious development of a durable press, light tan summer duty uniform. The shirt was to have seven military creases. At the time, available commercial production techniques for durable-press fabrics were inefficient in applying multiple sharp creases. Attaining the close shade tolerances required by the military also was a problem for commercial production. Natick Laboratories evolved new procedures to apply the shirt creases, overcome problems in shade control, and provide for the retention of permanent-press qualities.

The wash and wear rayon/polyester uniform, Tan army shade 445, was introduced in 1969. A summer test involving 600 drill sergeants throughout the United States rendered a 98 percent acceptability rate. Unfortunately, many soldiers experienced difficulties with these uniforms when purchased through the post exchange system. The *Army Personnel Letter* of 1 October 1969 reported, "Among the complaints has been the absence of truly wash and wear qualities in this clothing, even when it is laundered strictly in accordance with instructions."[16] The Army implemented actions to remedy these quality-control problems, and, although the uniform was not standardized until 21 June 1973, DA approved wearing the durable-press tan shirt and trousers commencing March 1970.

4.5 Service and Dress Uniforms

The Army's *tan uniform with coat,* which dated from 1942 and served as the Army's summer service uniform until 1964, was more commonly referred to as the tropical worsted or "TW" uniform, Tan army shade 61. The term,

Gen. William Westmoreland, the second MACV commander, wears the Army green uniform as the Army Chief of Staff. *U.S. Army.*

The Army blue uniform worn by the U.S. Army Vietnam Band (266th Army Band) with band distinctions. 1967. *USARV PIO.*

TW, was used officially until 1959 when regulations redesignated all uniforms by their color instead of their material. Most troops during the Vietnam era, however, continued to refer to this uniform as "TWs," regardless of its material content.

The uniform was usually manufactured of a lightweight wool weave called tropical worsted wool, but it was also made of wool/polyester and gabardine. This uniform's pattern served as the basis for the Army green uniform and fell out of favor after a lightweight green uniform became available. The "TW" coat uniform was permitted as optional wear in Vietnam until 31 December 1968 but could only be worn by officers and noncommissioned officers for events connected with travel to or from Vietnam, such as leave or R & R, temporary duty to other countries, or reassignment from Vietnam.

The Army adopted the *Army green uniform* on 2 September 1954, and it became available at quartermaster supply outlets two years later. After a transition period to allow wear-out of existing uniforms, the green uniform, army shade 44, became mandatory winter service attire in September 1961. The coat was a single-breasted, four-button coat with

The Army white uniform being worn with dress aiguillette by the Defense Attaché to the Republic of Vietnam, Maj. Gen. John Murray. *Author's collection.*

SSgt. Charles Morris of the 82d Abn Div wears the Army green uniform and garrison cap with airborne insignia. Note blue infantry discs beneath enlisted insignia on lapels, nameplate, ribbons, parachutist badge on background trimming, blue infantryman shoulder cord on right shoulder, and French fourragère on his left. *Author's collection.*

peaked lapels, was fitted slightly at the waist, and was worn with four-in-hand knot necktie and *tan shirt*. The shirt was initially long-sleeve and either cotton, Tan army shade 46, or polyester/cotton, Tan army shade 446. Optional wear of a short-sleeve poplin shirt, Tan army shade 446, with the green uniform was authorized by DA commencing 4 October 1967.[17]

The Army green uniform worn in Vietnam was the lightweight style adopted on 13 July 1964 as the new summer service uniform replacing the "TW" coat uniform. It was manufactured of 10-ounce polyester/wool blend fabric in tropical or gabardine weave, and became available for optional purchase through Army clothing sales stores on 1 July 1965. Soldiers in transit, however, could often be seen wearing the heavier Army green uniforms made of wool serge or gabardine.

In 1955, Gen. Maxwell D. Taylor had ordered black mohair braid for the trim on the Army green uniform. This was used in lieu of gold trim for the officer's coat-sleeve bands and trouser stripes. Russet was the shade originally proposed for the low-quarter shoes, cap visor, necktie, and socks. In 1954, this was changed to black in the interest of service standardization with the Navy and Air Force. These black accessories also harmonized with the Army blue and white uniforms and assisted supply and fiscal procurement, but they made the gold coat buttons and light tan shirt the only contrasting elements of the Army green uniform.[18]

The Army green uniform was considered the normal service uniform for the winter season, so its wear in Vietnam was restricted. Career Regular Army personnel were authorized to wear the Army green uniform for travel purposes to and from Vietnam, such as for R & R, temporary duty to another country, leave, or at the conclusion of their combat tour. Advisors assigned to the *Trường Võ-Bị Quốc-Gia* (Vietnamese Military Academy) at Dalat, however, were authorized to wear the Army green uniform on a year-round basis as their normal duty uniform throughout the war "as appropriate, considering both weather and activity."[19]

The *Army blue uniform* was the principal dress uniform of the Army during the war but was rarely worn in Vietnam. On some occasions, the USARV Band (266th Army Band) wore the blue uniform, but this was restricted to practice in preparation for wartime music tours of Australia.

The *Army white uniform* was manufactured of 8.2-ounce cotton twill, 11-ounce wool gabardine, or polyester/wool and polyester/viscose blended fabric. The coat was a single-breasted, peaked-lapel, four-button design, fitted slightly at the waist. The lower sleeve of officer and warrant officer uniforms was decorated with a 1.5-inch-wide band of white cotton or mohair braid. When worn with a bow tie, the Army white uniform was a dress uniform corresponding to civilian summer tuxedo or "black tie dress." With the four-in-hand tie, the white uniform was considered a service uniform. Both versions were authorized as optional wear on appropriate occasions, such as

U.S. Army *(left)* and Corps of Engineers, Officers *(right)*, pierced-design, 36-line-type buttons for the Army green, blue, tan, or white uniform coats were either gold plated, gold color, or anodized aluminum. *Author's collection.*

high-command social functions in Laos or Vietnam. Army advisors stationed at Dalat with the Vietnamese Military Academy and members of the Defense Attaché Office wore the white uniform as formal "after-six" attire.

In Thailand, the green uniform was equivalent to the Royal Thai blouse uniform, while the white uniforms of both nations were comparable. The Army white uniform was worn with sword and full medals at the annual Thai Ceremony of Taking the Oath before the Colors and at the Trooping of the Colors on His Majesty's Birthday. The white uniform was also appropriate at three other Thai events: (1) military weddings, for the water pouring ceremony; (2) cremations, when the deceased was a military person, or when Their Majesties were present, with addition of sword and mourning band preferred; and (3) other military functions as protocol demanded.

4.6 Female Attire

Army female personnel in Vietnam were primarily members of the Women's Army Corps (WAC), Nurse Corps, or medical service branches. In Vietnam the female service uniform was the Army *green cord uniform* fabricated of 4.3-ounce polyester and cotton cord,

Green Striped army shade 160. The complete uniform consisted of the Army green cord garrison cap or Army green hat, short-sleeve coat, skirt, nylon or silk stockings, and black pumps made of fine-grain calfskin or poromeric material with a leather finish.[20]

The *green cord coat* was hip length, single-breasted, and unlined. The coat had a rounded, open collar, short cuffed sleeves, sewn-down shoulder loops, slanted hip pockets, and a four-button front closure. The collar and cuffs were trimmed with a dark-green polyester edge braid. The six-gore *skirt*, with concealed slide fastener closure at the left side, had a sewn-on waistband with a single-button left-side closure. Skirt length was established by following Table 1 in Technical Manual 10-229, which, ideally, kept skirt hems just below the knees. In Vietnam, the skirts were often shortened, despite these regulations, and worn above the knees.

Accessories for the green cord uniform included black leather service *handbag*; nylon/cotton *gloves*, Gray-Beige army shade 270; and acrylic fiber and rayon flannel *scarf*, Gray-Beige army shade 273. On parade occasions, the USARV WAC Detachment wore the green cord uniform with gloves and yellow ascots, decorated with USARV organizational shoul-

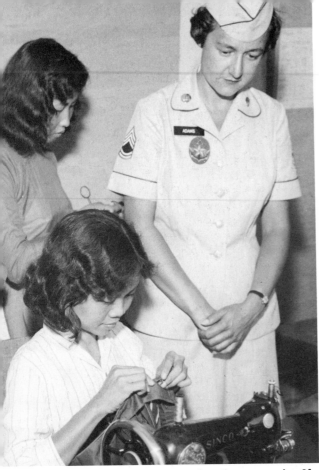

The Army green cord uniform worn by Sfc. Betty Adams, the first enlisted WAC military advisor to Vietnam. Note the red and silver *Quân-Đội Việt-Nam Cộng-Hòa* (RVNAF) advisory pocket patch below nameplate. Saigon, 9 March 1965. *U.S. Army.*

der sleeve insignia sewn on the ascot's center. Commencing 1 February 1967, female military personnel could wear the detachable patch of their shoulder sleeve insignia, enclosed in plastic and fastened below the right collar of the Army green cord uniform.

The *raincoat, green, with removable havelock,* was Green army shade 274, cotton and polyester poplin, styled in a belted and double-breasted pattern with plain buttons. By regulation, the raincoat bottom was one inch longer than the uniform skirt hem. The detachable havelock fit over the headgear and was visor-styled with an adjustable front closure.

USARV ordered female personnel to wear the woman's *hot weather field uniform* as their principal duty uniform commencing 7 February 1969. This relegated the Army green cord uniform to optional attire at the discretion of the commanders who had female personnel in their units.[21] The hot weather field uniform was composed of the utility cap; cotton poplin field shirt and slacks, Olive Green army shade 107; and women's black leather service boots or black leather oxford shoes.

The *hot weather field shirt* was single-breasted with side vents and had two breast patch pockets with buttoned flaps and a patch pocket on the left sleeve. The shirt also had buttoned shoulder loops, a convertible collar, and a five-button front closure with a protective flap to prevent areas between buttons from being exposed. The hot weather field *slacks* were tapered with two front or side, bellows-type pockets; front and back waistbands; and a two-button closure with protective gusset at each side.

Female troops in Vietnam expressed general dissatisfaction with the utility cap and pressed for adoption of the tropical hat with their hot weather field uniform. MACV policy permitted this substitution, reasoning that it contributed to their military appearance and promoted the maintenance of proper hair styles. The U.S. Army Garrison of Long Binh Post, where the USARV WAC Detachment was

SSgt. Charlene Kahl and SSgt. Catherine Kahl, twins who joined the Army together in January 1966, wear Army green cord uniforms in the USARV Personnel Actions Branch at Long Binh, 19 June 1969. *Army News Features.*

The hot weather field uniform and green cord uniform worn by women personnel visiting FSB Blaze, July 1969. *101st Abn Div PIO.*

stationed, changed its regulation to reflect this policy on 26 June 1970: "The tropical combat hat may be worn by all female military personnel at any time."[22]

When General Abrams began considering the restriction of tropical hats, senior USARV WAC officer Lt. Col. Shirley Barnwell recommended, on 20 April 1970, that the rules for WAC personnel should match the rules for male personnel.[23] Senior MACV officers, however, desired to eliminate the wear of the tropical hats and felt that continuing female wear of this headgear might diminish its acceptance among male soldiers. This attitude, combined

The hot weather field uniform is worn by an officer of the 22d Surgical Hospital *(left)*. Another officer wears the green cord uniform *(right)*. I CTZ, July 1969. *101st Abn Div PIO.*

The first female field uniform worn in Vietnam consisted of cotton herringbone twill (HBT) shirt and cotton, sateen carded slacks. The hot weather field uniform was developed to provide a suitable and functional replacement for this antiquated outfit. Because the hot weather field uniform did not complete quartermaster service tests until November 1963, the older garment continued to be worn until 1968. But it was rarely seen after 1966. *Author's collection.*

An Army nurse of the 45th Surgical Hospital at Tay Ninh wears the hot weather field uniform with pocket pen slots, used here to hold keys and scissors. *Author's collection.*

with strong female preference for the tropical hat, caused MACV to grant a special exception for WAC and nurse personnel on 17 September 1971, while restricting the tropical hat in other units. (For more on the Tropical Hat, *see section* 3.5, Military Hats.)

The *white hospital duty uniform* consisted of a 4.5-ounce cotton poplin, one-piece, single-breasted dress. The bodice was secured by three buttons, and the lower skirt portion had a fly-fastened front closure. The separate belt, made of the same dress material, was worn with the tab pointing to the wearer's left. The sleeves were quarter-length and had cuffs worn with cuff link closures. The white, cotton broadcloth *hospital duty uniform cap,* authorized

A Women's Army Corps captain wears the hot weather field uniform while attending a USARV ceremony in Long Binh. *U.S. Army.*

Nurses and officers of the 3d Surgical Hospital at Bien Hoa, October 1966, wear the hot weather field uniform, tropical combat uniform, and utility uniform. Note first-pattern utility uniform (center) and buttoned sleeves on utility shirt (second from right). *Author's collection.*

only for officers and warrant officers, was centered high on the back of the head.[24]

Female appearance tended to follow civilian fashion, independent of military directives. By regulation, the hair was to "be neat and well groomed, and will not extend below the bottom edge of the collar nor be cut so short as to present an unfeminine appearance. Makeup and nail polish will be in good taste." MACV directives stated, "Hair ornaments such as ribbons will not be worn. Pins, combs, or barrettes similar in color to the individual's hair may be worn."[25]

Off-duty female civilian attire varied con-

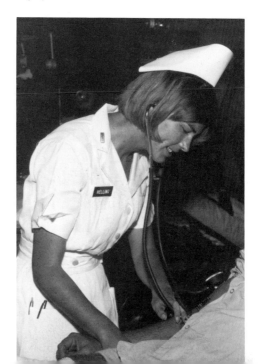

The white hospital duty uniform worn by 1Lt. Margaret Helling, the general duty nurse of the surgical ward at the 8th Field Hospital in Nha Trang, 23 February 1966. *U.S. Army.*

siderably from MACV command directives. For instance, T-shirts, tank tops, or halters as outer garments were prohibited, but, because of the tropical climate, these items were worn despite the regulations. MACV also restricted shorts to bermuda-length pants with straight hemmed or cuffed edges, but shorter shorts became popular as wartime fashions followed civilian trends.[26]

Notes

1. USARV Memorandum 670-1, 27 Oct 67.
2. MACV Directive 670-1, Change 2, 17 Nov 65, Para d.1.
3. Author's conversation with Jeffrey L. Junkins, 20 Jan 88.
4. Quartermaster Research & Engineering Command, *Clothing & Equipment Development Branch Series Report No. 26,* Feb 62.
5. U.S. Army Military History Institute File #2021-6, Base Hall Vietnam War Documents Collection, Carlisle, Pennsylvania.
6. RVN Ministry of Defense, *Annual Inspection Report #3730: TTM/TTQL/NCCT/KH,* 7 Aug 70.
7. Conversation with John C. Andrews, 1 Jan 88.
8. Dr. S. J. Kennedy, *Preliminary Evaluation of the Individual Clothing and Equipment of Vietnamese Military Forces,* Natick Laboratories, 15 Jul 63.
9. Advanced Research Projects Agency Research and Development, *Field Unit Report: Proj 2K-453,* 2 Jan 65.
10. RVN Ministry of Defense, *Annual Inspection Report #3263: TTM/TTQL/NCCT/KH,* 29 Aug 70.
11. USARV Reg 670-5, 26 Feb 68.
12. USARV Memorandum 670-1, 27 Oct 67.
13. MACV Directive 670-1, 12 Apr 72, 2.
14. MACV Directive 670-1, 20 Jun 66, 4.
15. MACV Directive 670-1, Change 2, 17 Nov 65.
16. *Army Personnel Letter #18-69,* 1 Oct 69.
17. MACV *Observer,* Vol. 6, No. 22, 4 Oct 67, 2.
18. Stephen J. Kennedy and Alice F. Park, *The Army Green Uniform,* Army Materiel Command, Mar 68.
19. MACV Directive 670-1, 2 Jul 64 and subsequent editions.
20. DA Reg 670-30, Aug 66, with Change 1, 11 Jun 68.
21. USARV Memorandum 670-1, 7 Feb 69.
22. U.S. Army Garrison, Long Binh Post, Vietnam (Provisional) Reg 670-5, 1 Sep 69, with Change 2.
23. USARV AVHGA-SM Disposition Form, Subj: Headgear for female personnel from Lt. Col. George C. Hoffmaster, Jr., 20 Apr 70, with Tabs A-D.
24. DA Reg 670-30, May 69, 13-1.
25. DA Reg 670-30, Aug 66, 5, and May 69, 1-2; MACV Directive 670-1, 5 Jan 73, Annex A.
26. MACV Directive 670-1, 5 Jan 73, 4.

5

Protective Gear

5.1 Basic Body Armor

The Army's individual protective armor, available at the start of the Vietnam conflict, was developed out of the experience of World War II and the Korean war when fragmentation wounds caused the majority of casualties. This protective armor proved inadequate against the higher velocity of small arms fire in Vietnam. Additionally, the body armor was cumbersome, relatively heavy, and hot to wear. The sweltering tropical heat retained by the vest sapped body strength and caused severe sweating, dehydration, and even heat prostration. Throughout the war, body armor was seldom seen on Army personnel, unless they were in mechanized units like the 11th Armored Cavalry or were manning positions that required little movement.

Although body armor had many disadvantages, it did save lives. SSgt. John O. Huffman of the 39th Engineer Battalion rappelled to clear a jungle landing zone near Chu Lai in August 1968. He was hit in the back as he reached the ground, and the impact knocked

him about six feet. "Just as I was about to get my balance, I was hit again and flew another six feet. Five more times I was thrown forward. Finally, I got under cover and directed the fire of the patrol in the sniper's direction. I don't know if we got him, but I was OK. I just had a long arc of bruises up my back." Huffman's vest was struck by seven-7.62mm bullets fired from a captured U.S. weapon.[1]

A host of frantic wartime research and engineering programs attempted to make protective gear more lightweight and to improve the ballistic performance of textile armor, but the results were disappointing. Developers realized that only a small fraction of their fabrics' energy-absorbing potential was being utilized. The military remained unaware of the advantages offered by DuPont's 1965 invention of Kevlar fiber, which formed the basis of postwar body armor.[2]

The first Army units arriving in Vietnam were well furnished with individual armor, but the equipment was relegated to the rear where it was neglected and became difficult to retrieve. Many units arriving later did not bring

Members of the 11th Armored Cavalry wear M1952 fragmentation protective body armor in typical combat fashion. The trooper *(right)* carries grenades on the vest hangers over each pocket. *Author's collection.*

Demolitions expert wears M1952 fragmentation protective body armor as he removes a VC mechanical ambush device from the path of a Rome Plow dozer in the Iron Triangle. 3 September 1967. *Author's collection.*

body armor with them; body armor stocks became depleted and shortages persisted. For instance, in 1966, the 1st Infantry Division expended its supplies of protective vests, which were not satisfactorily replenished until 1968.[3] Sometimes senior commanders refrained from ordering body armor even where situations demanded increased personal protection. An example was the sanguinary Battle for Hill 937, or "Hamburger Hill," which started 11 May 1969.

The two assaulting battalions (1st Battalion, 506th Infantry and 3d Battalion, 187th Infantry) fought uphill against entrenched bunker lines for five days before helicopters dropped protective masks and personal armor to them on 16 May. On the previous day a battalion commander, Lt. Col. Weldon F. Honeycutt, was wounded by rocket-propelled grenade fragments that lodged close to his spine. Only then was body armor dispensed to the troops as a "preventive measure against the increasing amount of shrapnel" striking the soldiers on the mountain.[4]

The *body armor, fragmentation protective, vest with 3/4 collar, titanium/nylon com-*

The T66-1 lightweight ''felt vest'' worn in experimental testing at Camp Pickett, Virginia, under the supervision of Aberdeen Proving Grounds. 17 April 1967. *U.S. Army.*

posite, was developed just before the Vietnam conflict to protect against flechettes and high-velocity fragments. In November 1964, the composite titanium-nylon vest, weighing 9 pounds in the medium size, was classified Standard A issue within the Army, although production tests were not completed until December 1965.[5]

The titanium-nylon vest's ballistic composite filler consisted of three layers of ballistic nylon. Two of these layers were completely covered with overlapping, 0.032-inch titanium metal plates, which were attached by stapling. The protective collar was composed of six layers of ballistic nylon, and the vest's tear-resistant ballistic cover was made of 3-ounce protective nylon cloth. For proper fit, the side flaps were laced together. The front was closed by a Velcro fastener. Pivot shoulder pads with foam rubber undersides were sewn to the vest at the neckline and laced on the other sides, allowing

Decorated tank crewmen and officers of the 1st Bn, 69th Armor (4th Inf Div), wear the fragmentation protective body armor, ¾ collar. West of Pleiku, January 1970. *Author's collection.*

the shoulder pads to move when either arm was raised. For assistance in weapons firing, cotton duck *rifle patches* were sewn to the shoulder padding and chest. This armor was not used often in Vietnam because of its greater stiffness, inflexibility, and heat retention than other variants of personal armor.

The armor most often issued to Army combatants in Vietnam was the standard B M1952 *fragmentation protective body armor.* This 8.5-pound armor contained three panels of ballistic filler, each using 12 plies of nylon ballistic cloth with yarns comparable to those in tire cords. These panels were spot-bonded with laminating resin. The filler was encased in a waterproof vinyl film and inserted into the outer nylon fabric cover. The cover had two bellows patch pockets, a front slide fastener covered by a snapped flap, elastic side laces, grenade hangers over each front pocket, and shoulder loops.

The *body armor, fragmentation protective, 3/4 collar,* was a slightly improved 1969 modification of the vest with stitched interior panels and an added protective neck collar. Unfortunately, the collar interfered with normal helmet wear. Both versions of the M1952 body armor had numerous design and construction problems. These included filler that bunched and migrated and a nondurable outer shell, which could be punctured, causing a reduction in ballistic protection. Also, the armor absorbed moisture and became heavy. A "Vietnam quick-fix" consisted of adding plastic stiffeners to alleviate the bunching and migration of the filler, but this increased the vest's weight, bulk, and stiffness.[6]

5.2 Lightweight Body Armor

The Army considered standard ballistic, nylon armor vests too heavy for LINCLOE purposes and ordered development of a lightweight body armor on 23 February 1966. Natick Laboratories adopted the "layer principle," a compromise that offered less protection overall but improved protection for the heart and spinal areas, since extra armor pieces could be attached to a basic layer for better protection of these vital body regions.[7]

The Army's variable type body armor. *Natick Laboratories.*

The exposure of armed helicopter crew members, such as this door gunner, necessitated the development of protective vests beyond the inadequate M1952 body armor worn here. *Author's collection.*

The basic layer, developed under this concept, was the *T66-1 lightweight body armor* nylon "felt vest." A lighter version of the standard M52 vest, weighing 4 pounds, 8 ounces, it gave equivalent protection to vital areas and 15 percent less protection to other areas. The new vest was fabricated from one layer of 6-ounce ballistic needle-punched nylon felt and two layers of ballistic nylon woven material. The panel-edge overlapping and elastic restraints of the felt filler eased body movement. The filler was enclosed in a polyethylene casing to prevent moisture absorption. Four plies of 4-inch-wide ballistic-protection nylon were stitched over the heart and spine portions.

The outside cover and collar were made of tear-resistant ballistic-protective nylon with drainage eyelets at the bottom seam. Shoulder patches of cotton duck assisted in positioning shoulder-fired weapons. The vest had two nylon, bellows patch pockets and cotton webbing grenade hangers. The front closure and elastic side laces were identical to standard vests.

Samples of the prototype lightweight felt vests were demonstrated in Vietnam by a special Army Materiel Command team during February and March 1966. USARV requested 200 lightweight felt body armor vests for combat testing on 21 March. Natick Laboratories air delivered the first 200 vests to Vietnam under ENSURE priority on 17 September 1966. Most of these vests were sent to the 1st Cavalry Division at An Khe for appraisal. ACTIV's final report of 22 June 1967 was noncommittal, recommending further testing of the lightweight felt vest by armor and mechanized troops.[8]

The second production quantity of 200 lightweight felt vests was extensively tested at Aberdeen Proving Grounds, Maryland, from 27 March to 19 July 1967. During this evaluation, the basic T66-1 vest was compared to the

The curved Pilot's torso shield was developed for Vietnam helicopter crewmen in 1963 but interfered with aircraft instrument operation. *Natick Laboratories.*

entire torso. Front and back ceramic-fiberglass plates for small arms protection could be worn with the felt vest. The vest with removable plates gave five protective options to the wearer.

Army Materiel Command ordered 42,000 *body armor, small arms, protective ground troops, front-back plate with vest,* in May 1968, at a cost of $800 per vest. Natick Laboratories dispatched the first 500 vests to USARV under ENSURE priority on 16 August. By the end of September, 913 vests reached Vietnam, and 2,000 vests were in country by 30 November. ACTIV tested the degree of ballistic protection offered, the ability of the ceramic plates to withstand rough handling, and the durability of the vest with or without plates. One of DA's greatest concerns was the combined weight of the ceramic plates, each of which weighed 7.5 pounds. On 21 May 1969, the final ACTIV report concluded, "increased protection of ceramic plates offsets extra weight for personnel engaged in physically undemanding duties."

From June 1969 through March 1970, between 1,500 and 4,500 variable-type body armor vests were shipped to Vietnam each month. In accordance with ACTIV instructions, these were employed primarily in motorized, boat unit, and stationary operations. The ENSURE priority was terminated on 31 March 1970 as the Army initiated action to make further resupply routine.[10]

5.4 Body Armor for Air Crewmen

It was fortunate that in 1962, just as low-flying Army aviation crews became dramatically exposed to direct rifle and machine-gun fire in Vietnam, Goodyear Aircraft Corporation was developing armor that utilized a ceramic shield laminated to a dozen layers of glass-reinforced plastic. Further development introduced monolithic ceramic plates that eliminated the bending and breaking of the small squares, previously used in construction and reduced overall weight by 20 percent. Technical advances in material development reduced the weight of the first body armor front and back plates from 27.5 pounds to 17 pounds.[11]

Until mid-1964, the development of air crew personal armor and aircraft armor were

standard 12-ply nylon vest and gave a mixed performance in areas designed for full protection, being superior in only two out of the five technical testing conditions. The inconclusive Aberdeen testing and lukewarm USARV analysis caused DA to lose interest in further development of lightweight felt vest designs.[9]

5.3 Variable-type Body Armor

Development of personal protection for ground troops in Vietnam was redirected toward variable-type body armor systems, using ceramic-fiberglass technology. The system featured a 5.5-pound ballistic-nylon felt vest that gave fragmentation protection for the intertwined. This arrangement produced some unsuitable combination protective systems. In August 1964, the Army assigned aircraft armor design to the Aviation Materiel Command, and air crew body armor development to Natick Laboratories. This separation streamlined future developments.

Initially, Army air crewmen in Vietnam relied on either the World War II Army flyer's flak vest and groin armor, or the standard M52 fragmentation protective vest. The flak vest was composed of overlapping manganese steel plates inserted into a cloth carrier, weighing 17 pounds, 6 ounces. At first, CH21 Shawnee helicopter pilots in Vietnam laid two of the armor flak vests in the nose bubble of their aircraft, while their crew chiefs and gunners sat on extra armor vests, but even this arrangement proved inadequate against the penetrating power of small arms fire.[12]

The Army Transportation Research and Engineering Command (TRECOM), the forerunner of Aviation Materiel Laboratories, sent a team to Vietnam from 1 August to 20 September 1962. The team surveyed ballistic protection for air crews and designed the *pilot's shield and tipping plate kit,* which weighed 17.5 pounds. By January 1963, 150 kits were sent to Vietnam-based CH21 Shawnee and UH1-series Huey helicopter crews from TRECOM.

The kit consisted of a shield that was placed in front of the aviator's chest and rested on his thighs, and tipping plates that were banded to the aircraft's interior sides. Theoretically, the plates decreased the bullet's penetrating power by tipping the projectile so it would hit the pilot's shield with larger surface area. The one-inch-thick pilot's shield was made of Doron, a World War II fiberglass fabric, plied and bonded together with polyester resin. This heavy shield, however, put too much weight on the pilot's legs, and the system was discarded as impractical.[13]

Lighter composites were used in the TRECOM *chest protectors,* composed of ceramic-reinforced plastic, which also arrived in Vietnam during 1963. Unfortunately, the chest protectors were designed to be used in the same manner as the unsatisfactory Doron shields. As a result, they were so uncomfortable that they were rarely used as intended. Instead some crew chiefs wired the shields to troop seats.

Sp5 Herbert Donaldson, a medical evacuation crewman, wears the small arms protective Aircrewmen armor. Long Binh, 1967. *U.S. Army.*

"The pilots complained that the weight and positioning of the shield on their laps caused such discomfort and restriction that they preferred exposure to small arms fire."[14]

The *curved pilot's torso shield* was introduced to Vietnam in May 1963. This 18.5-pound torso shield was made of 13 curved ceramic tiles bonded to a shell that extended from the wearer's collarbone to the groin area. It was held in place by shoulder straps and a lower supporting extension. The shield was more comfortable than its predecessors but interfered with operation of aircraft instruments.[15]

The *T65-1 small arms protective torso armor carrier,* or "armor carrier," was produced by Natick Laboratories for Vietnam service late in 1964. The cloth carrier had large pockets that contained a front torso plate for the pilot and co-pilot or front and back plates for

Helicopter crewmen, wearing small arms protective aircrewmen armor, front and back with carrier, refuel their UH1D. 14 March 1966. *U.S. Army.*

armor height than the earlier straps with snaps. The new carrier opened only on the right rather than on both shoulders, so the front and back units remained joined for ease in removal. Ballistic nylon felt was added to the shoulder padding and inner lining of the plate pockets. Instead of multiple ceramic tiles, which were intrinsically weak at the joints, monolithic, curved, rigid plates made of alumina-oxide ceramic glass-reinforced plastic were used. The resulting armor carrier offered much better protection and comfort. It began reaching Vietnam during March and April 1966.[17]

The *body armor, fragmentation, small*

Pilot of an O1 Bird Dog dons his ''chicken plate'' small arms protective fragmentation body armor, pilot/co-pilot version at Bien Hoa. *Army News Features.*

the gunners, who exposed their backs as they moved about the aircraft. The front and back units were attached by snaps at the padded shoulder sections. The sides of the carrier were closed by wrap-around Velcro flaps.

In March and April of 1965, a five-man team from Army Materiel Command visited all Army aviation units in Vietnam and modified the 500 TRECOM chest protectors that were still available. These were shortened by three inches in order to be placed inside cloth carriers, which were based on the T65-1 design of Natick Laboratories and produced in Vietnam. Both this field-expedient carrier and the regular T65-1 carrier were enthusiastically received by Army aviation crews, especially crew chiefs and door gunners.[16]

The improved *aircrewmen armor, small arms protective, front and back with carrier,* or "chicken plate armor," was introduced at the beginning of 1966. Elastic webbing replaced the nonstretch fabric at the sides, and sliding shoulder straps allowed better adjustment of

arms protective, aircrewmen (as it was later redesignated) was improved throughout the war. Later the armor plates were incorporated into the *spall reduction pockets* of a pullover vest, made of plies of lightweight ballistic nylon that covered the torso. Vest adjustment and removal was expedited by two quick-release snap fasteners on the shoulders and a Velcro front flap. An open weave, fire-retardant, raschel knit back was provided for the *pilot/co-pilot front*

Improved body armor with better adjusting and quick release apparatus, worn with the AFH1 ballistic flying helmet and Nomex flyer's gloves, 1970. *Natick Laboratories.*

version, which cost $120 and weighed 15 pounds, 12 ounces. The *gunner/crew chief, front and back plate* version was a complete vest with a molded polystyrene neck unit attached to the top of the armor plate. This vest in the medium size cost $215 and weighed 34 pounds, 3 ounces[18]

The armor carriers created a problem that initially bedeviled aviators. Serious wounds occurred when rounds impacted on the chest protector and shattered, causing ricocheting, secondary metallic fragments that tore into other parts of the body. In one 12th Aviation Group incident, a copilot's chest protector was hit by a round that blasted through the left chin bubble of his UH1 helicopter. Although his life

Aircrewmen leg armor developed during the Vietnam conflict, as displayed by Natick Laboratories. *Army Aviation Command.*

Front and rear view of body armor, air crewmen, small arms protective, front, back plates, and leg armor. Helicopter pilots and co-pilots wore only the front torso protector, while door gunners used the back plates and leg armor. *Natick Laboratories.*

was saved, metallic fragments tore away his knee joint. Shortly afterwards, in the same group, a round struck the right-seat pilot's chest protector. Instead of penetrating, the round splattered and sent jagged pieces of red hot metal through the eyes of the copilot.

The frequency of such mishaps caused Col. Raymond P. Campbell, Jr., the 12th Aviation Group commander, to investigate possible solutions. He supervised a series of experiments in early 1967 that proved that body armor worn underneath the chest protector served no useful purpose because rounds penetrating the chest protector would also penetrate the normal body armor. Secondary fragments

could be effectively trapped, however, by standard M1952 body armor worn *over* the chest protector. (Other vests were not suitable because their collars inhibited wearing of the flying helmet.)

With this arrangement, rounds penetrated the vest, struck the chest protector, and burst into fragments, which were absorbed by the standard body armor.[19]

Air crew body armor carriers became scarce during several critical periods of the Vietnam conflict. Supplies were exhausted in late 1967, and stocks in Vietnam were at zero balance for months. Small quantities finally began arriving during March 1968. At the time,

Lightweight buoyant vests being used by a riverine patrol of the 3d Bn, 7th Inf (199th Inf Bde), while boarding an Aircat airboat near the Y-Bridge in Saigon, 2 August 1968. *U.S. Army.*

the 4th Aviation Battalion possessed only 62 of the 176 armor carrier sets authorized. The 1st Aviation Brigade did not consider supply adequate until December, when the Army Inventory Control Center, Vietnam, was directed to maintain a stocked level of 2,500 sets for replacement purposes, combat losses, and initial issues.[20]

Another area of personal air crew protective development was leg armor. *Small arms protective leg armor* consisted of frontal-thigh and lower-leg units that were joined at the knee by an articulating hinge. Since composite ceramic tiles did not initially lend themselves to critical shaping, the first leg armor was fabricated from dual-hardness steel. It resembled medieval knight leg armor, and a pair weighed 38 pounds. Approximately 500 pairs of the steel full-leg armor were delivered to Vietnam in early 1965. Air crews reported that the devices were clumsy and hindered their mobility.[21]

During 1969, experimental single-piece lower-leg armor, weighing 18 pounds, was developed by eliminating the thigh section. The device was anatomically shaped to differentiate between right and left leg curvature. The outward flare of this single leg piece gave an oversized knee boot appearance, but it prevented knee contact with the armor. A foot bracket stabilized the armor on the leg and transferred some of the weight to the helicopter flooring.[22]

5.5 Buoyant Protective Gear

In May 1967, the Navy Research and Development Unit, Vietnam, distributed 30 *buoyant-ballistic fragmentation protective vests* to Coastal Task Forces 116 and 117 for evaluation. These were similar to the M1952 armor vest with ¾ collar, except for the replacement of the ballistic nylon fabric layers with layers of polypropylene felt enclosed in a separate heat-sealed vinyl bag to increase buoyancy. Three layers of quarter-inch closed-cell polyethylene foam were incorporated for additional positive buoyancy. This Navy testing resulted in an im-

Capt. Wesley Jacobs of the 175th Medical Detachment (Veterinary Service) wears a body apron as he vaccinates the pet of Sp4 Russell Conger, 2d Bde, 101st Abn Div, at Camp Sally, 15 December 1969. *101st Abn Div PIO.*

41st Engineer Company Specialist Fifth Class Petersen wears standard collared life preserver, vest, during wharf construction at Cat Lai, July 1969. *Author's collection.*

After intensive research, Natick Laboratories produced a full-leg armor using composite ceramic that conformed to limb curve. These devices were flight tested in Vietnam in February 1966. The top thigh unit, which required a hip harness, was uncomfortable and only useful if the crew chief or gunner was standing, since the thigh and underside of seated crewmen were still exposed to ground fire. Over 300 pairs of this composite leg armor were supplied to the 1st Aviation Brigade during 1967.

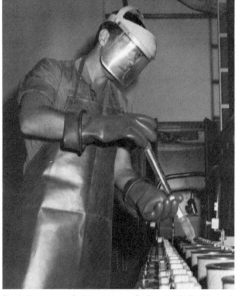

Industrial safety coveralls are worn by a 1st Transportation Bn mechanic checking a helicopter turbine aboard the USNS *Corpus Christie Bay*, **off Qui Nhon.** *Author's collection.*

Sp4 Raymond Mageau of the 107th Signal Company wears black rubber-coated duck impermeable apron; neoprene rubber gauntlet gloves; and industrial hinged-window face shield while repairing a dial telephone exchange at Long Binh, 3 October 1969. *U.S. Army.*

A soldier constructing the 2d Bn, 138th Artillery, mess hall at FSB Anzio, wears typical worker coveralls, 4 January 1969. *U.S. Army.*

proved variant with added shoulder shotgun pockets, snap fastener attachment of leg straps, and Velcro fasteners to replace zippers and snaps.[23]

This Navy *MOD II buoyant-ballistic fragmentation protective vest* reached Vietnam in October 1968. The vest was very buoyant, but the weak leg-strap fasteners came unfastened in the water, causing the vest to ride up on the wearer. As a positive displacement vest, it was very bulky, flared around the midsection, and was prone to catch on protuberances within the boat. The 28-pound vests were also extremely heavy and hot to wear.

The Army transportation corps procured a number of these buoyant-ballistic fragmentation protective vests for its boat crews in July 1969. Army personnel manning watercraft found them just as hot, bulky, and uncomfortable as Navy users and protested that the vest collar tended to push the wearer's face downward into the water while swimming. As a result, both Army and Navy judged the vests impractical for Vietnam combat.[24]

5.6 Aprons and Coveralls

Protective aprons and coveralls were designed to protect against specific hazards, such as concentrated acids, flying chips, hot sparks, or sharp-edged tools. Other aprons and coveralls rendered protection against less hazardous liquids and acids or food substances so that they did not permanently stain or damage military uniforms.

The *explosive handlers' coveralls* were made of fire-resistant, non-static, 8.5-ounce cotton sateen in natural color or tinted neutral gray. They contained a zippered closure and lattice-type hip pocket. The *industrial safety coveralls,* worn by electronic repairmen in areas requiring dust-free and lint-free conditions, were Tan army shade 448 polyester with an anti-static finish. Troops in Vietnam did not use Army *general purpose coveralls,* designed to fit over the uniforms of mechanics and maintenance personnel, because they were too hot for the tropical environment. In February 1966, however, DA adopted white cotton *safety coveralls* for such jobs as medical equipment repair or spray painting where sanitation was important.

Aprons were more common in Vietnam than coveralls. Waist-size and larger cotton *construction worker's aprons* had waist ties and pockets for holding small tools or nails. The black, full-body *rubber-coated duck impermeable apron,* with shoulder straps and waist ties, was typically worn in rear maintenance shops. The colorless plastic *laboratory apron* was preferred by personnel, such as mess attendants, who frequently contacted water or steam. Welders used either the *bib-type welder's leather apron,* or the *leg-length asbestos welder's apron.* These large aprons protected against sustained direct or reflected heat and flying sparks.

A variety of synthetic fabric knee- or hip-length *industrial protective leggings* protected the front of the legs from heat, splash, and moderate impact. Hip-length rubber leggings had belt straps and covered the entire leg. Heavy rubber or leather *industrial knee pads* gave protection against prolonged pressure or heat and were commonly used by soldiers working in a kneeling position when welding or riveting.

5.7 Protective Suits

Lethal Viet Cong booby trap devices hindered Army operations throughout the war. Many VC mines and booby traps were manufactured from grenades or dud American artillery shells and bombs. The VC rigged these with improvised fuses and turned them into extremely dangerous, highly explosive, mechanical ambush devices against U.S. troops.

Enemy booby traps were discovered by point men, Vietnamese Kit Carson scouts, or mine-detection dogs. The profusion of these traps and the shortage of explosive-removal experts forced most Army troops to disarm or destroy such VC devices by using techniques developed in the field. Often a grappling hook or an artillery shipping plug was tied to one end of a line and tossed out in front of the unit by a point man. The hook was pulled in slowly and smoothly, activating the trip wires in its path.[25]

The field-expedient *fragmentation suit,* or "special flak suit," of the 199th Infantry Brigade (Light) was one of the most resourceful innovations employed in Vietnam. The protec-

The 199th Inf Bde fragmentation suit, type I, with wrap-around apron, hooded head protector, and grapnel for anti–booby trap operations in ''The Pineapple'' area west of Saigon, 1968. *Author's collection.*

The padded 199th Inf Bde type I fragmentation suit trousers, fabricated of armored fragmentation vest material, were held up by suspenders. *Author's collection.*

tive suit was developed in September and October 1968 by the brigade's 7th Support Battalion under the direction of Lt. Col. Jack Gray. The Type I version used a body apron extending from the chest to the knees with reinforced trousers and a hooded head protector. The improved Type II assembly consisted of a wraparound body apron fabricated from the backs of six armor fragmentation vests, a standard protective vest worn over the chest, and a hooded head protector made of similar material for wear over the helmet.

The Vietnam-produced fragmentation suits were worn by point men who used modified grapnels to explode enemy mechanical ambush devices. The outfits were used extensively

105

The 199th Inf Bde type II fragmentation suit being demonstrated by a point man who hurls the grapnel forward to snare a Viet Cong mechanical ambush device. *Author's collection.*

The 199th Inf Bde fragmentation suit, type II, with protective vest, apron, and hooded head protector over helmet, worn during clearing operations west of Saigon, 1969. *Author's collection.*

in the booby-trap infested areas north and west of Saigon from the fall of 1968 until 1970. The weight of the suit in the tropical heat, however, necessitated the rotation every thirty minutes of men wearing this gear.

Maj. Rudolf Levy, the 199th Infantry Brigade intelligence officer, stated, "The suit is heavy and hot but effective. Several units have come back with numerous pieces of shrapnel in it. The men wearing it are not injured at all. From this, we judge that the suit is effective. The troops carry one of these every time they go on an operation. The forward people and the point element always carry this suit with them and put it on the minute they start finding booby traps."[26]

Explosive ordnance disposal personnel utilized the *M3 ensemble, toxicological agents protective,* or TAP suit, for handling munitions under dangerously vaporous conditions or while working in contaminated areas. The suit was a one-piece garment fabricated from double Butyl, a rubber-coated cotton sheeting,

A 199th Inf Bde point man wears the fragmentation suit while deploying a grapnel to disarm a Viet Cong booby trap in "The Pineapple" area west of Saigon, 1968. *Author's collection.*

with double-sewn, cemented, and strapped seams. The integral hood contained a large, frontal, plastic lens. A small, commercial half-mask respirator was mounted below the lens in case of supplied-air failure. The suit was donned by stepping through a slash-opening extending from the left hip to the right side of the hood, and was closed with a special rubber pressure-sealed zipper.

The suited man depended on low-pressure breathable air. Compressed air inflated his suit through a hose extending from the back. This kept the suit fabric away from the body and

The M3 toxicological agents protective ensemble or TAP suit, was worn under cooling suit coveralls by explosive ordnance disposal teams in Vietnam. *Army Chemical Center.*

107

Sp5 Paul Stoke and Capt. Arben Cordes of the 98th Ordnance Detachment (Explosive Ordnance Disposal) with cooling suit coveralls over their TAP suits in Southeast Asia, 19 March 1970. *U.S. Army.*

facilitated air circulation. A cut-off valve on the air-line hose permitted quick disconnection. Plastic and rubber cuffs on the legs and sleeves formed leak-proof seals with the gauntlet-type Butyl rubber *M4 TAP gloves* and the knee-high Butyl rubber *M2A1 TAP boots.* Undergarments consisted of long cotton *drawers, vesicant gas protective, impregnated* and *undershirt, vesicant gas protective, impregnated,* worn with *chemical protective socks.* The *TAP air fed cloth coveralls* and the *TAP double*

coated gas mask hood completed the outfit.[27] The TAP suit was disliked because assistance was required in donning and removal, and its "stay time" in contaminated areas was limited to less than 15 minutes. The ensemble was so uncomfortably hot in Southeast Asia that cotton Olive Green army shade 107 *TAP cooling suit coveralls* and the cotton duck *D7 TAP cover cooling gas mask hood* were worn over it.

In 1963, Natick Laboratories developed an experimental *thermalibrium clothing sys-*

The impermeable layer worn over the spacer system was part of the thermalibrium clothing system developed for explosive ordnance disposal experts in Vietnam. *Author's collection.*

This specially modified tropical combat uniform was the outer garment of the thermalibrium clothing system used by explosive ordnance disposal experts in Vietnam. *Author's collection.*

tem for explosive ordnance disposal specialists working in toxic or hazardous conditions. The system isolated the soldier from contaminated areas, and its heat-regulating device provided complete thermal protection from −40° to over 110° F. The system consisted of a spacer system, an impermeable layer worn over the spacer system, and an outer layer fabricated of a specially modified tropical combat uniform, which gave the thermalibrium suit utility consistent with standard Vietnam attire.[28]

A direct spin-off of this system was the man-lock thermal protective coverall designed for NASA's manned spacecraft center. During the war, however, the thermalibrium suit remained only a prototype design, and its Vietnam service was limited. More advanced pro-

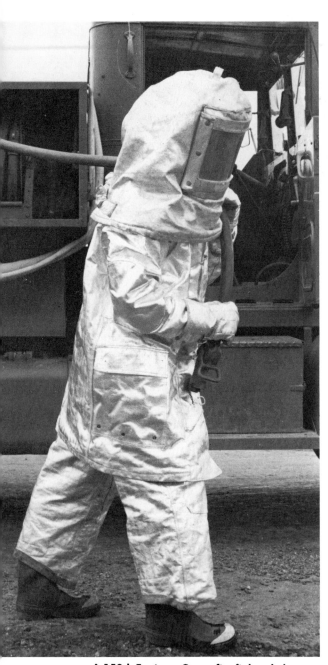

The Army fire fighter ensemble worn by Pfc. Roger Ruiz of the 114th Engineer Detachment (Fire Truck) after an aircraft crash at Vung Tau, 1967. *U.S. Army.*

A 159th Engineer Group fire fighter helps control an ammunition blaze at FSB Mace, 1971. He wears the aluminum asbestos fire fighter's ensemble. *Author's collection.*

Pacific Architects and Engineers fire fighter wearing an Army continuous-flow air-line respirator and "turnout coat." Cam Ranh Bay, 14 January 1970. *U.S. Army.*

tective systems for explosive ordnance disposal personnel did not reach the engineering phase of development until 1971 and were not employed in Vietnam.[29]

The Army's fire fighter ensemble consisted of several components. The *fireman's plastic shell helmet* was a shaped, reinforced plastic shell with adjustable shock-absorbing head harness and extended brim for shedding of water. The fireman's helmet in Vietnam was usually black with the red letters "FD" (for fire department, such as the U.S. Army Fire Department, Lai Khe, manned by the 85th Engineer Detachment). The FD letters were centered on the front of the crown, and firemen

were encouraged to inscribe their names in smaller block-style red lettering above.

The *fireman's coat,* or "turnout coat," and *fireman's trousers* were fire-resistant and water-repellent cotton sateen, dyed Olive Green army shade 107. The *fireman's boots* were 29-inch-high, black rubber boots with white toe caps and non-slip, puncture-proof soles.

The *aluminum asbestos fire fighter's clothing ensemble* was used in extinguishing high-intensity fires or conducting rescue work around burning structures or aircraft. The outfit consisted of fireman's coat, gloves, hood, and trousers fabricated of aluminum-coated asbestos.

Notes

1. Dr. S. J. Kennedy, *Clothing and Equipment Support to Our Troops in Vietnam,* Natick Laboratories, 24 Jun 69, 31–32.
2. Frank Rizzo, *Textiles Save Lives in Vietnam,* Natick Laboratories, 24 June 69, 14.
3. 1st Infantry Division, *Operational Report,* 31 Jan 68, Incl 7.
4. 22d Military History Detachment, *Operation Apache Snow,* 10 May–7 Jun 69, 11–14.
5. Army Materiel Command Memorandum for Record, Subj: Personal Armor Standardization Meeting, 15 Mar 65.
6. U.S. Army Test and Evaluation Command, *Annual Report FY 74,* Vol. II, 300.
7. Army Materiel Command, *Clothing & Equipment Support to U.S. Army in Vietnam,* Feb 67, 45.
8. Defense Supply Agency, ACSFOR DS Status Report, 31 Jan 68.
9. Aberdeen Proving Ground, *Final Report on Engineering Test of Lightweight Body Armor: Basic Vest T66-1,* Aug 67.
10. Defense Supply Agency, ACSFOR DS Status Report, 31 Mar 70.
11. Dr. S. J. Kennedy, 28–31.
12. Aviation Materiel Command Aircraft and Aircrew Armor Team, *Report of Visit to South Vietnam, 10 Feb–21 Mar 65.*
13. Transportation Research & Engineering Command Memorandum for Record, 5 Feb 63.
14. Army Materiel Command, *Technical Report 69-43-CE,* Jan 69, 8.
15. Natick Laboratories, *Annual Historical Summary FY 63,* 83.
16. Army Materiel Command, *Report of Visit to South Vietnam, 10 Feb–21 Mar 65.*
17. Army Materiel Command, *Report of Visit to South Vietnam, 14 Feb–4 Apr 66.*
18. *Aviation Digest,* Aug 69, 50.
19. USARV Aviation Pamphlet 95-2, 30 Jun 67, 9.
20. 4th Infantry Division, *Operational Report,* 21 May 68, 21; *1st Aviation Brigade Commander's Notes #20,* 19 Mar 68, and *#28,* 9 Dec 68.
21. Army Materiel Command, *Report on Body Armor for Aircrewmen,* Jan 69, 11.
22. Edward R. Barron, Anthony L. Alesi, and Alice F. Park, *Body Armor for Aircrewmen,* Natick Laboratories, 1969.
23. U.S. Navy Research and Development Unit, Vietnam, *Final Report: NRDU-V Project 7-67,* Suppl Report 1, 13 Aug 69.
24. 1st Logistical Command, *Operational Report,* 20 Aug 69, Incl LL-9.
25. II Field Force Vietnam, *Booby Trap Seminar,* 30 Apr 69.
26. 44th Military History Detachment, *Special Report on Booby Traps,* 9 Nov 68.
27. DA Pamphlet 385-3, 10 Sep 68.
28. Natick Laboratories, *Annual Historical Summary FY 63,* 64.
29. Natick Laboratories, *Technical Report 69-48-CE,* Nov 68, 1.

6

Clothing Accessories

6.1 Neckerchiefs and Scarves

The *tropical combat neckerchief sweat cloth* was a one-square-yard piece of highly absorbent dark green cotton, originally developed during hot-weather clothing experiments of the Korean war era. Natick Laboratories expedited 200 of these neckerchiefs to Vietnam in April 1966 for testing. ACTIV completed favorable evaluation on 30 December 1966, stating, "The troops usually tied them loosely around the neck, like cavalrymen of the Old West, or wrapped them around the head as protection against the hot tropical sun."[1]

In response, the *neckerchief* was standardized to a 36-by-24-inch size, in Olive Green army shade 409 to match the undershirt. This cloth became popular for wiping perspiration and dirt from the brow and hands and for cleaning weapons and ammunition. It was worn over or around the head in a variety of bandanna, cravat, and sweatband styles. Muslin field dressings or triangular bandages were also worn in this fashion.

Several units employed varicolored or dec-orated scarves for esprit. Black scarves were the most popular. This practice originated with the South Vietnamese use of scarves as a token of battlefield valor, and Army troops accepted them as items of special merit. Additionally, standard Army rayon or nylon scarves were often worn with the Army khaki uniform in ceremonial formations. These either reflected the branch color (red for artillery, light blue for infantry, for example) or were of nylon camouflage fabric.

6.2 Coats, Knitted Shirts, Safety Shirts, and Cape Sleeves

Units operating in Vietnam's rugged western mountains sweated in searing daylight temperatures of over 100°F and shivered through the nights when the temperatures plunged to 50°F. The 1st Battalion, 8th Infantry, wrote, "When the sun went down, fatigue jackets were necessary to combat the cold."[2] Coats were issued, one per individual soldier, in Highland areas of I and II CTZ. (*See* Army Uniform Map of Vietnam.) The coat was also supplied

Lt. Col. Carmen Negaard, commander of 1st Bn, 28th Inf (1st Inf Div), wears a typical scarf cut from camouflage parachute nylon. He stands beside a captured NVA heavy machine gun at FSB Picardy, 19 March 1969. *121st Signal Bn.*

by Central Issue Facilities to all Army personnel returning from Vietnam to the United States or other duty assignments.

The M1951 *field coat*, or "Field Jacket," was 9-ounce cotton, wind-resistant sateen, Olive Green army shade 107. The coat had waist and hem draw cords, breast patch pockets, and lower front hanging pockets. The M1965 *cold weather field coat with hood*, standardized on 29 September 1966, was fabricated of nylon-cotton sateen, Olive Green army shade 107, with rounded collars, snap pocket closures, and Velcro sleeve closures. The newer coat lacked the trim appearance of the other

garment but was more durable and had a hood zippered into the collar.

Sweaters were also needed during colder weather in certain areas in Vietnam. The Pleiku-based 4th Infantry Division reported, "Sweaters are a necessity for troops operating in the Central Highlands during the dry season. High altitudes and strong winds create an abnormally high wind-chill factor. While field jackets are satisfactory for rear base camp areas, they are too bulky for use in the forward areas and impede troop agility."[3]

The Army's initial *lightweight knitted shirt,* or "jungle sweater," was an olive green

Troops of the 2d Bn, 1st Inf (1st Inf Div), wear battalion-authorized black scarves near Binh Long, 1 August 1967. Man *(center)* holds PRT-4 transmitter, while radioman *(right)* has PRC-25 radio with spare batteries on his lightweight rucksack. *U.S. Army.*

Sgt. Wayne Olds, a section chief with the 6th Bn, 29th Artillery, wears the neckerchief just after the battle of 26 March 1968, when he fired his howitzer point-blank into an NVA battalion charging American positions near Polei Kleng. *James Olmstead.*

knitted, wool, shrink-resistant garment dating from World War II when it was used in the Burmese highlands. It resembled a pullover sweater and had full-length sleeves with knitted cuffs and a convertible collar with button closure. In 1966, the wool version was replaced by the nylon or acetate *lightweight knitted shirt,* called the "sleeping shirt," which rendered over 50 percent insulating improvement and also dried more rapidly when wet. Late in the Vietnam conflict, this item was redesignated as the *heat retentive and moisture resistant sleeping shirt.*

The lightweight knitted shirt was provided on the basis of one per soldier stationed in Highland areas of I and II CTZ. (*See* Army Uniform Map of Vietnam.) Many soldiers in other regions also possessed them. For exam-

Members of the 3d Bde, 82d Abn Div, disembark from a C141 at Chu Lai wearing cotton sateen field coats, or "field jackets," to ward off the monsoon cold of I CTZ, 17 February 1968. *U.S. Army.*

114

The M1951 field coat *(right)* and M1965 field coat *(left)* worn at Fort Hood Texas, 1969. Note the Nomex flyer's gloves worn by the aviation officer *(right)*. Also note the difference between Army-issue utility cap *(left)* and PX-style utility cap *(right)*. Service cap *(center)* was not worn in combat theaters like Vietnam. *Author's collection.*

ple, the 1st Cavalry Division brought their knitted shirts with them during redeployment from I CTZ to Phuoc Vinh in III CTZ in October through November 1968. Although issue of the wool, knitted version stopped in 1966, it was preferred by aviators because the natural-fiber material was safe to wear under Nomex flight clothing. Throughout the war, air crewmen were warned against wearing lightweight knitted shirts made of nylon or acetate because they easily caught fire and rapidly melted in aircraft mishaps.[4]

The *safety shirt, oil- and water-resistant, fire- and water-resistant,* was made of Dacron, Dynel, or Orlon and worn in combination with matching trousers. With the permission of commanding officers, this shirt was worn in

Soldier of the 101st Abn Div wears a lightweight knitted shirt *(center)* during a mission near FSB Saber, 12 October 1969. This use of the shirt as an outer garment was officially prohibited because of its inability to withstand rugged wear. *U.S. Army.*

101st Abn Div officer, holding 12-gauge pump shotgun, wears a lightweight knitted shirt underneath his tropical coat, 1969. *101st Abn Div PIO.*

lieu of protective overalls or similar protective clothing by machinists and some equipment operators. It protected against hazards such as radiant heat, sparks, acids, grease, alkalis, abrasions, and minor impacts.

The *sleeve, cape, and bib welder's: flameproof* was a leather cape sleeve with snaps in front for quick removal. This was used by Army personnel on jobs requiring complete protection against sparks or flame for the upper body, including chest and back.

6.3 Raincoats and Rain Suits

Army raincoats were worn with formal uniforms and were not normally approved to

Sp5 Gary Ferguson wears the cape sleeve and welder's bib as he welds two metal panels together. 5 January 1970. *U.S. Army.*

Foremost soldier of a 1st Bn, 502d Inf (101st Abn Div), patrol near FSB Arsenal wears lightweight knitted shirt under his tropical coat. Sleeve of soldier in center was probably cut off after having been ripped. *Chuck Kahn.*

be worn with work and field clothing. The poncho was the standard garment for wear with the field or tropical combat uniform in inclement weather. (*See section 9.2, Poncho.*) In Vietnam, however, the standard raincoat could be worn over tropical combat and utility uniforms, if those uniforms were not being used for field or fatigue duties.

At the beginning of the Vietnam conflict, the Army's standard raincoat was the *taupe raincoat,* army shade 179. This raincoat was fabricated of 1.6-ounce, taupe, nylon twill that was coated on the inside with polyvinyl butyral for complete waterproofing. Unfortunately,

Burial detail wears taupe raincoats, army shade 179, as they carry the remains of a captain killed in Vietnam, 11 October 1967, to his grave site in the United States. *American Red Cross.*

Artilleryman of the 5th Bn, 27th Artillery (center), wears the pullover wet weather parka at Phan Thiet, 1970. *U.S. Army.*

Sp5 Charlie Grace wears the raincoat, Green army shade 274. 12 January 1968. *Fort Lewis Photo Facility.*

like all coated-fabric raincoats, the garment was impermeable to perspiration and subjected the wearer to the discomfort of moisture condensation inside the coat. The treated outside discolored when wet; the soft fabric clung to the wearer's legs when he walked; and the coat puckered at the seams.

Artillerymen of the 2d Bn, 40th Artillery (199th Inf Bde), wear rubberized nylon waterproof parkas at FSB Verna, June 1970. *Author's collection.*

A prototype lightweight two-piece rain suit field tested in Vietnam during 1967. *Author's collection/Melissa Priest.*

Sp4 Denny Horn and Sp4 Bob Blackwell (101st Abn Div) wear waterproof parka and bib coveralls as they put Christmas decorations on their bunker line. 11 December 1970. *John Ivy.*

The search for a new raincoat was made possible by a 1959 breakthrough in rainwear research by the Army Quartermaster Research and Development Laboratories. Chemists produced a new water-repellent treatment called Quarpel — for "Quartermaster-developed repellent" — that eliminated the need for coated raincoat fabrics. After extensive testing, a new Quarpel-treated Army *green raincoat* was adopted on 18 August 1964.[5]

The raincoat was army Green shade 274 and harmonized with the army Green uniform, draped better over the coat, and washed well, insuring greater longevity. It was made of a single layer of 5-ounce cotton-nylon fabric with an inside shoulder yoke. The new raincoat was not commonly worn in Vietnam until 1 July 1967, when the Army began individual sales and issue to recruits. On 1 July 1969, the raincoat became mandatory wear in Vietnam, although the Army taupe raincoat was not officially declared obsolete in the rest of the Army until 1 July 1971.

A lightweight two-piece *rain suit* was fabricated by Army Materiel Command as a re-

Lt. Richard Haley, 266th Chemical Platoon commander, wears a rain parka purchased from the Long Binh post exchange. He carries the 34-pound E8 35mm 16-tube launcher. Di An, 27 May 1968. *U.S. Army.*

The Australian military raincoat folded into its own pocket and was very popular with Army Special Forces and senior officers. *Author's collection/Melissa Priest.*

Helicopter door gunner wears Nomex flyer's gloves while landing soldiers of the 101st Abn Div, 21 August 1970. *Gordon Burton.*

sponse to DA directives of 21 June 1966. Based upon previous research when various materials had been tested under tropical conditions, Natick Laboratories chose three different garments to send to Vietnam. These afforded three levels of rain protection and heat retention. All of the rain suits consisted of a trouser-jacket combination. One suit was fabricated from impermeable material, polyurethane-coated nylon. Another suit type was made from cotton-nylon oxford fabric, which was treated with a water repellent. The final suit was made of the same material but contained reinforcing patches across the shoulders, and on the elbows, knees, and seat.[6]

On 20 January 1967, Natick Laboratories shipped 100 rain suits of each type (300 total) to Dover Air Force Base, Delaware, and these were airlifted into Vietnam for ACTIV evaluation. According to a USARV interim report of 26 August, "preliminary results indicate combat service support units like them and combat units dislike them." ACTIV completed testing on 22 September 1967 with a negative report, which cancelled further rain suit procurement.[7]

Late in the war, about 1971, a prototype *wet weather parka and trousers* suit, made of 2-ounce water-resistant, polyurethane-coated nylon, reached the front in limited quantities. A combination of zippers and Velcro closures provided ventilation, so moisture would not build up inside the garment, and allowed the apparel to be easily donned and removed. The entire suit weighted 2.26 pounds.

A recon member of MACV-SOG wears flyer's sheepskin glove shells for a sterile weapons mission. *Army News Features.*

6.4 Gloves and Protective Hand Wear

The Army used a wide variety of gloves in Vietnam. General-purpose gloves were made of cotton or canvas with band, knit, or gauntlet wrists. Some gloves provided protection for specific needs. For instance, rubber gloves were worn around acids, caustics, and other chemicals, oils, and solvents. Special rubber gloves insulated against electrical shock. Asbestos gloves and mittens protected against sparks, heat, or hot material. Plastic-coated gloves were good for work involving steam or water, as well as some acids and caustics.

Army aviation requirements led to adoption of the *flyer's gloves, nylon, fire retardant.* Flight personnel in Vietnam were initially supplied with dark brown and gray sheepskin *flyer's glove shells.* USARV requested flame-protective flight gloves with Nomex backing on 5 June 1967, and the flyer's glove design was chosen. The glove contained a knitted high-temperature-resistant simplex jersey (Nomex) on the back of the hand for flame protection. The glove's thin leather palm gave hand dexterity and sweat resistance with "second skin comfort." Approximately 300 pairs were airshipped to Vietnam on 13 August 1967 for comparative thermal-protective testing.

USARV completed evaluation on 31 January 1968, and recommended some minor improvements. DA approved the slightly altered glove, costing $6.50 per pair, at the end of March. On 31 May 1968 a total of 17,225 pairs were ordered under the ENSURE priority program, and 8,500 pairs reached USARV by the end of June. During July, the flight glove was reclassified as standard Army issue, although the cost per pair had increased to $11.39. By 1 October 1968, USARV had received 16,000 pairs through priority channels and had switched to normal resupply. Nomex flight gloves remained in short supply, however, until mid-1969.[8]

Gloves were extremely important in many ground operations as well. Two special glove types were available for Army troops working around barbed wire or tape, German razor wire, or tanglefoot. The *heavy barbed tape-wire handler's gloves* were cowhide gauntlet-cuffed gloves with metal clips on the palm and finger. The *leather glove, barbed wire,* was a variant cowhide or horsehide glove with gauntlet cuff and reinforced palm. These gloves were common in Vietnam because all fire support bases and most camps depended on wire barriers as part of their main perimeter defenses.

One of the Army's most commonly issued gloves in Vietnam was the M1950 *leather glove,*

Black leather glove shells with truncated fingertips were widely used in Vietnam by reconnaissance personnel and known as "recon gloves." These protected hands from thorns and other jungle hazards while permitting unhampered use of weapons. Here Sgt. Gary Poppell (*standing*) of Company C (Ranger), 75th Inf, discusses NVA target with team member Pfc. Mike Thompson during a mission, 26 February 1970. *U.S. Army.*

strap closure. This was a general-purpose, heavy work glove that was cream colored. It was worn by equipment operators, construction engineers, boat handlers, parachute and aerial equipment riggers, and even reconnaissance troops while rappelling. This type was favored in Southeast Asia because it was lightweight and extremely comfortable. Although not as widely used, the *cotton work gloves* with leather palm and knit cuff or gauntlet were also employed.

Two types of heavier leather gloves with steel stitching were available for such tasks as animal training or machinery operation, although they could not be used around electrical equipment. The first was the *steel sewed heavy leather glove.* For heavy work requiring extreme protection against sharp or rough edges, the *steel reinforced leather glove* was provided. This was a leather, gauntlet-type,

Members of the 326th Engineer Bn wear barbed tape-wire handler's gloves with gauntlet cuffs while stringing defensive wire. East of Hue, February 1968. *MACV PIO.*

A 173d Abn Bde trooper uses seat rappel with carabiner and M1950 leather gloves, strap closure, April 1970. *Author's collection.*

Machine gunner Pfc. Larry Lovette (left) and radioman Sp4 Rufus Green both carry M1950 leather gloves, strap closure, as part of their combat equipment. 27 November 1970. *U.S. Army.*

steel-stitched glove, which had its palm and finger areas reinforced with steel ribbons.

Welders used a range of gloves for protection against heat or sparks, from cowhide, lined gloves to gauntlet-cuffed *asbestos cloth gloves* and *asbestos cloth mittens.* Welders also used leather sleeves with tie strings for protection of the upper arms. Asbestos hand wear was popular with mortar crews and machine gunners because of the heat that their weapon barrels generated in sustained combat.

Film handlers used white cotton work gloves, which gave a snug fit for maximum dexterity. Lightweight, protective *goatskin work-type gloves* with safety cuffs permitted finger dexterity in other situations, although they could not be worn around moving machinery. Latex *surgical gloves* were amber-colored,

Sgt. Henry Zimmerle of the 497th Engineer Company wears welder's asbestos cloth gloves while checking pipe weld of a 21,000-gallon water storage tank at Cam Ranh Bay, 23 May 1971. *Louis Tourgee.*

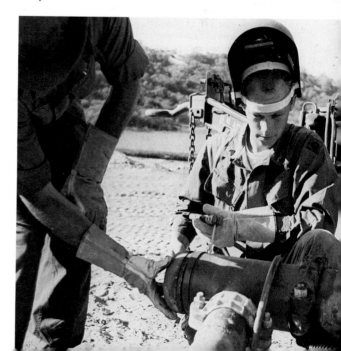

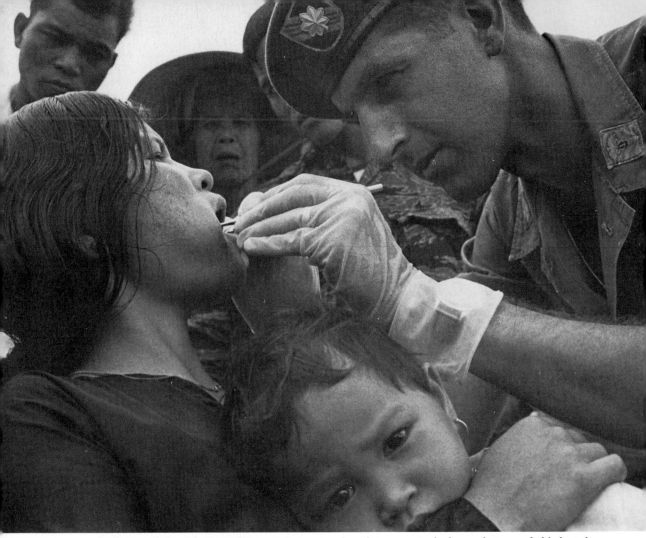

A dentist of the 5th Special Forces Group employs latex surgical gloves during a field dental mission, 1968. *Author's collection.*

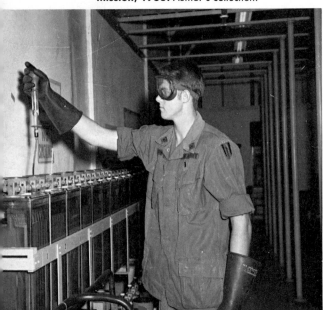

lightweight gloves used in laboratories and medical areas. Personnel handling frozen food and meats in cold storage facilities in Vietnam used *waterproof cloth gloves*. These canton flannel gloves, coated with either latex or synthetic rubber, had a gauntlet cuff.

The *plastic coated impermeable glove* was utilized by military personnel working with live steam, water, acids, or caustics such as in steam cleaning, sand blasting, and operations

Sp5 Danny Dinnebeck of the 52d Signal Bn wears acid-resistant black rubber gloves while checking wet cell batteries at the Can Tho Dial Telephone Exchange. Note subdued cloth insignia of rank sewn on collar. 22 June 1970. *U.S. Army.*

Sp4 John O'Daniel of the 6th Bn, 29th Artillery, wearing V-neck undershirt, defended his howitzer in close combat against the NVA west of Polei Kleng, 26 March 1968. *Author's collection.*

Artilleryman of the 2d Bn, 320th Artillery, holding a 105mm round *(center)* wears the green cotton crew-neck undershirt. *Army News Features.*

where oil was an irritant. *Type I rubber gloves, acid and alkali resistant,* were pliable synthetic black rubber gloves of medium weight for general industrial and laboratory applications. *Type II rubber gloves, aromatic, fuel resistant,* were 14-inch-long, heavyweight, black rubber gloves used by battery workers. Late in the war, neoprene rubber gloves became available within Vietnam.

The *lineman's leather gloves* were gray or cream-colored, work-type leather gloves worn by telephone installers, wiremen, electricians, and linemen to protect *class B rubber gloves*

A 1st Bn, 506th Inf (101st Abn Div), soldier wears the olive green towel draped around his neck, a common field practice to prevent sores while carrying equipment on the shoulder. Helicopter has just crashed near Hue, 1968. *101st Abn Div PIO.*

Flame-thrower of the 1st Bn, 508th Inf (82d Abn Div) uses soaked towels to ward off heat near Trung Lap, June 1969. *U.S. Army.*

worn underneath. The black class B rubber gloves had a 3,000-volt rating and were worn while working around medium-high voltages. A strong, durable rubber glove with high dielectric strength for protection against electrical shock was worn by Army personnel working with voltages higher than 3,000 volts.

Linemen also used *leather glove shells, gauntlet type* with five finger sheaths, Gunn cut, in brown or cream color. These were slipped over the linemen's rubber gloves for additional protection in high voltage work. The *lineman's glove shells* were pliable leather gloves, Gunn cut, and cork colored, for wearing over lineman's rubber gloves to protect them from physical damage. Finally, the *lineman's sleeve, rubber,* was worn by electricians handling tools or rough surfaces. It insulated

Artillerymen of the 1st Bn, 92d Artillery, wearing the white undershirt (center) and V-necked green undershirt as they fire a 155mm howitzer near Dak To. *Army News Features.*

the wearer from contact with energized lines and prevented deterioration of the gloves.

6.5 Underwear and Socks

Olive-green shades for towels and underclothes were revived in November 1965 as the Army announced initial clothing allowances for enlisted personnel being assigned to Vietnam. During the interim between ordering and production of green-shaded items, field units were directed to dye white underwear and towels by expeditious commercial means preparatory to Vietnam deployment. White underwear was reserved for Army khaki and tan uniforms.

In 1966, new underwear—dyed a deep green to blend with the jungle—was manufactured out of absorbent cotton that would not bind or chafe in hot, humid weather. The *boxer-style drawers* were made of cotton muslin, either bleached or dyed Olive Green army shade 107, and had elastic-webbing waistbands.[9] The cotton *quarter-sleeve undershirt* was a bleached white or Olive Green army shade 109 combed cotton.[10] Each soldier in Vietnam was issued five drawers and five undershirts by authority of USARV Regulation 735-1 or MACV Directive 735-2.

The wool stretch-type, cushion-sole *socks*, Olive Green army shade 408, which maintained resiliency even when wet, were standard issue during the Vietnam conflict. Clean socks were especially important because of the myriad foot diseases in Vietnam, and daily sock changes were emphasized. Socks sometimes doubled as field-expedient carriers for metal C-ration cans. During combat in the swamp forests of the Rung Sat Special Zone throughout November 1966, each 3d Battalion, 22d Infantry, infantryman carried ten C-ration meals in two socks tied to load-bearing equipment.

Several varieties of lightweight socks, designed to reduce disabling fungal and bacterial problems experienced by the 9th Infantry Division in the Mekong Delta, were field tested. On 5 January 1968, one thousand pairs of net-type socks were flown to Vietnam for evaluation, but these were judged unsatisfactory and USARV cancelled further action on 18 November. USARV requested 500,000 pairs of a newer "Delta footwear" sock on 2 June 1969. Because

Field expedient towel-shirts worn by combat engineers of the 31st Engineer Bn who guard the bridge across the Song Be near Bu Dop. January 1971. *Author's collection.*

of the withdrawal of the 9th Infantry Division, 285,000 pairs of both thin nylon and stretch cushion-sole nylon socks were furnished. The nylon cushion sock was well received, and the Army classified them as standard issue on 15 January 1970. A total of 23,870 pairs were air delivered to Vietnam on 9 March 1970.[11]

The all-nylon boot socks possessed one serious flaw: they melted at relatively low temperatures and posed such a great hazard to flight personnel that USARV prohibited their wear in aviation units in 1971. Unfortunately, the Army stocked so many nylon socks, once they became standard issue, that wool socks were very scarce in Vietnam. This severe shortage of wool boot socks, especially in medium sizes, was not alleviated until December 1971.[12]

127

Notes

1. Army Concept Team in Vietnam, *Final Report, Proj ACL-84/67*, 30 Dec 66.
2. 1st Battalion, 8th Infantry, *Annual History, 1967*, 1 Mar 68, 31.
3. 4th Infantry Division, *After Action Report: Battle of Dak To*, 3 Jan 68, 65.
4. *Aviation Digest,* Nov 72, 40.
5. Natick Laboratories, *Technical Report 68-41-CM,* Mar 68, 19–20.
6. Army Materiel Command, *Clothing & Equipment Support to U.S. Army in Vietnam,* Feb 67, 15.
7. Defense Supply Agency, ACSFOR DS Status Report, 31 Jan 68; Army Concept Team in Vietnam letter, 22 Sep 67.
8. Defense Supply Agency, ACSFOR DS Status Report, 31 Dec 68.
9. Military Specification MIL-D-40099E, 27 Aug 69.
10. Federal Specification JJ-U-513B, 13 Apr 67.
11. Defense Supply Agency, ACSFOR DS Status Report, 30 Jun 70.
12. *Aviation Digest,* Mar 72, 50.

7

Footwear

7.1 Tropical Combat Boots

The Army's *tropical combat boot,* or "jungle boot," was one of the most successful clothing innovations of the Vietnam conflict. Its development was begun in 1955 as an attempt to overcome a major problem in the footwear used in World War II and in Korea. Because of the failure of the Goodyear welt stitching in that footwear, the sole often separated from the boot. This problem was particularly prevalent in jungle climates, commonly occurring after a month's exposure to constant dry-wet conditions. To overcome this stitching defect, the Army Quartermaster and Engineering Research Command adopted the vulcanized sole process, first developed in Europe.[1]

The first three types of direct molded sole (DMS) tropical combat boots were tested in Panama during 1960 and 1961. The boots were styled after World War II, 1943-pattern combat boots with buckled cuff, except that a screened eyelet was added at the inside shank of each boot and a Swiss Vibram-pattern mountain-climbing sole was used. The three types varied only in their upper materials. An all-leather, an all-nylon, and a combination style were tried. The all-leather uppers proved uncomfortably hot and heavy, and the all-nylon uppers did not provide enough support or protection against external objects. The combination style—nylon duck upper with the leather foot portion (vamp and counter-pocket) vulcanized directly to a rubber-cleated sole—was the most satisfactory and retained its superiority in all subsequent boot-design tests.[2]

The first-pattern DMS tropical combat boots were very popular because they were lightweight, quick drying, and long wearing, and the cleated sole gave satisfactory traction. Unfortunately, the sole still had a 37 percent bonding failure, and the two leather straps and buckles snagged on vegetation and jingled as the wearer walked. These problems were corrected in 1962 when a new adhesive was developed that was more compatible with the rubber sole compound and that prevented bond failures, the buckled cuff was replaced by a full-laced closure, and the all-nylon upper fabric was changed to cotton-nylon to reduce flam-

Foot care was critical in Vietnam. This sergeant of the 1st Bn, 46th Inf (Americal Div), powders his feet after removing tropical combat boots near Chu Lai, January 1968. *Author's collection.*

mability. This tropical combat boot was officially adopted by both the Army and Marine Corps on 23 January 1965.[3]

Natick Laboratories started developing spike-protective boots after October 1961 when it was informed that VC guerrillas were planting poisoned punji stakes and sharp, contaminated metal or bamboo spikes in ground traps and under water. The spikes penetrated the footwear of military advisors, causing numerous injuries that sometimes proved fatal. Fortunately, previous work with fire fighting boots enabled the Army to develop a slip-in protective insole.

The first-pattern tropical combat boots, worn here by Maj. Frederick Woerner of the Jungle Warfare School, had leather straps and buckles at the top. These were issued to some units in Vietnam from 1962 to 1965. *U.S. Army.*

The DMS tropical combat boot with integral spike resistant insole. *U.S. Army.*

The initial *spike-resistant insole* was made of overlapping strips of steel, encased in fabric, which could be slipped into the DMS boot in the same way it was used in the fireman's boot. These insoles were not entirely satisfactory but did offer some protection, and 30,000 pairs were shipped to Vietnam in June 1963.[4] Natick Laboratories also produced a 0.011-inch-thick stainless slip-in steel plate, which was shaped to fit the bottom of the foot and was laminated with woven plastic screening for ventilation. Vietnam testing, however, indicated that the insole became hot and caused blistering and chafing of the feet after prolonged walking.[5]

The Vibram-design sole of the early-style standard tropical combat boot *(bottom)* contrasts with the Panama sole of the 1966-pattern tropical combat boot *(top)*. Note difference in drainage eyelets. *Author's collection.*

Early DMS tropical combat boot with Vibram sole had leather bands across the top of the nylon duck upper fabric. *Natick Laboratories.*

Typical lower trouser lacing and blousing of trousers in tropical combat boots was essential to keep insects off the legs during jungle movement in Vietnam, as worn here by a 1st Bn, 12th Cav (1st Cav Div), trooper cleaning his M16 rifle. *Thomas Crawford.*

The Color Guard of the 39th Signal Bn at Vung Tau wear white lacings in their tropical combat boots, typical of distinctive uniform items worn by ceremonial elements. *Author's collection.*

As a result of these complaints, Natick Laboratories tested the incorporation of spike-protective insoles as an integral component of the boot. The leather insole of the boot was split into two pieces and the 0.011-inch steel insole was inserted between these layers. The test results were satisfactory, and a new specification for DMS spike-protective tropical boots was completed in May 1966.

The improved tropical combat boot was fabricated of a mildew-resistant nylon duck upper portion with leather toe box, vamp, counter, and flaps. This combination of leather and nylon was lightweight and quick drying. In addition, the boot contained better drainage eyelets. The direct, or injection, molded sole with steel insert featured a Panama anti-mud traction design, replacing the earlier Vibram sole, which muddied too easily. The boot was very durable and its long serviceability eliminated the need for field repair and maintenance.[6]

The intensified anti-personnel mine and booby trap warfare of Vietnam caused a large number of foot and lower-leg amputations. The Army needed blast-protective combat boots. During the Korean war, soldiers wearing insulated rubber boots received less severe injuries after stepping on mines than those with conventional combat boots. Natick Laboratories altered some tropical combat boots to incorporate a stainless steel wedge (investment cast) filled with aluminum honeycomb and covered on the top with alumina plate. The wedge covered the heel and arch areas with a V-shaped transverse cross-section, which deflected a blast outward from the sole of the foot. The protective shank weighed approximately 7 ounces per boot, and the first 1,000 pairs were sent to Vietnam during 1967.[7]

The jungle combat boot used by South Vietnamese military forces was of poor quality and fit poorly. The Special Forces procured a more durable boot in Japan for its indigenous forces in the summer of 1966.[8] Following an extensive joint effort by the MACV J46 Office, with the technical guidance of Natick Laboratories, the Bata Shoe Company office in Saigon succeeded in developing a suitable boot. This became known as the *new ARVN combat boot,* and the South Vietnamese government signed the first contract for limited procurement in December 1968. Commencing in March 1969, Natick Laboratories developed casting patterns with Vietnamese anthropo-

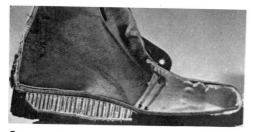

Cross-section view of composition and placement of aluminum honeycomb wedge in blast-protective combat boot first sent to Vietnam in 1967. *Army Materiel Command.*

The pieces of a blast-protective combat boot after detonating a land mine in Vietnam, showing extent of energy absorbed by the protective wedge that prevented foot amputation in this incident. *44th Medical Bde Photo Lab.*

Military police of the 716th MP Bn, preparing to counterattack VC occupying the American Embassy grounds in Saigon. The tropical combat boot with all-nylon duck uppers is worn at left; the black leather combat boot at right. 31 January 1968. *U.S. Army.*

metric foot measurements and fabricated steel molds incorporating the Panama sole design. The project was completed in June 1971.[9]

7.2 Boots and Shoes

After adopting the DMS process for the tropical combat boot, Natick Laboratories began a program to apply the vulcanized sole to the leather combat boot as well. The major problems were traction and the adequacy of the DMS bond at low temperatures in ice and snow. In January 1967, a new rubber compound and a chevron tread design were adopted as part of the black leather combat boot. This DMS version was lighter than pre-

During training, a Vietnamese CIDG recruit wears the Special Forces—procured indigenous combat boot made by Bata Shoe Company. 30 March 1967. *U.S. Army.*

Sgt. Robert Swick, 148th Supply & Service Company, resoles welt-stitched black leather combat boots, which required frequent shoe repair in Vietnam. Nha Trang, 19 November 1966. *U.S. Army.*

This DMS black leather combat boot featured a chevron tread-design sole adopted in January 1967. *Natick Laboratories.*

Color Guard of the 96th Supply & Service Bn at Cam Ranh Bay wear white leggings over their combat boots during memorial services for Pfc. Sammie Howell, 31 January 1967. *Author's collection.*

vious welt-construction models. The improved boot was worn in Vietnam, especially in aviation and other tasks where nylon tropical combat boots were unsuitable because of fire hazard.

The *leather combat boot, black, mildew resistant,* was also produced in a women's pattern, and in a special version for men who required footwear with orthopedic corrections.[10]

The *blast-protective overboot* was developed as a result of research on the blast-protective combat boot. The test data indicated that when a blast-protective combat boot was supplemented by a blast-protective overboot, the potential save of the foot increased from 45 percent to 90 percent and bone damage was minimized. The overboot's upper section was made of easily stretched rubber, which secured the overboot outer sole to the combat boot. The thick rubber sole of the overboot contained a metal shank in the heel and arch sections. The shank was a V-shaped, transverse cross-section made to deflect the blast from anti-personnel mines away from the sole of the foot. Natick Laboratories procured the first 1,200 pairs of overboots for Southeast Asia during early 1967.[11]

Special Forces honor guard members wear privately purchased Corcoran "jump boots," with reinforced foot and ankle support preferred by airborne troops, during ceremonies for a fallen comrade at Tan Son Nhut Air Base, 9 May 1963. *U.S. Army.*

Vietnamese Armor School advisor Lt. James Doherty (center) wears privately purchased "tanker boots" with double-wrap leather straps, storm welting, and reinforced stitching. Thu Duc, 27 August 1964. *U.S. Army.*

Combat engineers of the 79th Engineer Group construct a bridge in III CTZ while wearing insulated protective boots. *Author's collection.*

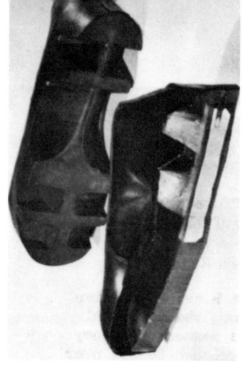

Cross-section of placement of V-shaped metal shank in the thick rubber sole of the blast-protective overboot. *Army Materiel Command.*

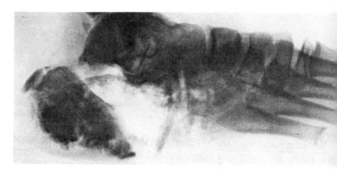

X-ray view of an Army soldier's foot that was severely shattered by blast effects of an anti-personnel mine in Vietnam. This person was not wearing blast-protective boots. *44th Medical Bdg.*

The blast-protective overboot, when worn over the blast-protective combat boot, increased protection against amputation by 45 percent to 90 percent. *Army Materiel Command.*

First experimental version of the "Delta foot-wear" boot, shown here during a 9th Inf Div patrol on 9 November 1968, was an open mesh design that proved unsatisfactory. *U.S. Army.*

Army signalman at the Long Binh Dial Telephone Exchange wears special lint and dust-free overshoes. *Author's collection.*

The standard *overshoe* had five buckles and was non-skid. Soldiers wore these overshoes while performing tasks such as port or barge security, river patrol, or other waterborne duty. The women's overshoe versions were either ankle height and made of gray

Experimental rubberized waterproof "Delta footwear" sock being field tested in the 9th Inf Div, 9 November 1968. *U.S. Army.*

vinyl, or a higher style and made of black vinyl.

Late in the war, a *lightweight overshoe* was developed as part of the LINCLOE program. This overshoe was fabricated from plasticized polyvinyl chloride and was moisture impermeable. The boots were made in whole sizes, which fitted over the standard leather combat boot, and had full bellows openings, which eased both donning and removal. The overshoe had a button-and-loop closure and was less expensive than the standard five-buckle overshoe but never became readily available in Vietnam.

White nylon *overshoes, lint and dust-free* had drawstrings for tightening around the shoe. Even in Vietnam, some areas demanded a degree of cleanliness that necessitated these overshoes. Such areas included the precision-instrument maintenance areas of sophisticated signal sites and the computer control rooms within the Inventory Control Center, Vietnam.

7.3 Delta Footwear and Lace-in Zippers

During the war, the Army concentrated on developing footwear that might reduce the alarming number of foot fungus disease (dermatophytosis) cases among U.S. troops operating throughout the Plain of Reeds and Mekong Delta. As a result, boots, shoes, and slippers manufactured for wear in such inundated areas (*See* Army Uniform Map of Vietnam) became known as "Delta footwear."

USARV requested 400 specially designed combat boots to promote the foot hygiene of 9th Infantry Division mobile riverine force soldiers on 16 October 1967. The division surgeon visited Natick Laboratories at the end of October, and on 17 November the Army Materiel Command was directed to purchase 400 test boots under ENSURE priorities. These were air expressed to Vietnam on 5 January 1968 but proved unsatisfactory. Further action on this design was cancelled 18 November 1968.[12]

The *taplin boot* was the next prototype developed for Army use in extremely wet terrain. The boot had uppers made of all-fabric, fine-mesh Nomex, a slide fastener closure, six drain holes, fiberglass heel counter-toe caps, and a Panama sole. The first batch of 750 pairs

The Army's experimental "barefoot boot" was designed to leave the imprint of native feet by Special Forces patrol members. *U.S. Army.*

reached Vietnam during March 1969. Since the withdrawal of the 9th Infantry Division lessened operational requirements for this boot, only 1,200 more pairs were sent to Vietnam for evaluation in October. The taplin Nomex boots were not significantly better than tropical combat boots, and further procurement was terminated 30 June 1970.

The "Delta footwear" *canvas shoe* and a *comfort shoe* were both designed so soldiers could get out of wet boots and socks whenever practical and yet have some degree of foot protection. On 25 May 1968, USARV requested 20,000 pairs of canvas shoes for 9th Infantry Division evaluation. All were air mailed to Vietnam by 15 January 1969 but proved unsatisfactory.

USARV requested the comfort shoe on 2 June 1969. This *comfort shoe, type II,* or "bivouac slipper," was Velcro fastened and could be folded and put in the pocket. The Army ordered 47,200 pairs under ENSURE priority on 30 September 1969, and reclassified them as standard issue on 15 January 1970. The first batch of 14,688 comfort shoes was flown to Vietnam on 13 March, and another 11,022 pairs arrived at the end of the month.[13]

Pfc. Arthur Jordan, a 1099th Transportation Company LCM crewman on the Song Vam Co Tay, wears the crepe sole canvas shoe, required for safety reasons on Army inland watercraft. 18 August 1967. *U.S. Army.*

In 1969, as part of the "Delta footwear" program, the Army ordered 47,200 pairs of nylon lace-in zippers for tropical combat boots as a quick-release mechanism. *Lace-in boot zippers* were reclassified as a standard Army issue for selected units on 15 January 1970, and 15,000 pairs were flown to Vietnam on 20 February. Another 30,000 pairs arrived by air express 27 March 1970, but after that date USARV procured them through normal supply channels.[14]

MACV restricted lace-in zippers for tropical combat boots to Special Forces, ranger companies, advisory teams, combat tracker and scout dog platoons, and infantry or mechanized infantry battalions operating in water inundated regions. (*See* Army Uniform Map of Vietnam.) These restrictions were tightened by MACV on 23 September 1972: "Lace-in zippers for tropical combat boots are authorized for wear only by personnel assigned to units working in or around ports and water inundated areas."[15]

7.4 Experimental Boots

Late in the war, advanced development in boots was centered on a fabric for fire-resistant uppers and on micro-cellular rubber soles to further reduce boot weight. For example, a lightweight, insulated boot was considered. It was made of micro-cellular blown urethane, which provided durability and had an outer Vibram-design sole and molded upper portion. The pull-on jackboot style fit close to the ankle.

An experimental attempt to fool NVA/VC trackers by making footprints look like ground debris produced the unusual *footprintless shoe.* This shoe was actually a boot that disguised the distinctive footprint of the tropical combat boot with leaf-type imprints on the sole. USARV requested 2,270 pairs of these boots on 6 June 1967, and DA approved the requirement on 29 June under ENSURE priority. At a cost of $4,000, Natick Laboratories produced two dozen pairs of the prototypes. The footprintless shoes were sent to Special Forces for combat evaluation in August, but the project was cancelled on 26 August 1967.[16]

Another type of unusual Army footwear of the Vietnam conflict was the "barefoot boot." These boots were made with soles designed to leave the footprint of Vietnamese peasants or the print of Viet Cong sandals. Anatomically correct molds of typical Vietnamese feet and molds of Viet Cong sandals were used to produce the imprint on the bottom of the boot. This secret development program rushed 120 pairs (60 of each type) to Special Forces in Vietnam during early 1965. The experimental boots were extremely rare and apparently unsuccessful.[17]

7.5 Protective Guards and Safety Footwear

A variety of protective footwear was used in Vietnam for special purposes. The black rubber *hip boot* was sometimes used in bridge construction or other work. The black neoprene rubber boot provided resistance to solvents, oil, and grease, which normally destroyed boots or rubber-composition footwear. Black, rubber-cleated *knee boots* were used in outdoor storage facilities for steam cleaning equipment or handling certain fuels. The *safety knee boot* contained a safety toe and removable innersole steel shank for work in muddy or wet areas where hazards from falling heavy objects also existed.

The *safety boot* was worn by heavy equipment operators engaged in ground maintenance work and who were exposed to hazards from which they could not be protected by standard safety shoes or combat boots. The boot was 8 inches high, and had a steel cap and toe and neoprene sole and heel.

Linemen and other soldiers requiring protection from electric shock wore *safety boots: non-sparking sole and heel, nonconductive*. This 8-inch-high boot was suitable for working with electrical equipment on poles or trees. The *lineman's safety shoe* was a high-top leather shoe with insulated bottom and neoprene soles and heels for work on power lines.

Linemen and other soldiers whose work required ascending and descending high poles and trees were equipped with the *climber's set, tree and pole*. This pair of adjustable, metal leg

A lineman of the 1st Signal Bde puts on his tree and pole climber's set. *Army News Features.*

1st Transportation Bn personnel fire M79s from the *Corpus Christie Bay*, an Army floating aircraft-maintenance depot ship near Qui Nhon. They wear required non-skid, non-sparking boots. *Author's collection.*

irons, with leather-retaining strap and drop-forged gaff and tang, attached to the leg for climbing. The *lineman leg climber's protective guard* was a cork or plastic protector that covered the gaff on the climber's set.

The *guard, protective foot* was a curved, hard fiber or metal shield shaped to fit over the shoe or boot for additional protection. The *guard, protective shin* was a heavy fiber guard that could be strapped to the lower leg to protect against cuts, flying objects, sparks, and bruises. For security duty, the Military Police possessed heavy, leather-covered *shin and leg protective guards*, reinforced with steel stays. This guard was the same type used by forest rangers and timber cutters in the United States.

A number of different safety shoes were utilized in Vietnam. Conductive or spark-proof soles and heels were used in areas where static or friction sparks might ignite hazardous materials. One sandal type with fabric straps featured a special composition sole that dissipated static charges. The *industrial safety shoe* was rubber with steel toe and shockproof insole. Its outer sole tread was designed for traction. The *non-sparking safety shoe* was a regular oxford style, with a safety toe and non-sparking, composition rubber sole. Finally, a russet, leather *safety shoe, oil and acid protective,* with conductive sole, was worn in gas handling sites, ammunition breakdown points,

maintenance shops, or wherever explosive gases or vapors were present and explosions caused by static sparks were possible.

The *non-sparking shoe: traction tread sole and heel, mildew resistant* was used by mechanics of the 1st Transportation Battalion aboard the Army's floating aircraft-maintenance depot, *Corpus Christie Bay.* Other personnel working around oil or diluted acid, where the hazard of falling objects also existed, wore this non-sparking shoe. The general use, high-top leather shoe with neoprene sole and safety toe was another non-sparking shoe variety. This version was not suitable where a high degree of hazard from static discharge existed.

Notes

1. Dr. S. J. Kennedy, *Preliminary Evaluation of the Individual Clothing and Equipment of Vietnamese Military Forces,* Natick Laboratories, 15 Jul 63, 5.
2. Quartermaster Field Evaluation Agency, *Engineering Test of Boots, Combat, Tropical: T59-1, -2, -3,* 12 Jan 62.
3. Natick Laboratories, *Technical Report 68-20-CM,* Sep 67, 10.
4. Army Test and Evaluation Command, *Integrated Engineering and Service Test of Boot, Combat, Tropical, DMS, with Sole Shield, Spike Resistant,* Jan 64.
5. Army Quartermaster Research & Engineering Field Evaluation Agency, *Historical Summary, 1 Jan–31 Mar 64,* 9–10.
6. Military Specifications MIL-B-43154C, 24 Jan 67; MIL-B-43154D, 26 Sep 69, and MIL-B-43154E, 16 May 72.
7. Army Materiel Command, *Clothing & Equipment Support to U.S. Army in Vietnam,* Feb 67, 7.
8. 5th Special Forces Group, *Operational Report,* 10 Aug 66, 7.
9. Vietnam Laboratory Assistance Program, *Report: VLAPA Project #9,* 31 Mar 70.
10. Army Materiel Command, *Clothing & Equipment Support to U.S. Army in Vietnam,* Feb 67, 1.
11. Army Materiel Command, *Clothing & Equipment Support to U.S. Army in Vietnam,* Feb 67, 9.
12. Defense Supply Agency, ACSFOR DS Status Report, 31 Dec 68.
13. Combat Research and Development Command, *Footgear for Inundated Areas,* 1 Dec 69.
14. Defense Supply Agency, ACSFOR DS Status Report, 30 Jun 70.
15. MACV Reg 670-5, Change 2, 3 Jun 70; MACV Directive 670-1, Suppl 1, 23 Sep 72.
16. Defense Supply Agency, ACSFOR DS Status Report, 31 Aug 67.
17. *Soldiers,* Feb 79, 29–32.

8

Individual Equipment

8.1 Load-Carrying Harnesses, Slings, and Belts

The Army's M1956 *individual load-carrying equipment* was manufactured of cotton webbing fabric. The material readily absorbed water, became heavy when wet, and dried slowly. On 26 October 1965, ACTIV requested that quick-drying, lightweight nylon gear be fabricated for testing purposes in Vietnam. Natick Laboratories manufactured six experimental sets of nylon equipment. They approximated the design of eight standard items in the set: individual equipment belt, intrenching tool carrier, canvas combat field pack, sleeping equipment carrier, two small arms ammunition cases, field first-aid dressing/compass cases, water canteen covers, and suspenders. This prototype lightweight load-carrying system weighed only 3.3 pounds. It was sent to ACTIV on 14 January 1966.[1]

The reception of this individual nylon gear in Vietnam was enthusiastic. On 13 February 1967, USARV requested that 550 sets of "M56-design nylon load-bearing equipment"

be expedited to Vietnam for further ACTIV evaluation. These sets, which cost $82 each, were made of nylon fabric or webbing in lieu of cotton wherever possible, and aluminum hardware was substituted for the standard steel and brass. Some functional design changes were incorporated, such as new sleeping bag carriers and quick-release buckles on individual equipment belts. The sets were flown from their production site at Richmond, Virginia, to Vietnam on 13 April 1967. The 5th Special Forces Group and most divisional recon companies received 40 sets in May.[2]

USARV reported on 26 August 1967 that field receptivity to the lightweight load-carrying system was excellent. The final ACTIV evaluation report, of 24 January 1968, was also very favorable. The Army ordered 204,650 sets under ENSURE priority on 8 April 1968, but manufacturing difficulties prevented complete sets from reaching Vietnam until 1970. Instead, the system components were sent as they became available. For example, the first 25,000 belts were airlifted to Vietnam on 8 August; 16,000 first aid packets on 30 August; 16,000

The M1956 individual load-carrying system being worn by arriving 11th Inf Bde soldier with duffel bag at Qui Nhon, 20 December 1967. *U.S. Army.*

Maj. Joe Shankle (left), Army liaison officer to the 35th Security Police Squadron, wears cap, with appropriate Air Force insignia, and individual equipment belt, with suspenders and two ammunition cases. Phan Rang, June 1969. *Army News Features.*

water canteen covers on 20 August; and 14,000 sleeping gear carriers on 29 August 1968. As a result, the equipment was distributed unevenly, and, by 1971, individual load-carrying systems in Vietnam were a mixture of cotton and nylon components.[3]

The *universal load-carrying sling* designed to complement the M1956 individual equipment system, was a 6.5-foot-long adjustable web strap, containing buckles, slide loops, and snap fasteners, which could be shifted to various positions for attaching loads. Each sling could carry about 35 pounds of special loads, including three 3.5-inch rocket rounds or four 81mm mortar rounds. Two slings could be combined to carry a 5-gallon water can.

The standard Army cotton webbing, Olive Drab M1956 *individual equipment belt,* or "pistol belt," was produced in long and medium sizes and was adjustable at both ends with a heavy, brass wire ball-type fastener. The belt with its field combat-pack suspenders provided the foundation of the load-carrying system. Other equipment was attached to this foundation. The suspenders could either be snapped to the field combat pack, which was clipped to the individual equipment belt, or be snapped directly to the belt. The suspenders were made of olive drab cotton webbing and

The M1956 sleeping equipment carrier used to strap poncho (with poncho liner rolled inside) to the load-carrying harnesses of 1st Cav Div troopers at An Khe, 25 January 1966. Note the M1956 combat field pack *(left)* and M1961 combat field pack *(center)*. *U.S. Army.*

drill cloth and could be adjusted by means of clamp-style buckles.

The new nylon webbing M1967 *individual equipment belt* with a quick-release metal fastener was adopted 7 July 1967. The seat-belt-type fastener with an ingenious T-slot was designed by Davis Aircraft Products. Unfortunately, it tended to unfasten at inopportune times. The nylon individual equipment belts began arriving in Vietnam in August 1968, and quantitative supply stocks were achieved during 1969. The belt was not standardized, however, until 23 November 1970.[4]

The standard, cotton webbing *trousers belt* was black with a brass or black-finish roller buckle. During the Vietnam conflict, a frame buckle was also produced for field use.

The universal load-carrying sling, used here to carry mortar ammunition above the combat field pack, was largely replaced by the lightweight rucksack in Vietnam. *U.S. Army.*

A soldier of the 2d Bn, 28th Inf (1st Inf Div), pauses during action in the Michelin Rubber Plantation, 14 November 1965. Note the suspender attachment to the individual equipment belt and first aid packet. *U.S. Army.*

1Lt. John Doane of the 1st Bn, 503d Inf (173d Abn Bde), wears the lensatic compass case *(left)* and first aid packet *(right)* on his suspenders near An Khe. Note insect repellent bottle in helmet camouflage band. *Arnold Fischer.*

The *general officer's belt* had a 2.3-inch round, 24-karat-gold-plated buckle that was lacquered and embossed with the American coat of arms and wreath. The general officer's belt with gold-plated belt buckle was often worn over the tropical coat by generals who helicoptered frequently to field units.[5]

The Army employed three basic types of safety belts in Vietnam. The *safety belt, body type* was a nylon-cotton or leather belt reinforced with padding and D-Rings, which prevented falls while engaged in high work. The *lineman's safety belt with safety strap* was an adjustable web or leather body belt with tool holders and two D-Rings. This belt was used

The rear suspender attachment to the M1956 combat field pack is displayed by this trooper of the 1st Bde, 101st Abn Div, questioning Vietnamese villagers, 8 May 1966. *U.S. Army.*

SSgt. Frank Walker of the 299th Engineer Bn wears the M1942 first aid packet/lensatic compass case (redesignated from "pouch" in the Vietnam era). General Westmoreland presents Distinguished Service Cross for Walker's actions of 11 November 1967. *Author's collection.*

SSgt. George Steinhoff of the 199th Inf Bde wears the anglehead flashlight on his load-carrying harness. He is carrying the combination tool upside down and hooked to his lightweight rucksack. 1968. *U.S. Army.*

by wiremen, electrical linemen, and repairmen to prevent falls from elevated positions. The *ladder safety belt* was a padded waist belt equipped with a large, drop-forged snap with keeper for snapping over round ladder rungs when going up high, straight ladders. A lanyard, which consisted of a tail line of manila, nylon, or steel tied onto a stationary object and equipped with snaps for fastening to the safety belt, was often recommended for additional protection from falls.

8.2   Extraction Harnesses

The *McGuire rig*, named after Sgt. Maj. Charles T. McGuire of Project DELTA from 1964 to 1965, was an extraction device used to retrieve up to three patrol members at a time

from areas where jungle growth or enemy fire prevented normal helicopter boarding. The rig, consisting of a 2-inch-wide webbing sling, attached to the end of a long nylon rope, was dropped from a hovering helicopter. The individuals to be extracted placed the webbing around their buttocks to form a seat and, at the same time, slipped their hands through wrist loops attached to the web sling. The wrist loops tightened and helped prevent the dropping of injured or fatigued personnel.

The rig was unsatisfactory because it had to be donned and activated while in a standing position, and the hands were not free to un-

The combat field pack suspenders (with first aid packet attached at upper right) linked into M1956 small arms ammunition cases on the individual equipment belt. The M1967 individual equipment belt with Davis fastener is below. *Author's collection.*

The general officer's belt worn by Brig. Gen. Richard M. Lee, the deputy senior advisor to II CTZ. Note parachutist's chin strap. July 1967. *U.S. Army.*

The limitations of the McGuire rig shown in training of Company L (Ranger), 75th Inf, near Phu Bai. Personnel must be seated in the harness and use both hands during extraction. *Author's collection.*

The improved extraction ability of the Stabo extraction harness, allowing both hands to remain free, is demonstrated at Nha Trang by three 5th Special Forces Group NCOs. On right is Sfc. Clifford Roberts, one of the Stabo extraction harness inventors. *Author's collection.*

Sp4 Thomas Ippolito wears the lineman's safety belt while installing lighting as part of the Dau Tieng Bridge defense system. *25th Inf Div PIO.*

tangle lines or use a weapon. Because of discomfort and impairment of blood circulation, the McGuire rig was normally used only for emergency recoveries involving short periods of actual flight.

The Special Forces MACV Recondo School developed a more efficient extraction harness that was first demonstrated on 1 October 1968. This rig was developed by Maj. Robert L. Stevens, Cpt. John D. H. Knabb, and Sfc. Clifford L. Roberts, who were all instructors at the Nha Trang base course, in response to a number of tragic operational mishaps involving the McGuire assemblies. The new rig was called the Stabo rig, a designation derived from the names of its creators. After rigorous combat testing with a handful of locally produced Stabo extraction harnesses, the 5th Special Forces Group requested 1,000 rigs under emergency ENSURE priority on 30 June 1969.[6]

The Stabo extraction harness modeled by a Special Forces sergeant at the MACV Recondo School, 27 November 1968. *Author's collection.*

The Stabo extraction harness, modeled by a Special Forces instructor of the MACV Recondo School, with carabiner attachment to the lift rope. Nha Trang, 31 October 1970. *Author's collection.*

The *Stabo extraction harness* was superior to the McGuire rig because it could be used to extract a man who was unconscious, and it permitted an individual to be lifted out while still firing his weapon or using his radio. The Stabo gear was fabricated of nylon webbing sewn into a configuration of the parachute harness and standard load-bearing equipment. The main lift harness formed an "X" across the back with leg straps. These straps were retained by tape or rubber bands to keep them from dangling loose. The harness was completely buckled around the legs with metal D-Rings only when extraction was imminent. Otherwise, secured leg straps would bind against the inner thighs during movement. The harness was linked into a nylon individual equipment belt, and the assembled combination carried

combat gear such as canteens, ammunition cases, and other items. The two carabiners on the upper shoulder straps of the main lift harness attached to helicopter-dropped ropes.

There were two types of Stabo extraction harnesses, which differed primarily in the construction of the helicopter-mounted rope deployment bag and in the method of attaching the individual equipment belt. In the first version the belts were sewn into the harness and necessitated individualized tailoring for proper belt adjustment. The improved harnesses, introduced in 1970, had two loops, one positioned above the other, sewn into the webbing, that enabled the belt to be slipped into whichever position afforded the best fit for the wearer. This method also enabled recon personnel to wear the belt styles they preferred and to easily replace damaged ones.

The Army instituted long, arduous stateside safety tests, which were not completed until 31 March 1970. During this time, Special Forces personnel relied on a very limited supply of approximately 500 Stabo extraction harnesses that were produced by the 2d Logistical Command on Okinawa and were purchased through the Counterinsurgency Support Office. Regular Army funds were made available on 30 June 1970, and Natick Laboratories began procurement procedures. Approximately 3,300 Stabo extraction harnesses were produced and sent to the 5th Special Forces Group and MACV-SOG in Vietnam and to the 46th Special Forces Company in Thailand (for use in Laos and Cambodia), from 16 October to 31 December 1970.[7]

8.3 Ammunition Cases, Bandoleers, and Bags

The standard *universal small arms ammunition case,* or pouch as it was termed prior to 1962, was a box-type case made of cotton webbing and duck and was 6.25 inches high. It was sized deliberately in order to carry the ammunition for a "universal" variety of weapons as used in 1956 when the case was standardized. The pouch was designed to hold two BAR magazines, or one bandoleer of six M1 clips, or four 30-round carbine magazines. The cover was shut by a canvas tab fitting through a metal loop, which was riveted to a billet sewed on the front of the case. On the outside, hand grenades could be carried in side slots and were safeguarded by two web straps on each side. Two universal small arms ammunition cases were ordinarily secured to the individual equipment belt by slide lock keepers, and their supporting straps were snapped to the suspenders.[8]

In Vietnam, during sustained fire fights, large quantities of ammunition had to be carried and reached quickly. The universal small arms ammunition cases were stiff and their depth hindered ready accessibility to M16 magazines, even though plastic stiffeners in the

back of the cases eased ammunition removal. Soldiers resorted to putting extra field dressing or rolled-up socks in the cases to raise the magazines for easy reach.[9]

The M1967 equipment assembly design envisioned a nylon small arms ammunition case for carrying two M14 rifle magazines. This item was not adopted until 13 July 1971 and was never issued in Vietnam.

The canvas *small arms ammunition case, M16A1, 20 rounds,* was developed to carry four M16 magazines each and was standardized on 29 August 1967. On 15 March 1968, the specification was modified for nylon fabrication and redesignated as the *small arms ammunition case, M16, 20 rounds.* These nylon cases featured plastic squeeze catches that were originally designed for arctic operations where mittens were required.[10]

In late 1965, the Army Weapons Command informed Natick Laboratories that a new 30-round magazine was planned for the M16 rifle. The Army Materiel Command requested development of a suitable ammunition case on 19 January 1966. Natick Laboratories designed a nylon fabric case capable of accommodating three 30-round magazines. The case contained a riveted metal insert and opposing stainless steel leaf springs that maintained pressure against the magazines to keep them from rattling. Although prototype cases were ready by 1967, they were not standardized until 30 January 1969, as the *30-round small arms ammunition case (M16 and M16E1 Rifle).* Utilization of the cases in Vietnam was sporadic because of developmental problems in producing satisfactory 30-round magazines.[11]

An interesting concept, which might have disposed of ammunition cases altogether, was the expendable plastic M16 magazine that USARV requested on 31 December 1965. The substitution of plastic for metal was envisioned as a means of eliminating noise and the need for reloading in the field. In addition, potentially, it offered a cheap material that would neither corrode in the jungle atmosphere nor provide useful material if recovered by the enemy. DA approved expedited design of the disposable magazine as an ENSURE priority item on 16 May 1966. Several designs were selected on 1 December, and preliminary testing commenced at Aberdeen Proving Grounds,

Top, *left to right:* Folded shelter half; 3-section tent pole; 5 tent pins; guy line; combat field pack; folded wool blanket. *Center, left to right:* M1956 individual equipment belt with 2 small arms ammunition cases, first aid packet, combination tool and carrier, canteen cover; combat field pack suspenders; M1950 leather gloves, strap closure. *Bottom, left to right:* Field mess kit; polyethylene 1-quart canteen and canteen cup; trouser suspenders; overshoes. *U.S. Army.*

The soldier *(center)* of the 2d Bn, 506th Inf (101st Abn Div), carries an M16 ammunition bandoleer during the attack on Binh My, 1 February 1968. *USARV PIO.*

M79 ammunition bandoleers and field expedient grenade carrier vest worn by parachutists of the 2d Bn, 327th Inf (101st Abn Div), 14 January 1966. *U.S. Army.*

Maryland, on 22 March 1967. The project was terminated on 20 January 1968, however, because of the high cost of the plastic magazines.[12]

The two ammunition cases normally attached to the individual equipment belt carried an inadequate supply of ammunition in sustained fire fights. Soldiers on the battlefield resorted to carrying the seven-pocket, cotton bandoleers in which the M16 ammunition was packaged. On 9 November 1967, the 1st Cavalry Division favorably concluded evaluation of stripper clip ammunition: pre-packaged *5.56mm ball M193 10-round clip bandoleers,* which allowed soldiers to load their ammuni-

Pfc. Raymond Allmon of Company F (Ranger), 75th Inf, charges forward with his M60 machine gun and ammunition carrier boxes during the skirmish at Hieu Thien, 2 April 1970. *Author's collection.*

tion quickly and easily. Although the bandoleers were very flimsy, ripped easily, and wore through rapidly, the popularity of the clips and bandoleers was quickly manifested throughout Vietnam. Platoon leader Lt. Joel M. Shreenan of the 9th Infantry Division stated, "We don't use many ammo pouches over here because magazines are easier to carry and get at in an empty claymore bag or bandoleer."[13]

The *M18A1 antipersonnel mine carrier,* or "claymore mine bag," became popular as a sack for spare rifle magazines. The bag contained two large compartments, offered protection from moisture, and was very durable. When the 173d Airborne Brigade parachutists assaulted Hill 873 in November 1967, they carried claymore mine bags filled to the brim with extra magazines and strapped double over their chests. As they charged toward the summit,

Sp4 Charles Hines' M16 magazines stopped an NVA bullet from entering his stomach during a Company N (Ranger), 75th Inf (173d Abn Bde), fire fight that killed 8 NVA soldiers. *Joe Oden.*

"Claymore mine bag," under the arm of soldier in front, carried during the 11th Inf Bde destruction of My Lai, March 1968. *Peers Commission Inquiry.*

they could easily reach ammunition and rapidly slam it into their automatic rifles.

The claymore mine bag was also used to carry M79 grenade rounds. The basic load for grenadiers was 27 rounds, but the capacity of the issued M79 ammunition bandoleer was only 6 cartridges. Thirty rounds could be carried in one claymore bag, however, and grenadiers could double that amount by lashing two bags across their chests.

The *grenade bag* was developed by Natick Laboratories in response to an urgent USARV message of 7 June 1966, which reported safety problems with carrying grenades suspended from the ammunition cases or suspender harnesses. The handles of the grenades were not strong enough when carried in this fashion, according to the USARV message, and often broke, causing accidental detonations. The message concluded, "A grenade bag capable of holding six to eight grenades, similar to the type used in World War II, is required."[14]

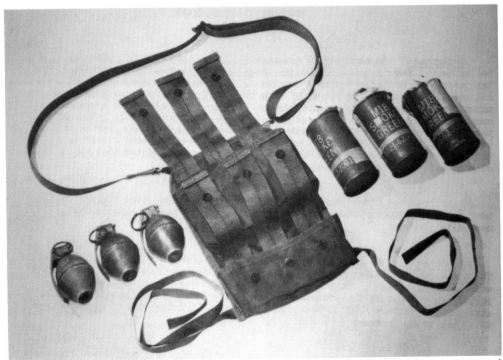

The M26 Grenade bag developed by Natick Laboratories and used in Vietnam during 1966 and 1967. *Natick Laboratories.*

The improved M79 grenade carrier vest worn by a grenadier patrolling the Central Highlands. *Army News Features.*

A grenadier *(right)* of the 2d Bn, 3d Inf (199th Inf Bde), wears the early-version grenade carrier vest, with difficult-to-reach back pockets, 18 June 1967. *U.S. Army.*

Natick Laboratories designed a water-repellent, nylon duck grenade bag with two pockets. The upper pocket could hold three canister or three fragmentation grenades, and the lower pocket could accommodate only three fragmentation grenades. The grenades were positioned upright in the pockets and were spaced by handle retaining straps using Velcro closures. The bag could either be attached to the belt or suspended from the shoulders with a shoulder strap.

DA approved procurement on 21 July 1966, and the grenade bags were manufactured in Richmond, Virginia, under ENSURE priority. Approximately 100 grenade bags were airlifted to Vietnam on 28 September 1966, but ACTIV reported that the item was unsuitable on 21 February 1967. On 4 August, further

This 4th Inf Div grenadier wears the improved M79 grenade carrier vest, which carried 24 rounds in three rows of grenade pockets. West of Pleiku. *U.S. Army.*

Soldier of the 2d Bn, 327th Inf (101st Abn Div), armed with an M203 40mm semiautomatic grenade launcher, wears the M79 grenade carrier vest. *Author's collection.*

action was delayed while the Army considered a general-purpose vest in lieu of the grenade bag. The M26 grenade bag was finally cancelled on 26 August 1967 when USARV decided that M79 ammunition carrier vests would satisfy any grenade-carrying needs.[15]

8.4 Ammunition Carrier Vests

Ammunition for the M79 grenade launchers was issued in six-round bandoleers, which consisted of two three-round pockets and a shoulder strap. The bandoleer was unsatisfactory in Vietnam because the straps often were snagged by vegetation and they twisted, causing the rounds to drop out. Grenadiers complained that carrying several bandoleers also created uncomfortable weight imbalances and hindered easy one-handed access to the rounds in their bandoleer pockets.

A Special Forces sergeant in Vietnam assembled a makeshift vest in early 1965 and showed his prototype model to a Natick Laboratories' representative. The sergeant's vest was taken back to the United States and copied. Following a 14 October 1965 directive from Army Materiel Command, 6,687 of these *grenade carrier vests* were fabricated for Vietnam-

The M60 ammunition carrier vest was developed in November 1969 and service tested in Vietnam in 1970 and 1971. *Natick Laboratories.*

The need for an M60 ammunition carrier vest is demonstrated by this machine gun crew of the 2d Bn, 27th Inf (25th Inf Div), crossing a canal near the Cambodian border, 1969. *Author's collection.*

wide utilization. Approximately 10,195 smaller vests were also produced for the ARVN forces. These were airlifted to Vietnam in May and June 1966.[16]

The grenade carrier vest was well received in Vietnam, but USARV requested modifications in the design on 3 January 1967. Natick Laboratories then produced 500 improved

Sp5 Thomas Rhodes wears the M16 ammunition vest as he holds a Viet Cong bamboo fish trap. 18 November 1970. *U.S. Army.*

The lightweight rucksack worn by Sp4 Patrick Harding of the 1st Bn, 5th Inf (25th Inf Div). Southwest of Bear Cat, 2 October 1970. *Author's collection.*

vests. To minimize heat stress, the grenade carrier vest was fabricated from nylon netting. The vest could be adjusted by three elastic cross straps down the center of the back and by drawstrings along each side below the armholes. The front closed with a Velcro tape fastener. The vest contained six three-grenade pockets, two on each side of the front and two on the back. This provided an 18-round carrying capacity. These improved vests were flown to Vietnam on 28 March 1967.

An extensive evaluation of the grenade carrier vest under Vietnam combat conditions was begun by ACTIV on 17 April 1967 and revealed that the vest was rather clumsy and the back carrier pockets impractical. As a result, on 27 September 1967, ACTIV suggested another redesign to be followed by further testing. USARV agreed that the grenade carrier vest should be modified but wanted any improved vests expedited onto the battlefield, without the need for further testing inside Vietnam. DA compromised on 9 October 1967 by agreeing to accelerate testing of the redesigned vest at Fort Benning, Georgia. This was successfully completed on 28 December. The vest was approved by DA on 19 February 1968 and procured for Vietnam utilization under EN-SURE priority. The first 2,000 vests reached Vietnam in September, and 14,400 vests were in the combat theater by 13 December 1968.[17]

The improved M79 grenade carrier vest could carry 24 rounds in the three rows of grenade pockets on each side of the front, 12 to a side. The front of the vest was made of nylon duck, while the shoulders and back were of porous nylon mesh for ventilation. Following a USARV evaluation report on 30 September 1969, Natick Laboratories again redesigned the vest. This time, the entire vest was fabricated of raschel knitted nylon fabric, and the nylon duck portions were eliminated. This final version, the grenadier carrier vest, reached Vietnam in 1971 and 1972.[18]

One continual problem in Vietnam was the need for plenty of machine gun ammuni-

Soldiers of the 1st Bn, 35th Inf (4th Inf Div), add rope coils to their lightweight rucksacks. Note M17 protective mask centered on rucksack at center. Near Kontum, 21 April 1968. *U.S. Army.*

The 1st Bn, 8th Inf (4th Inf Div), use lightweight rucksacks to carry personal gear, ammunition, machetes, and combination intrenching tools on Hill 742 northwest of Dak To, 15 November 1967. *U.S. Army.*

tion with no handy way to carry it except in belts crisscrossing the body. Because the cartridges became wet, soiled, and corroded, there were misfires in combat. In November 1969, an *ammunition carrier vest* for M60 machine gun ammunition was developed by Natick Laboratories and was service-tested in Vietnam the next year. The shoulder and back area of the vest were fabricated from a nylon Raschel knit netting. The vest's lower front, made of nylon fabric, had two pockets sewn on each side of the front closure, each capable of carrying a full assault packet of M60 ammunition. The Velcro closure in front was reinforced with two snap closures.

During the spring of 1969, the Vietnamese 25th Infantry Division requested a specialized, lightweight ammunition carrying vest from the Army Materiel Command's Customer Assistance Office in Vietnam. On 16 June 1969, the request was passed to Natick Laboratories, which agreed that a convenient ammunition

vest for twenty M16 magazines and two canteens would permit the removal of unnecessary equipment during a fire fight. This would dispense with the multitude of bandoleers and claymore mine bags that were ordinarily used for carrying ammunition. The *lightweight ammunition carrying vest* prototype was finished 16 October 1969, and 400 vests were sent to Vietnam for evaluation on 26 January 1970. More vests were ordered for the Vietnamese after successful testing, and American troops were also using them by the end of the year.[19]

8.5 Lightweight Rucksack

The *lightweight rucksack* was first produced as the T62-1 lightweight rucksack, which was originally developed for arctic utilization and adopted in 1962. The rucksack was standardized on 2 November 1965. The rucksack assembly, weighing 3 pounds, included a riveted aluminum tubular frame designed to

Airmobile assault of the 2d Bn, 14th Inf (25th Inf Div), 20 August 1969. The problem of paint flaking off the lightweight rucksack frame can be seen here. This problem was not resolved until the successor frame was anodized after the war. *Author's collection.*

keep the load off the back and provide for air circulation. The sack and all other components, including shoulder, cargo, and back straps, were strapped to the frame. An optional cargo support shelf could be added if the frame was used as a packboard. The rucksack was also furnished with a waist strap, intended for keeping the rucksack centered on the back while skiing, and an M14 rifle carrier strap assembly, also used only while skiing.

The lightweight rucksack was made of water-resistant nylon, Olive Green army shade 106. It had over twice the capacity of the M1961 combat field pack, and had two side pockets, a back flap pocket, and double eyelet web tabs for the attachment of canteens, ma-

Soldiers of the 4th Bn, 9th Inf (25th Inf Div), convert their lightweight rucksacks into pack frames for mortar rounds while operating in War Zone C in 1969. Center soldier wears the M79 grenade carrier vest. *25th Inf Div PIO.*

chete sheaths, and other equipment. The rucksack could be freely moved and reattached to different parts of the frame to create upper or lower space for carrying sleeping gear, mortar rounds, radios, or other equipment. The removable, metal cargo shelf helped to secure these items. Without the pack, the rucksack could be transformed into a load-carrying frame for larger items. The complex, emergency quick-release system, initially mounted on the left shoulder strap, was later replaced by shoulder strap quick-release devices, which allowed the wearer to easily discard the entire rucksack assembly.[20]

During combat operations, the soldiers carried most of their supplies in lightweight rucksacks. In the event of a fire fight, the rucksacks were usually dropped to increase the soldier's mobility and decrease his profile when moving on the battlefield. As soon as the fire fight ended, troops retrieved their rucksacks. Sometimes, rucksacks were not carried by the troops during long marches but were brought to the field by helicopter before RON (Remain Overnight) positions were established. The lightweight rucksack was vital to Vietnam operations and was kept in good supply, although local shortages sometimes existed. The 1st Infantry Division, for example, lacked enough rucksacks during 1966. On 19 July 1973, after the last Army units were withdrawn from Vietnam, production of the lightweight rucksack was cancelled.

8.6 Indigenous Ranger Pack (ARVN Rucksack)

In 1961, the Combat Developments and Test Center was directed to make an indigenous rucksack for the South Vietnamese Army rangers. The intention was to produce an item that could be made locally from materials readily producible in Vietnam. The rucksack was designed by Eldon C. Metzger of Natick Laboratories. He based his prototype on the Vietnamese ability to carry three- to ten-days'-worth of rice, vegetables, and ammunition on typical missions, which he observed in July 1963.[21]

The resulting *ranger pack,* or "indigenous rucksack," consisted of a large cotton duck pack, with drawstring closure and two outside pockets, mounted on a rattan "X" frame (later

An aidman of the 3d Bn, 503d Inf (173d Abn Bde), uses his lightweight rucksack to carry an additional medical instrument and supply case, with 2-quart canteen attached. Near Bao Loc, 1969. *U.S. Army.*

made of spring steel), which kept the load off the back for air circulation. On the top of the pouch cover there was an equipment hanger for attaching the intrenching tool carrier. The handle of the tool was secured to the pouch by a strap with buckle sewn between the pockets. Other equipment could be secured to the six loops sewn on the pack's side and bottom.[22] A similar rucksack that did not have a frame was used by the NVA.

The indigenous ranger pack was handy and compact, with few projections to catch on undergrowth. The indigenous load-bearing system, including the specially developed belt and suspenders, weighed 5 pounds. The Vietnamese used the ranger pack to carry a host of

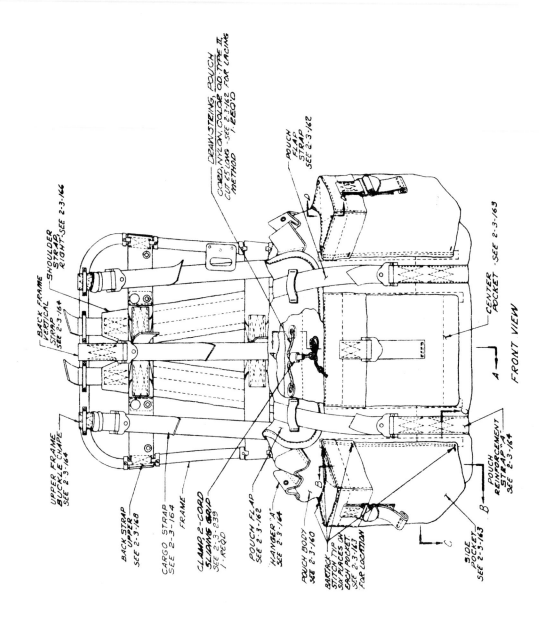

DRAWSTRING, POUCH
CORD, NYLON, COLOR OD, TYPE II,
CUT 65 LONG - SEE 2-3/62 FOR LACING
METHOD 1.25 OLD

POUCH
FLAP
SEE 2-3-/62

BACK FRAME
VERTICAL STRAP
RIGHT - SEE 2-3-/66

SHOULDER
STRAP
SEE 2-3-/64

BACK FRAME
VERTICAL
STRAP
SEE 2-3-/64

UPPER FRAME
BUCKLE CHAPE
SEE 2-3-/64

BACK STRAP
UPPER
SEE 2-3-/68

CARGO STRAP
SEE 2-3-/64

FRAME

CLAMP 2-CORD
SLIDING GRIP
SEE 2-3-239
1-REQD

POUCH FLAP
SEE 2-3-/62

HANGER 'A'
SEE 2-3-/64

POUCH BODY
SEE 2-3-/60

BARTACK
STITCH TYP
SIX PLACES ON
EACH POCKET
SEE 2-3-/43
FOR LOCATION

CENTER
POCKET - SEE 2-3-/63

POUCH
REINFORCEMENT
STRAP 'A'
SEE 2-3-/64

SIDE
POCKET
SEE 2-3-/63

FRONT VIEW

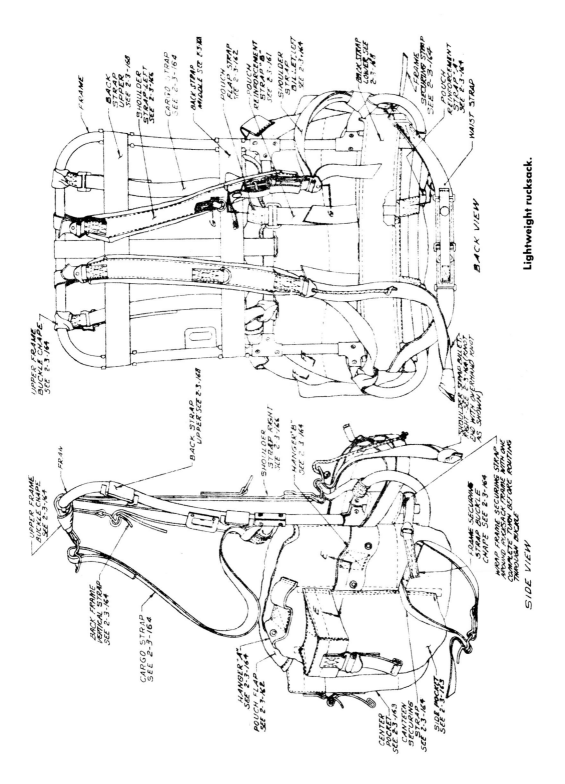

FRAME

BACK STRAP UPPER SEE 2-3-168

SHOULDER STRAP LEFT SEE 2-3-165

CARGO STRAP SEE 2-3-164

BACK STRAP MIDDLE SEE 2-3-163

POUCH FLAP STRAP SEE 2-3-162

POUCH REINFORCEMENT STRAP "B" SEE 2-3-161

SHOULDER STRAP OIL LET LEFT SEE 2-3-165

BACK STRAP LOWER SEE 2-3-168

FRAME SECURING STRAP SEE 2-3-164

POUCH REINFORCEMENT SEE 2-3-164

WAIST STRAP

UPPER FRAME BUCKLE CHAPE SEE 2-3-164

BACK STRAP UPPER SEE 2-3-168

SHOULDER STRAP RIGHT SEE 2-3-165

HANGER "B" SEE 2-3-164

SHOULDER STRAP OIL LETS RIGHT SEE 2-3-164 END WITH OVERHAND KNOT AS SHOWN

BACK VIEW

UPPER FRAME BUCKLE CHAPE SEE 2-3-164

FRAME

BACK FRAME VERTICAL STRAP SEE 2-3-164

CARGO STRAP SEE 2-3-164

HANGER "A" SEE 2-3-164

POUCH FLAP SEE 2-3-162

CENTER POCKET SEE 2-3-163

CANTEEN SECURING STRAP SEE 2-3-164

SIDE POCKET SEE 2-3-163

FRAME SECURING STRAP BUCKLE CHAPE SEE 2-3-164

WRAP FRAME SECURING STRAP AROUND RUCKSACK FRAME WITH ONE COMPLETE TURN BEFORE ROUTING THROUGH BUCKLE

SIDE VIEW

Lightweight rucksack.

Vietnamese infantrymen wearing ARVN rucksacks prepare to board helicopters for an airmobile operation against the VC in the Mekong Delta, 1970. *U.S. Army.*

articles. For instance, on ARVN field operations, it was not unusual to see a live chicken sticking his head out of the pack.

Limited production commenced 31 August 1964 at a U.S. cost of $8.39 in materials per ranger pack. Testing of the ranger pack included a harrowing eight-day MACV-SOG mission from Kham Duc and was concluded 7 October 1964. By mid-1969, over 1,500,000 ranger packs had been manufactured for Vietnamese consumption. In 1970, they were designated *ARVN rucksacks* and continued in use until the fall of Saigon.

Despite the good reception that the rucksack received, two problems remained. One was that wartime conditions inside Vietnam prevented any sizable local production of the rucksack and forced manufacture to the United States. The other was that the rucksack was not water repellent—in mid-1969, the indigenous rucksack was treated with a waterproofing compound, but the treatment was judged unsatisfactory after extensive testing by Special Forces Mobile Strike Force troops throughout Vietnam.[23]

The indigenous ranger pack received so much favorable attention that Natick Laboratories was ordered to produce one for Thai troops. The resulting Thai version was 1.5 inches higher, allowing for the difference in body height, and was accepted by their forces on 16 November 1965. During 1965, 1,500 Thai ranger packs were sent to their Border Patrol Police and were later mass-produced by Thai quartermaster facilities. The Thai versions were used in Laos by 46th Special Forces Company and MACV-SOG commandos operating out of Thailand. Large quantities reached Vietnam with the Thai Expeditionary Division at Bear Cat.[24]

8.7 Tropical Rucksack

A larger, nylon *tropical rucksack* was designed by Natick Laboratories for U.S. troops, based on the indigenous ranger rucksack design. Four of these prototypes were sent to

Tropical rucksack being carried by a trooper of the 2d Bn, 8th Cav (1st Cav Div), during the Cambodian invasion, May 1970. *Author's collection.*

Sgt. Terry Lambert *(left)* and Sgt. Ed Agle *(right)* carry the tropical rucksack during a reconnaissance patrol in I CTZ, 1971. *Author's collection.*

Vietnam for ACTIV consideration on 2 December 1965. USARV expressed interest in the item and ordered 500 more tropical rucksacks for further evaluation on 20 June 1966. The rucksacks were manufactured under ENSURE priority and flown to Vietnam on 13 February 1967. The 5th Special Forces Group secured their allotment on 21 March and concluded field tests on 10 May, noting that they were "a great improvement over existing rucksacks." The tropical rucksack was adopted on 11 July 1967, but no procurement was made until the ACTIV evaluation report of 10 October 1967 was reviewed.[25]

Based on the Vietnam testing, Army Materiel Command requested certain modifications on 17 November 1967. These modifications—strengthening of the bag and rounding the corners of the frame—necessitated a complete reworking of the item. Approximately 120,500 of the improved tropical rucksacks were ordered at $20 apiece on 21 December 1967 and standardized on 4 March 1968. Following this determination, the order was increased to a total of 204,650 rucksacks on 8 April 1968. The tropical rucksacks were air delivered to Vietnam as they became available, from 25 August to 22 November 1968.[26]

The tropical rucksack, or "jungle rucksack," was a frame-type pack about 4 inches higher than the indigenous ranger pack. The spring steel frame and large bag were retained. The larger size of the pack permitted a third outside pocket to be added. The fabric and webbing was water-resistant nylon duck, dyed Olive Green army shade 106, and the assembly weighed 3.5 pounds. The webbing strips on the exterior of the main bag contained eyelets and slots for attaching additional equipment. The main flap had a Velcro-closed pocket underneath. Reusable, waterproof, rip-stop nylon liners were provided for each outside pocket as

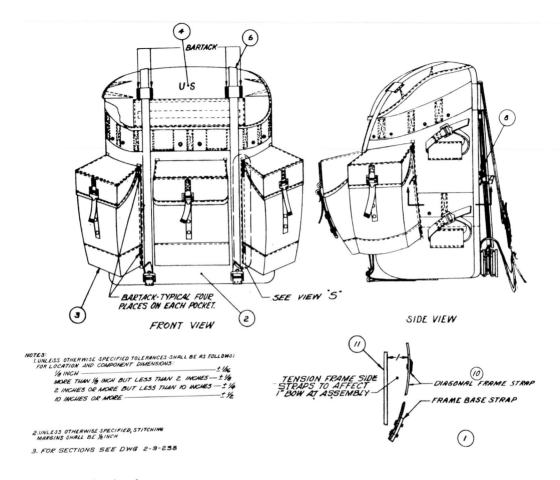

NOTES:
1. UNLESS OTHERWISE SPECIFIED TOLERANCES SHALL BE AS FOLLOWS:
   FOR LOCATION AND COMPONENT DIMENSIONS:
   1/8 INCH ——————————————————— ± 1/16
   MORE THAN 1/8 INCH BUT LESS THAN 2 INCHES — ± 1/8
   2 INCHES OR MORE BUT LESS THAN 10 INCHES — ± 1/4
   10 INCHES OR MORE ——————————————— ± 1/2

2. UNLESS OTHERWISE SPECIFIED, STITCHING
   MARGINS SHALL BE 3/8 INCH

3. FOR SECTIONS SEE DWG 2-9-238

BARTACK

U S

BARTACK-TYPICAL FOUR
PLACES ON EACH POCKET.

SEE VIEW 'S'

FRONT VIEW

SIDE VIEW

TENSION FRAME SIDE
STRAPS TO AFFECT
1" BOW AT ASSEMBLY

DIAGONAL FRAME STRAP

FRAME BASE STRAP

Tropical rucksack.

well as for the main bag. Quick release buckles, suggested by Special Forces, were incorporated on the shoulder straps to permit fast jettisoning in an emergency.[27]

8.8 Packboard

The plywood *packboard,* first introduced in 1943, was designed to carry bulky loads of considerable weight. The packboard consisted of a molded plywood frame and a cotton-webbing shoulder strap pulled through upper frame openings and buckled into billet straps at the lower sides of the frame. The packboard

was equipped with a canvas backrest laced to the frame with rope. The backrest held the frame away from the back, thus protecting the wearer against hard, irregular objects and providing air space for the evaporation of perspiration.

The load was secured with rope and lashing hooks. In Vietnam, however, the cotton-webbing quick-release strap was generally used instead of rope so that lashed loads could be unloaded quickly. A cargo attachment, made of electra-zinc-plated steel, was used to support heavier loads and was attached to the packboard by placing its flanges over the lower-

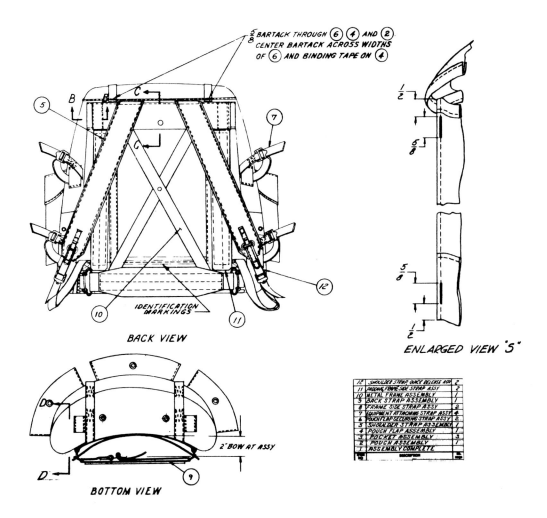

BARTACK THROUGH (6)(4) AND (2).
CENTER BARTACK ACROSS WIDTHS
OF (6) AND BINDING TAPE ON (4)

BACK VIEW

ENLARGED VIEW "S"

IDENTIFICATION MARKINGS

BOTTOM VIEW

2" BOW AT ASSY

12	SHOULDER STRAP, QUICK RELEASE ASSY	2
11	PADDING, FRAME SIDE STRAP ASSY	2
10	METAL FRAME ASSEMBLY	1
9	BACK STRAP ASSEMBLY	1
8	FRAME SIDE STRAP ASSY	2
7	EQUIPMENT ATTACHING STRAP ASSY	4
6	POUCH FLAP SECURING STRAP ASSY	2
5	SHOULDER STRAP ASSEMBLY	2
4	POUCH FLAP ASSEMBLY	1
3	POCKET ASSEMBLY	1
2	POUCH ASSEMBLY	1
1	ASSEMBLY COMPLETE	

frame edge. During the Vietnam conflict, the lightweight rucksack frame was often substituted for the packboard, which was relegated to carrying loads that the former would not accept.[28]

8.9 Combat Field Pack

When it was first developed, in the 1950s, the *combat field pack,* or "butt pack," was not designed for extensive multi-day infantry missions, but rather as a minimal "day pack" for mobile armored infantry operations.[29] In Vietnam, the combat field pack was compact enough to suffice for perimeter security duty, airmobile raids, and other situations where extended field duty was not required. The combat field pack was also preferred to the rucksack on some patrolling operations. (*See section 1.4,* Combat Load of the Infantryman.)

Several versions of the combat field pack were used in Vietnam as standard equipment. All packs contained a flap secured by web straps and buckles, two bottom web straps for attachment of a rolled poncho, a flap handle for hand-carrying, and a plastic card holder on the top or back for identification. The original M1956 *combat field pack* was made of cotton

The packboard being used as a PRC-25 radio carrier during a 199th Inf Bde mission in lower Bien Hoa Province. Officer in front carries a camera. *U.S. Army.*

The plywood packboard, here shown with electro-zinc-plated steel cargo attachment, was designed to carry bulky loads of considerable weight. *Author's collection.*

duck. This pack was modified and redesignated as the M1961 *combat field pack,* which differed from the earlier version primarily because it had a rubberized waterproof collar at the opening, derived from the 1944/45 field pack system. This collar kept the pack's contents dry in temporary immersions but was intended for amphibious or river assault purposes rather than for use in sustained monsoon storms.

The combat field pack design was modified and manufactured in nylon. It was adopted on 21 August 1967. Two versions existed. The first was a prototype nylon version similar to the M1961 combat field pack pattern. The other nylon version, which became standardized on 22 January 1971, contained D-rings instead of back eyelets, placed so that the snaps on the suspenders would not rip out. Two nylon webbing straps, sewn across the top of the pack, served to anchor the front flap

The M1961 combat field pack worn by a soldier of the 2d Bn, 27th Inf (25th Inf Div), in Hau Nghia Province, 6 July 1967. *U.S. Army.*

This machine gunner of the 1st Bn, 502d Inf (101st Abn Div), carries the M17 protective mask carrier (left) and M1961 combat field pack with two canteens attached at each side for easy access. *Paul Higgs.*

buckle and rear D-rings, and kept the handle from ripping out.

8.10 Canteens and Water Containers

The 1-quart plastic *water canteen,* standardized on 14 September 1962, was made of olive drab polyethylene and replaced the M1910 aluminum/stainless steel canteen. The new canteen had a plastic screw cap, attached with a strap, and fitted into a stainless steel *water canteen cup.* The canteen and cup were originally carried in the M1956 pile- or felt-lined, cotton duck water canteen cover. The improved M1967 nylon cover had a pocket for the snap-cap bottle of water purification tablets. USARV regulations authorized two plastic water canteens per soldier throughout the war,

but in the dry season this number was sufficient for only a few hours. Extra canteens were often attached by their cap straps to metal carabiners on the soldier's gear.

In February 1962, the Army Special Forces requested, for Southeast Asian operations, a 2-quart collapsible canteen that did not rattle. The Army Quartermaster Research and Engineering Command revived an obsolete specification, JQD 311A of March 1945, but several deficiencies were reported in the prototype bladder and cover, the fabrication of which required considerable hand work. A new model of the canteen was developed, using both blow-molding and thermo-forming manufacturing techniques, and the carrier was redesigned.[30]

The first 2-quart *collapsible canteen,* which became available in quantity during

Infantryman *(foreground, second from right)* carries the XM28 protective mask above his combat field pack as the 1st Bn, 27th Inf (25th Inf Div), board armored personnel carriers near Dau Tieng, 1969. *25th Inf Div PIO.*

The M1910 canteen carried by medic *(right)* of the 4th Bn, 23d Inf (25th Inf Div), was still being issued early in the Vietnam conflict. Cu Chi, 18 May 1966. *U.S. Army.*

This grenadier of the 1st Bn, 327th Inf (101st Abn Div), carries a 1-quart polyethylene canteen at Phan Rang, 25 June 1966. *U.S. Army.*

The 4th Inf Div rifleman (*upper left*) carries the first-pattern 2-quart collapsible canteen. *U.S. Army.*

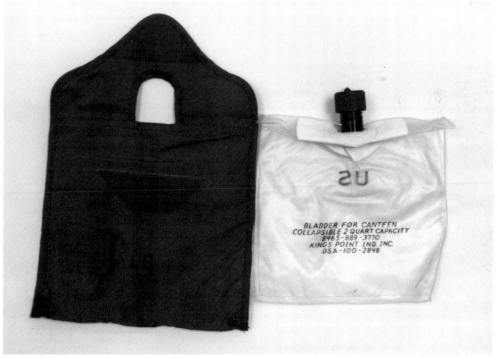

The first-pattern 2-quart collapsible canteen and carrier. *Author's collection/Melissa Priest.*

Parachutists of the 2d Bn, 503d Inf (173d Abn Bde), carry prototype 2-quart collapsible canteens high on the horizontal back straps of their lightweight rucksacks during an assault near Vo Dat, 1 December 1965. *U.S. Army.*

1966, consisted of a square, molded-vinyl bladder and an M1910-pattern cap with chain that was centered on the canteen body. The vinyl bladder was heat sealed on the edges and flattened when empty. The canteen lacked D-rings for a strap and could only be worn on the belt or in other awkward positions that took too much room (such as on the horizontal back straps of the lightweight rucksack). This fact, combined with sealing difficulties, rendered it unsatisfactory for rugged field utilization.

The standardized 2-quart collapsible canteen was a plastic bladder made of ethylene-

The 2-quart collapsible canteen with prototype plain nylon cover. *Author's collection/ Melissa Priest.*

vinyl acetate copolymer that measured about 7 by 7 by 3 inches, with a neck at one corner. Prior to standardization, this canteen was nicknamed the "LP (limited production) bladder," and this slang term was retained to differentiate it from other versions. Although DA approved development of this 2-quart canteen on 2 December 1965, actual funding did not become available until 1 January 1967. The canteen was intended to have a collapsible metal cup, but this concept was discarded during development.

The Pleiku-based 4th Infantry Division favorably evaluated 2,000 prototype collapsible canteens in the spring of 1967, but the canteen was not standardized until 11 October 1968 and not readily available until 1969.[31] The water-repellent nylon duck cover was Olive Green army shade 106, had a latch-fastener closure, and could be attached to the individual equipment belt with slide lock keepers or carried by its detachable shoulder strap. An outside pocket for a bottle of water-purification tablets was on both the prototype plain nylon cover and the standardized acrylic pile cover.

The *flotation bladder assembly* was first

Pfc. Russ Jones of the 1st Bn, 5th Inf (25th Inf Div), carries a 2-quart collapsible canteen on his lightweight rucksack. East of Xuan Loc, November 1970. *Author's collection.*

Using a 1-quart canteen, a soldier of the 3d Bde, 101st Abn Div, refills his 2-quart collapsible canteen from a mountain stream in the A Shau Valley. 17 August 1969. *101st Abn Div PIO.*

produced in 1968 and consisted of a 5-quart collapsible vinyl-film bladder with nylon cover. The bladder measured approximately 13.5 by 10.5 inches, with a canteen-like neck and a cap equipped with a rubber gasket. A removable strainer filter was inserted in the neck of the bladder. The cover contained retainer loops and tie-down cords at each corner. An opening with snap fastener was provided at the long side of the cover, and a fabric funnel-shaped pouch was sewn into the neck opening for attachment of the bladder to the cover and assistance in filling the bladder with water. A pocket for holding water-purification tablets was sewn to the cover's upper side. Instructional dia-

The 5-quart collapsible flotation bladder assembly. *Author's collection/Melissa Priest.*

A trooper of the 2d Bn, 5th Cav (1st Cav Div), drinks from his 2-quart collapsible canteen during a break in the Cambodian offensive. June 1970. *Author's collection.*

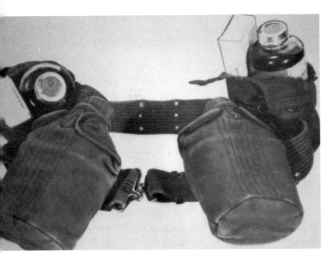

Medical specialists in Vietnam often carried blood volume expander in canteen covers attached to the individual equipment belt. *U.S. Army.*

grams for filling the bladder were printed on both sides of the cover.[32]

8.11 Intrenching Tools and Machetes

The Korean war–vintage M1951 *combination tool,* which folded once for carrying and for setting the blades at different angles, had a pick blade and a shovel blade. The tool was employed for a large part of the war, and many soldiers preferred its heavy cutting ability. The tool was sometimes used in hand-to-hand combat, since the M16-bayonet combination was unsuitable for clubbing and slicing at close quarters. The 4-pound tool with carrier was unsatisfactory, however, because it was awkward to carry, oversized for LINCLOE purposes, and the snaps rusted the carrier shut under rainy tropical conditions.

The Army achieved a significant breakthrough in the design of the soldier's intrenching tool when it developed an aluminum *light-*

The lightweight intrenching tool and carrier reached Vietnam in quantity during 1969 and 1970. *Natick Laboratories.*

A modified 1-quart canteen with special screen filter adapter and extended plastic strap for the cap was issued to Special Forces reconnaissance and long range patrol units. Although designed to filter out brackish swamp water, the author carried this one in the Laotian Mountains. *Author's collection.*

A radioman of the 2d Bn, 12th Cav (1st Cav Div) *(right)*, carries the M1942 machete in early Korean war sheath during tunnel reduction operations near Bong Son, 19 September 1966. *U.S. Army.*

weight intrenching tool and carrier in 1967. The new intrenching tool contained a hollow, triangular-shaped handle and single shovel blade. It folded twice for carrying. The tool was 9.5 inches long when collapsed and about 23.5 inches long when fully extended. One edge of the blade was sharpened for cutting, and the opposite edge was serrated for digging and chopping roots. The blade could be adjusted into appropriate positions by means of a locking nut next to the blade.

The Army contracted for 272,000 in-

A 25th Inf Div aidman wears the combination tool and carrier as he treats a soldier wounded by a mine explosion. 18 May 1966. *Army News Features.*

trenching tools for use in Vietnam in October 1968, but soldiers in the field complained that prototype models were not hefty or sharp enough for use as an ax. A strengthened version, weighing 35 ounces, was procured in February 1969. Approximately 600,000 improved intrenching tools were ordered, and these began arriving in Vietnam that summer.

During testing of the new tool at Fort Benning in early August, officials reported the failure of the thrust washer when the tool was in the pick position. Approximately 300,000 intrenching tools were already in Vietnam. In September 1969, Natick Laboratories solved the problem with the addition of a snap-on washer. This field modification of the intrench-

Soldier of the 1st Bn, 2d Inf (1st Inf Div), wearing black scarf as a unit emblem, charges off a helicopter north of Phuoc Vinh in 1967, carrying a machete and a full-size "pioneer tool" ax, probably taken off a vehicle. *U.S. Army.*

The AN/PRC-64 radio set being transported, slung from the shoulder with carrying strap. *Author's collection.*

Corp. Dick Busta of the 101st Abn Div prepares to destroy a captured NVA bunker 12 miles south of the DMZ, 16 October 1969. He carries a light anti-tank Weapon and the type IV survival ax. *U.S. Army.*

ing tool was only partially made as washers became available in Vietnam because many units were never alerted to this corrective action.[33]

The M1942 *machete* was a straight-backed, 18-inch knife with a smooth plastic handle. The machete was an effective cutting instrument only in soft, herbaceous jungle growth, for it depended on velocity and angle rather than weight of thrust for its effectiveness. The machete's design precluded its use in chopping bamboo and other hard vegetation. Instead, Army Special Forces troopers used shorter bolo-like knives, procured from sources outside normal military channels. The 9th Infantry Division requested a shorter machete for Delta operations. In response, an experimental, thicker, 14-inch LINCLOE machete was developed by 1971.[34]

The 1944-pattern machete sheath was

The AN/PRC-64 radio set being operated in the voice mode, which proved unreliable during Army Airborne, Electronics, and Special Warfare Board testing. September 1964. *Author's collection.*

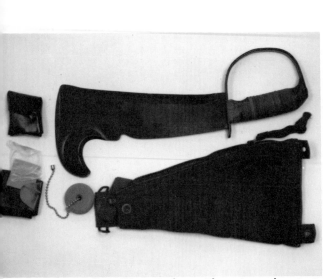

Type IV survival ax with carrier and contents of carrier pockets, which include a glass to start fires and a sharpening kit. The ax was favored as an engineer tool and also used in tunnel exploration. *Author's collection/Melissa Priest.*

A radioman of the 3d Bn, 7th Inf (199th Inf Bde), carries a AN/PRC-25 across a canal southwest of Saigon, 17 August 1967. *U.S. Army.*

made of a flexible, plasticized duck fabric with a metal throat, which incorporated a brass retaining spring. An olive green plastic machete sheath, or "self-sharpening sheath," with a built-in tungsten carbide blade sharpener, was produced in 1967.

8.12 Man-portable Radios

The *AN/PRC-64* radio set was a battery powered, crystal controlled, high-frequency transceiver weighing about 10 pounds. The radio was designed by Delco for long-range jungle patrols and tested in Vietnam by the 5th Special Forces Group from 3 October 1964 to 11 January 1965. The radio performed well in

Pfc. Harry Carter of the 25th Inf Div carries the AN/PRC-10 radio during an operation north of Cu Chi, 20 May 1966. *U.S. Army.*

Sgt. Louis C. Goehri of the 9th Inf Div with an AN/PRC-77 radio near Bear Cat, 6 July 1968. Note radio packboard attachment to lightweight rucksack. *U.S. Army.*

The AN/PRC-77 radio with KY-38 voice security device being carried in combination mode outside Tay Ninh. 16 October 1969. *U.S. Army.*

the continuous wave (CW) mode but was unreliable for voice communications. As a result, the radio was relegated to utilization by trained key operators of Special Forces teams in Southeast Asia.[35]

The Army's primary man-packed radio during the Vietnam conflict was the *PRC-25* short-range FM radio, which was modular and transistorized except for a power amplifier tube. PRC-25 radios began reaching Vietnam in the summer of 1965 after USARV expressed frustration over the short distance and restricted frequency range of the *PRC-10* voice FM radios. The first 1,500 PRC-25 radios went to advisors and Special Forces, and they did not become available to all Army units until May 1967. The range of the PRC-25 radio depended upon antenna-type and terrain but averaged 3.5 miles. Heavy combat losses in Vietnam during 1967 temporarily exhausted the Army's entire inventory of PRC-25 radios, forcing emergency production of 15,000 bushings used to adapt old PRC-10 antennas to the PRC-25.

The *PRC-77* radio was an improved version of the PRC-25, having a completely solid-state design that provided more reliability while requiring less power. The PRC-77 radios were ready in the fall of 1967, but the Army

Sgt. Wilbert LeMay of the 2d Bn, 8th Inf (4th Inf Div), uses the hand-held AN/PRT-4 transmitter and the helmet-mounted AN/PRR-9 receiver west of Pleiku, 27 June 1968. *U.S. Army.*

delayed shipping them to Vietnam until May 1968 because the National Security Agency needed time to correct deficiencies in the *KY-38* companion voice-security devices.[36]

Although the secure voice capability at company level enabled rapid, detailed discussion of plans without fear of enemy detection, the PRC-77/KY-38 combination had weight disadvantages, and the cables between the two instruments frequently broke. In Vietnam, two men were often used to carry the complete package—one carrying the radio; the other, the KY-38. Or units moved without the secure-voice communications device and had it flown in before assuming static or night defensive positions. Special replacement cables were manufactured to replace the unsatisfactory ones, but these were not available in the field until December 1968.[37]

The Army requirement for a handy compact radio to provide walkie-talkie-type, short-range communication between platoon and squad leaders was approved on 13 December 1965. The Army Materiel Command contracted for a proposed light, two-piece radio on 11 March 1966. This 29-ounce radio consisted of a hand-held transmitter, *AN/PRT-4,* and a miniature helmet-mounted receiver, *AN/PRR-9.* The unit cost was $1,100. On 22 April, USARV requested expedited procurement; and a hasty combat evaluation, completed on 3 February 1967, declared the set suitable for use in Southeast Asia. The first increment of 400 radios was shipped to Vietnam on 7 March, and by the end of the year it was available to most combat units.[38]

Some of the first squad radios were issued to the 1st Battalion, 12th Infantry, of the 4th Infantry Division. The battalion's tactical commo chief, SSgt. Howard A. Disharoon, related, "the manual states that it is designed to fit the soldier's helmet. However, since there's always a good possibility of losing your helmet or taking it off during a break, we prefer to have the radio operator attach it to his web gear."[39]

Regardless of where it was carried, the radio system fell well below expectations. On

The URC-10 emergency radio being used by Company E (Long Range Patrol), 50th Inf (9th Inf Div), near Dong Tam, July 1968. *U.S. Army.*

patrols in both hilly and flat terrain, transmissions were lost repeatedly at relatively minor distances, even at 40 meters straight across rice paddies. The sets were calibrated and recalibrated by maintenance personnel with no improvement in performance. Although the set was standard issue, most soldiers switched to the more reliable PRC-25 or -77 radios, and they relegated the two-piece miniature radio sets to static, defensive base perimeters.[40]

Notes

1. Army Materiel Command, *Clothing & Equipment Support to U.S. Army in Vietnam,* Feb 67, 31.
2. 5th Special Forces Group, *Combat Development Report,* 8 Aug 67, Incl 8-2.
3. Defense Supply Agency, ACSFOR DS Status Report, 31 Dec 68.
4. Military Specification MIL-B-43723, 23 Nov 70; U.S. Patent information researched by Carter Rila.
5. DA Quartermaster Corps, *Interim Purchase Description for Buckle, General Officers' Belt, Gold Plated,* 14 Mar 60.
6. 5th Special Forces Group, *Operational Report,* 15 Feb 69, 40; MACV Recondo School letter, Subj: Stabo Rig, 27 Nov 68.
7. Defense Supply Agency, ACSFOR DS Status Report, 31 Dec 70.
8. Carter Rila, "Accoutrements of the U.S. Army, 1921 to 1985" (unpublished manuscript, 1987), 25.
9. Author's conversation with Gordon L. Rottman, 2 Dec 87.
10. Both types were rare in Vietnam.
11. Army Materiel Command, *Clothing & Equipment Support to U.S. Army in Vietnam,* Feb 67, 37.
12. Defense Supply Agency, ACSFOR DS Status Report, 31 Jan 68.
13. 19th Military History Detachment, *Combat After Action Interview 11-67,* 4; 1st Cavalry Division, *Operational Report,* 17 Mar 68, 12.
14. Army Materiel Command, *Clothing & Equipment Support to U.S. Army in Vietnam,* Feb 67, 33.
15. Defense Supply Agency, ACSFOR DS Status Report, 31 Aug 67.
16. Army Materiel Command, *Clothing & Equipment Support to U.S. Army in Vietnam,* Feb 67, 35.
17. Defense Supply Agency, ACSFOR DS Status Report, 30 Sep 69.
18. Natick Laboratories, *Combined Infantry-Army Aviation Program Review,* 1971.
19. Vietnam Laboratory Assistance Program, *Report on VLAPA Project #20,* 26 Jan 70.
20. Military Specification MIL-4-43373, 2 Nov 65, and 43373A, 24 Sep 68.
21. Dr. S. J. Kennedy, *Preliminary Evaluation of the Individual Clothing and Equipment of Vietnamese Military Forces,* Natick Laboratories, 15 Jul 63, 16.
22. Advanced Research Projects Agency Vietnam, *Report of Evaluation: Ranger Pack,* 3 Jun 65.
23. 5th Special Forces Group, *Operational Report,* 15 Aug 69, 33.
24. Natick Laboratories, *Final Report on Development of Pack for Vietnamese and Thai Military Forces,* 30 Apr 64.
25. 5th Special Forces Group, *Operational Report,* 15 May 67, 20.
26. Defense Supply Agency, ACSFOR DS Status Report, 31 Dec 68.
27. Military Specification MIL-R-43574, 4 Mar 68, and MIL-R-43574A, 6 Nov 70.
28. DA Technical Manual 10-8465-202-23, Aug 63, 3.
29. Carter Rila, "The Development of U.S. Army Infantry Field Equipments, 1903–1956," *Military Collector & Historian,* Vol. XXI, No. 2, Summer 1969, 35–43.
30. Army Materiel Command, *Clothing & Equipment Support to U.S. Army in Vietnam,* Feb 67, 27.
31. 1st Logistical Command, *Operational Report,* 15 May 67, 140.
32. DA Technical Manual 10-276, 15 Aug 70, 35.
33. Combat Research and Development Command, Fact Sheet, Subj: Intrenching Tool, 1 Dec 69.
34. Army Limited War Laboratory Technical Report #68-10, *Final Report: Trail Cutting Machete,* Jun 68.
35. Army Concept Team in Vietnam, *Final Report: JRATA Proj 1A-105,* 15 May 65.
36. John D. Bergen, *Military Communications: A Test for Technology,* Dept. of the Army, 1986, 446–48.
37. 101st Airborne Division, *Operational Report,* 22 Nov 68, 39.
38. Defense Supply Agency, ACSFOR DS Status Report, 30 Jun 67.
39. *The Army Reporter,* Vol. 3, No. 29, 29 Jul 67, 3.
40. Americal Division, *Operational Report,* 7 May 68, 70–71.

9

Existence and Survival Gear

9.1 Sleeping Gear

The Army's field sleeping gear was essential to Vietnam survival because soldiers without proper rest were not fully alert to ambush situations and hidden booby traps. Sleeping arrangements were hampered by natural tropical conditions, and exhaustion was aggravated by the carrying of heavy individual loads.

The Chu Lai–based 23d Infantry Division (Americal) stated in May 1968, "It is essential that the combat soldier be provided lighter-weight sleeping gear. This could be accomplished very readily by a lightweight poncho and a lightweight hammock. Both items must be durable, waterproof, and have the capability of being folded into a pocket size package."[1]

The weight of sleeping gear had to be minimal for travelling purposes. Instead of sleeping bags, soldiers in Vietnam normally slept on poncho liners placed inside ponchos, which were rolled around them and snapped shut. Since this placed them on the wet jungle floor, pneumatic mattresses were often used to keep poncho combinations off the ground.

The *pneumatic mattress* or "air mattress" was an inflatable, coated-fabric sleeping accessory, ridged with side panels, and dyed Olive Green army shade 207. The 7.75-by-31.5-inch size was shaped to conform to the sleeping bag. The mattress doubled as a hand-towed float for keeping radios and other important equipment dry while crossing streams and flooded terrain.

The Army Combat Development Center began investigating lightweight Australian tropical sleeping gear on 24 February 1966. Australian components consisted of (1) an air mattress with an outer cover of coated nylon and three inflatable, replaceable inner tubes, which slipped into the cover sleeve; (2) a full length nylon-knit-mesh mosquito net; (3) a nylon sheet individual shelter; (4) a lightweight "inner bed" wool blanket; and (5) a lightweight "outer bed" permeable fabric blanket. The 1st Cavalry Division field tested this Australian sleeping equipment in the fall of 1966, and USARV completed evaluations on 31 January 1967. Logistical considerations ruled against adopting these items, but some Special Forces and other personnel preferred Australian sleeping gear whenever available.[2]

182

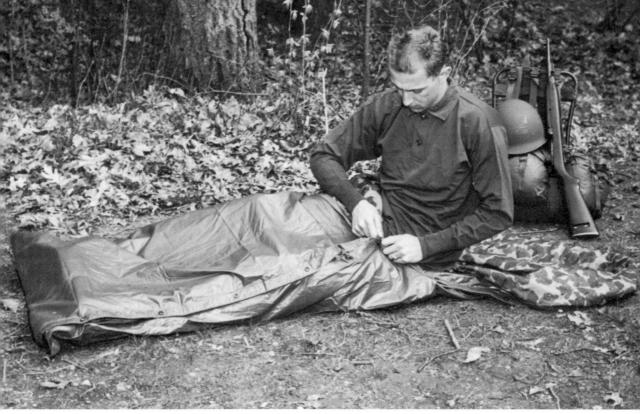

The tropical lightweight sleeping equipment consisted of a poncho liner laced into an outer poncho, here demonstrated for use in technical manuals. The soldier is wearing a lightweight knitted shirt. *U.S. Army.*

9.2 Poncho

The Army's standard nylon-coated *poncho* with hood, Olive Green army shade 207, had been adopted on 9 November 1961. The USARV Tropical Combat Uniform Board reported on 22 November 1965 that the poncho was inadequate for Vietnam, since it became relatively heavy when wet and had a shiny finish that gleamed in the rain. Natick Laboratories began development of a new lightweight poncho on 14 February 1966.

The *lightweight poncho* was almost identical in design to the standard poncho, measuring 91 inches long and 66 inches wide but weighing only 1.5 pounds, half as much as the standard version. The new poncho was fabricated from 1.5-ounce nylon-based fabric with a polyurethane coating. The poncho was compact and could be rolled small enough to fit into the tropical combat uniform's trouser cargo pocket. Approximately 200 lightweight ponchos were shipped to Vietnam on 9 September 1966.[3]

The pneumatic mattress being used to float equipment across a small river in the Mekong Delta by soldiers of 3d Bn, 39th Inf (9th Inf Div) in 1967. The mattress was normally placed under sleeping equipment to elevate it off the ground. *U.S. Army.*

Australian-type sleeping gear was field tested by Army forces in Vietnam during 1966 but not adopted because of logistical considerations. *Natick Laboratories.*

The poncho used as a rain garment by a 1st Inf Div MP guarding NVA weapons captured in Operation Attleboro, 1966. *1st Inf Div PIO.*

ACTIV completed testing this lightweight poncho on 19 June 1967. The final evaluation expressed the need for smaller snaps, less sheen in the material, and more durability. On 7 September 1967, USARV requested issue of 282,000 ponchos with the desired modifications. DA replied on 5 October 1967 that the item could be provided in alternative camouflage print with insect-repellent treatment, but that other modifications would negate expeditious ordering. USARV answered that the standard snap was acceptable, clearing the way for production on a priority basis under the ENSURE program. The poncho was reclassified as standard Army issue on 8 April 1968, and it began arriving in Vietnam in large quantities after June.[4]

The poncho with hood was made of lightweight rip-stop nylon that was polyurethane-coated. It was roughly rectangular, 92 by 66 inches; weighed 1.5 pounds; and cost $11.39 in 1968. A smaller size for Vietnamese consumption was 82 by 60 inches. The poncho was provided in both an Olive Green army shade 107 and an ERDL camouflage pattern. To give the poncho a greater softness and reduce the papery noise of the fabric, the transparent coating was applied after the fabric was printed or dyed to the desired color.[5]

The poncho could be slipped over the head, adjusted by waist and hood drawstrings, and worn as a rain cape. Or it could be rigged

Fallen paratroopers are covered with ponchos on a battlefield littered with M79 grenade shells and empty ration tins. *U.S. Army.*

as a one-man shelter by attaching it to tree branches, bushes, or sticks. It was useful as a waterproof ground cover; the side snaps could be fastened together making a sleeping bag; and it could be easily folded into a compressed roll and attached to load-carrying equipment.

Despite the poncho's versatility, it still fell short of expectations. Most critical in Vietnam was the poncho's high gloss, which intensified when wet. This gloss was extremely undesirable and nullified subdued or camouflage coloration. The poncho was also highly flammable. Additionally, the 4th Infantry Division complained that both poncho and poncho liner

offered little protection against the night cold of the western highlands.

9.3 Poncho Liner

Blankets were replaced in Vietnam by the lightweight, quick-drying, quilted *wet weather poncho liner,* which laced into the poncho. This was first provided to Special Forces in 1963, and its immense popularity led to procurement of over 2,750,000 by 1969. Later versions weighed 1.3 pounds when dry, compared to 1.7 when first produced, but they still retained an insulating value equal to a heavy

185

Troops of the 1st Cav Div rig a makeshift shelter with ponchos during Central Highland operations, 1966. *Author's collection.*

wool blanket weighing nearly 4 pounds. Poncho liners were not always available, however, in sufficient quantities to front-line troops. The 1st Cavalry Division reported on 22 November 1966, "Problems have continually been experienced throughout the reporting period [fall 1966] in obtaining adequate quantities of ponchos, mosquito nets, poncho liners, and GP medium tentage."[6]

The poncho liner's original resin-bonded batting was replaced in 1969 with a polyester batting, quilted to the 1.1-ounce rip-stop parachute fabric. Unfortunately, this development was unsatisfactory because when laundered the liner lost half of its thickness. The poncho liner became heavy when wet. After five minutes of draining, a soaked poncho liner still weighed over 4 pounds, although this was far less than a wet wool blanket.[7]

The poncho liner is used to warm a seriously wounded soldier of the 3d Bn, 187th Inf (101st Abn Div), as a medic applies intravenous fluid replacement from a saline bottle. June 1969. *U.S. Army.*

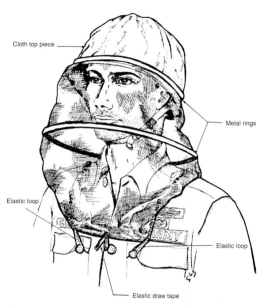

Cloth top piece

Metal rings

Elastic loop

Elastic loop

Elastic draw tape

Hat and mosquito net assembly.

The small bulk of the rolled-up poncho is visible on this soldier of the 2d Bn, 1st Inf (196th Inf Bde) during Operation Cedar Falls, January 1967. *Author's collection.*

9.4 Jungle Hammocks

The Army used several kinds of *jungle hammocks* in Vietnam. USARV was issued 1942-pattern jungle hammocks, even though they were no longer standard, for soldiers in bivouac situations. These World War II–style canvas hammocks weighed 15 pounds and had sewn-in mosquito netting and a rubberized nylon top. They were superior to newer types in which comfort and protection were sacrificed

The insect net, worn here with the T66-series prototype tropical hat being tested by Army Materiel Command in 1966, was a detachable accessory of the tropical hat during the Vietnam conflict. *Army Materiel Command.*

The Army multi-purpose net is used by aviators to take a quick nap between missions in the Central Highlands. July 1969. *Author's collection.*

in order to save weight. The older hammocks were preferred in artillery positions and Special Forces camps, and also served as mosquito-proof drapes over cots and beds in some barracks.

The Army's standard jungle hammock was designed for mobile operations and did not contain integral mosquito netting (the insect bar was used for such purposes). It weighed 3 pounds, 14 ounces but became heavier and quite bulky when wet. On 7 June 1966, USARV requested a lighter jungle hammock based on the design of a captured North Vietnamese Army hammock.

Natick Laboratories secured permission to produce an improved hammock under EN-SURE priority on 21 July 1966. The hammock was copied from the North Vietnamese model but was made of a single layer of nylon fabric, 108 by 34 inches, with a draw cord tunnel at

each end through which a 14-foot length of quarter-inch-diameter braided polyester rope was passed. The laboratories also produced a rectangular 4-by-8-foot nylon fishnet hammock. One hundred of each kind, for a total of 200 hammocks, were airmailed to Vietnam from 16 to 22 September 1966 for combat evaluation.[8]

Both prototype lightweight jungle hammock designs reduced bulk over the standard hammock by 65 percent and were simpler to erect and use. The new North Vietnam–type hammock weighed 1 pound, 6 ounces, and the fishnet hammock weighed 2 ounces more. The 5th Special Forces Group conducted extensive testing, and ACTIV completed its evaluation on 15 April 1967, reporting that Natick's North Vietnam-style hammocks were preferred. USARV ordered 128,000 improved jungle hammocks based on this test. DA approved the request on 12 August 1967 at a cost of $7.00 each, and these began arriving in Vietnam during February 1968. Priority shipments ceased on 16 August 1968 as the last ENSURE order reached Vietnam, and regular supply of the improved jungle hammock commenced.[9]

The *lightweight jungle hammock,* or "NVA-style hammock," was constructed of 4-ounce, water-repellent-treated nylon. The 3-by-8-foot hammock was supported by two 15-foot, quarter-inch-thick polyester draw cords. Rain stoppers, in the form of 2-inch-diameter rubber washers, were placed on each cord a short distance from the hammock to stop rain from running down the rope into the hammock. Short, elastic ties kept the poncho center ridge tied to the hammock line and made the two into an integrated assembly. The hammock could be compressed along with the lightweight poncho into a small bulk that weighed 2.6 pounds total. The multi-purpose net (*See section 9.5*, Netting and Insect Bars) could also be used as a hammock, although not as successfully.

9.5 Netting and Insect Bars

The *hat and mosquito net* assembly was first issued in 1961. It fitted over the helmet with a large cloth top piece. Two metal rings held the netting away from the face, and elastic loops on the bottom fastened the net to the

A tent shelter half, rigged next to a poncho used as a tent, forms a canopy for the 1st Inf Div position *(center)* at FSB Picardy, March 1969. In Vietnam, shelter halves were usually delivered by helicopter rather than carried by soldiers. *121st Signal Bn.*

front-pocket buttons. This cumbersome ensemble was replaced by a dark green, nylon tricot netting with elastic draw tape sewn into top and bottom hems. The lower elastic draw tape could be tightened to keep it closed, as the netting was normally pulled over the helmet or hat. The *insect net* was issued as a detachable accessory of the tropical hat, and the combination was officially reclassified as the *hat and insect net.*[10]

The Army *multi-purpose net* was developed in response to the April 1963 program to outfit South Vietnamese forces, but the net saw considerable combat service in American ranks as well. The 17-ounce, olive green net was 5 by 9 feet in size and constructed of a 3-ply nylon raschel knit netting. The long sides had nylon-bordered edges, and the edges of the short sides had been melted to prevent ravelling. The

net was strong enough to support a load of about 200 pounds.

In December 1963, 500 multi-purpose nets were distributed to the ARVN Trung Lap Ranger Center; 11th, 31st, and 42d Ranger Battalions, 77th Special Forces Group; and Marine Brigade. The net successfully passed testing on 22 December 1964. Throughout the war, it was used for a variety of purposes: hammock, litter, cache container, camouflage cover, sniper's roost, and man-packed cargo net for small loads. The Vietnamese often used the net as a fish seine and animal trap, especially when seining for the small crabs and fish that abound in the rice paddies of South Vietnam. It saw combat service in many U.S. Army advisory and Special Forces operations, as well.[11]

The *insect bar* was a canopy made of

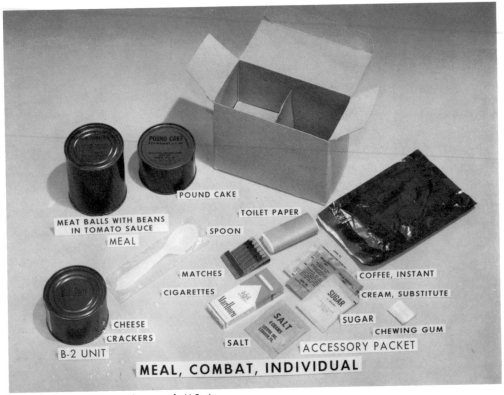

A typical individual combat meal. *U.S. Army.*

mildew-resistant, nylon, small-mesh netting. It was used with a bed, cot, hammock, poncho, or shelter half for protection against mosquitos and other insects. The bar could be suspended by tying the tapes to crossed sticks fastened to each end of the bed or cot, with the hem of the netting carefully tucked under, leaving no openings. The insect bar could also be fastened inside the shelter half.

9.6 Tent Shelter Halves

The *tent shelter half* was one-half of a small tent, a design dating from 1943. The shelter half was just over 154 inches long with triangular flaps at both ends. One shelter half was carried per individual, and these could be buttoned together to make a two-man tent with both ends closable. The shelter half was made of water-repellent and mildew-resistant cotton

duck, dyed Olive Green army shade 107. Early in the war, the fabric of the filling was changed to a highly water-repellent rayon filament yarn, while the cotton duck was retained to reduce weight and increase resistance to tearing.[12]

9.7 Mess Equipment and Individual Rations

The corrosion-resistant, individual *field mess kit* issued in Vietnam consisted of a stainless steel oval-shaped pan and cover, with *field mess spoon, fork,* and *knife,* which fitted inside the pan. In 1965, the Army adopted the new stamped, one-piece field mess knife without a cast aluminum handle. Vietnam's muddy jungle and dry-season conditions often prevented units from having the water or facilities necessary to properly clean metal mess kits and utensils. After successful testing of paper plates and plastic eating utensils in July 1966, most combat units used disposable items in lieu of mess kits whenever hot food was available.

The standard field ration was the *meal, combat, individual,* or "C-ration." The rations were packaged in 12-meal cases; each meal weighed about 2 pounds and was available in 12 different "menus." Each menu consisted of one canned meat item; one canned fruit or dessert item; one B-unit of crackers and the like; one accessory packet containing cigarettes, matches, chewing gum, toilet paper, instant coffee, cream substitute, sugar, and salt; and one plastic spoon. Each meal furnished approximately one-third of the minimum nutrient intake prescribed by Army regulations.

The individual combat meals presented

The stainless steel individual field mess kit issued in Vietnam. *Author's collection/Melissa Priest.*

composition-stability problems throughout the war, and Natick Laboratories expended a great deal of effort attempting to improve the quality and texture of the rations. The food was barely palatable if eaten cold, so most troops heated their meals or doused them with Tabasco pepper sauce before consumption. The peanut butter in the B-1 units tasted like clay, and since the substance burned, was often used for landing-zone markers at night.[13]

The *individual food packet, combat, supplemental (interim)* was proposed by the Special Warfare School on 25 May 1962. Natick Laboratories designed the small, lightweight packet to provide a high caloric content compatible with water intake of two quarts per day. Normal daily consumption was expected to be two packets. Ten menus, ranging from 680 to 818 calories, were packaged into plastic resealable packets. Assembly was completed in December 1963, and they were favorably field tested in Vietnam during 1964.[14]

This packet, which was modified and standardized as the *food packet, long range patrol,* or "LRP (pronounced lurp) ration," became the basis of the first freeze-dried combat ration in the military. The meal was designed for reconnaissance operations, where troops would operate up to ten days before being resupplied. The LRP ration was a precooked, freeze-dried main dish (typically beef hash, chicken stew, or pork) in a reconstitution package. The substance could be eaten dry or rehydrated, using cold or, preferably, hot water. The packet also included a cereal, candy, or fruitcake bar, and sundries such as coffee, cream, sugar, toilet paper, matches, and a plastic spoon. There were eight menus, each weighing 11.3 ounces and furnishing over 1,000 calories.

9.8 Emergency Survival Items and Vests

Individual aid and survival kits for Special Forces personnel were delivered to those departing for Southeast Asia commencing in early 1964. The kit provided emergency medical supplies and a shelter and foraging capability for up to ten days. The kit's 42 items were divided into 2 packets: an operational package for day-to-day use and a reserve package for use while evading the enemy. The operational

A wounded 9th Inf Div soldier is carried out of a Delta swamp. The battalion commander *(right)* wears a rope coil and carabiner commonly used in crossing inundated areas. *Army News Features.*

The use of rope in flooded regions was critical in moving vital equipment. Here a PRC-25 radio with spare batteries is moved across a stream near the Song Vam Co Dong by the 2d Bn, 27th Inf (25th Inf Div), 30 June 1969. *25th Inf Div PIO.*

The long range patrol food packet. *Author's collection.*

The individual survival kit packets 1 and 2 were a set that could be attached to the individual equipment belt or other equipment by Velcro fasteners. The contents of one packet are shown on the protective covering that fitted over the box. *Author's collection.*

Capt. William Dussling *(left)*, a helicopter pilot flying in support of the 4th Inf Div, wears the individual survival kit, leg holster, as he prepares for a mission at Pleiku. *U.S. Army.*

package contained a signal mirror, a saw, a flare, salt tablets, bandages and medication, water purification tablets, bouillon cubes, and insect repellent. The reserve package contained a fire starter, a fishing kit, a sewing kit, a compass, and a knife.

The *hot-dry lightweight survival kit* completed field testing in September 1966. The kit consisted of about 50 components. These included medicines for diarrhea and dysentery, antimalarial drugs, a painkiller, and treatment for fungus skin diseases. Nonmedical items included signal flares, a signal mirror, insect repellent, a head net and mitts for insect protection, a fish line and hooks, a razor knife, a head cloth, sun cream, and an instruction pamphlet. The kits began arriving in Vietnam during the spring of 1967, and the 506th Field Depot gave priority on issue to the 1st Aviation Brigade.[15]

The *individual survival kit, leg holster,* was classified as standard issue for Army aviation personnel in April 1968. It never became readily available, however, and was disliked by many pilots since it caused weight imbalance on one leg and impeded walking. This made aviators who wore it appear to be hobbling or lame. Procurement was cancelled during late 1969 when the Army decided to adopt the Air Force SRU-21/P survival vest.[16]

The *SRU-21/P survival vest* was a survival garment that could be worn by aviation per-

Capt. Clement Wickett *(second from left)*, 1Lt. Stephen Maness *(second from right)*, and 1Lt. Ronald Szurek *(right)* of the 23d Inf Div (American) wear SRU-21/P survival vests inside an Air Force AC119 gunship. December 1969. *U.S. Air Force.*

sonnel on most types of Army aircraft. The vest was adopted directly from the Air Force, being modified only by the enlargement of one pocket to accept the URC-68 radio. It was not in general supply, however, until 1972. Special Forces long-range patrol members sometimes used SRU-21/P survival vests as convenient, lightweight carriers for survival and other items but acquired most of their vests during the Vietnam conflict from the Air Force because of the vest's late adoption by the Army.[17]

The survival vest was constructed of raschel knit nylon cloth with pockets attached to hold the prescribed survival components. The vest also accommodated a .38-caliber pistol holster, which could be snapped into position on the lower left side. Other vest components included a SDU-5E distress marker and flash guard, a lensatic compass, a fishing grill net, a pocket knife, a plastic water bag, a signalling mirror, a butane lighter for starting fires, a set of foliage penetrating "pen flares," a first aid kit, a tourniquet, and a radio pocket with antenna cover. This pocket could hold the AN/PRC-90, ARC/RT-10, or AN/URC-68 survival receiver-transmitters as applicable. The vest was closed with a slide fastener and could be adjusted using Velcro tabs.

Notes

1. Americal Division, *Operational Report,* 7 May 68, 85.
2. Army Materiel Command, *Clothing & Equipment Support to U.S. Army in Vietnam,* Feb 67, 41; 1st Cavalry Division, *Operational Report,* 22 Nov 66, 23.
3. Army Materiel Command, *Clothing & Equipment Support to U.S. Army in Vietnam,* Feb 67, 21.
4. Defense Supply Agency, ACSFOR DS Status Report, 8 Apr 68.
5. Military Specification MIL-P-43700, 16 Apr 70.
6. 1st Cavalry Division, *Operational Report,* 22 Nov 66, 28.
7. Dr. S. J. Kennedy, *Clothing and Equipment Support to Our Troops in Vietnam,* Natick Laboratories, 24 Jun 69, 9–12.
8. Army Materiel Command, *Clothing & Equipment Support to U.S. Army in Vietnam,* Feb 67, 39.
9. 5th Special Forces Group, *Combat Development Report,* 8 Aug 67, Incl 8-5; Defense Supply Agency, ACSFOR DS Status Report, 30 Sep 68.
10. Military Specification MIL-I-43746, 30 Jul 71.
11. Advanced Research Projects Agency, Vietnam, *Report for Evaluation,* 22 Dec 64.
12. Military Specification MIL-S-3725C, 11 Apr 69.
13. Natick Laboratories Production Engineering Program, *Quarterly Reports,* for FY 70.
14. Natick Laboratories, *Annual Historical Summary FY 63,* 71–72.
15. 1st Aviation Brigade, *Operational Report,* 15 May 67, 11.
16. *Aviation Digest,* Dec 69, 63.
17. *Aviation Digest,* Nov 72, 40.

10

Special Purpose Uniforms and Equipment

10.1 Advisors

Army advisory duty was one of the most dangerous assignments in Vietnam. Service with Vietnamese units began to invite selective

Viet Cong reprisal during 1963, and advisor casualties increased to alarming levels in 1964. It became increasingly obvious that American personnel were being deliberately targeted, and MACV directed advisors to wear South Vietnamese military clothing as a means of "personal camouflage." On 2 July 1965, MACV reiterated this guidance:

Special Provisions for Personal Camouflage. Personnel serving as advisors or assisting Vietnamese forces are authorized to deviate from service uniform regulations for the purpose of personal camouflage whenever the wearing of the distinctive U.S. uniform will make them a conspicuous target in the event of enemy action. Wearing of the Vietnamese uniform, in whole or in part, is strongly encouraged during combat operations, when living in isolated areas with Vietnamese units, and at such times, places, and under circumstances where the U.S.

Three Army advisors (left), lightly armed with pistols and wearing first-pattern utility uniforms with unsubdued insignia, discuss a helicopter mission with Vietnamese officers. July 1962. *Norman Sklavowitz.*

MACV Advisory Team 95 Capt. Don Christensen *(right)* wears first-pattern tropical combat uniform with 52d ARVN Rgt, 27 August 1964. Note metal pin-on branch insignia with Korean war regimental numbering affixed. Sfc. John D. Cali *(second from right)* wears first-pattern utility uniform. *U.S. Army.*

advisor would be placed in jeopardy by virtue of being clearly distinguishable from other military personnel in the area.[1]

Large Army formations were inside Vietnam by 1966, and advisors were ordered to wear tropical combat uniforms to promote recognition by other American units. Advisors, however, were "encouraged to wear Vietnamese badges awarded or issued by the Vietnamese government. These badges will be worn as prescribed by Vietnamese regulations while on

Special Forces Capt. Edwin Rybat, holding an M16A1 rifle, wears a *Beo-Gấm* dapple-type camouflage suit with matching mountaineering-style cap, procured with counterinsurgency funds in Okinawa and brought to Vietnam. He commands a CIDG strike force, although technically classified as an advisor to the LLDB, in the Iron Triangle, 12 November 1964. *USARPAC Photo Facility.*

Sgt. Roy Allen, advisor to the 44th ARVN Ranger Bn, wears the Vietnamese airborne camouflage tunic with red ascot, the *Biệt-Động-Quân* recon pocket patch, Ranger Service Badge (above name tape), and decorated helmet. He has been presented with the Presidential Unit Citation (worn above badge). 1 June 1965. *U.S. Army.*

Sergeant Major Hoover, an advisor to the ARVN Airborne Division, wears camouflage French parachutist jacket with Vietnamese jump status designator on pocket at Cat Lai, 23 March 1967. The shoulder sleeve insignia is sewn on pencil pocket. *Author's collection.*

duty in Vietnam. In addition, Vietnamese insignia of rank may also be worn by U.S. advisory personnel while on duty, in the manner prescribed by senior advisors reporting directly to this (MACV) headquarters." Metal or cloth Vietnamese rank badges were normally worn centered along the front of the tropical coat or hat, or on the side of the beret, so as not to interfere with standard Army insignia of grade.[2]

10.2 Aviation Personnel

At the war's outset, the international orange flight suit was the only fire-retardant aviation outfit in the Army system. The suit lost its fire-protective properties after being laundered 14 times. The Army's gray *K2B flying coveralls or* "flight suit" could be treated with a borax solution as a field expedient. This made the fabric fire retardant but offered only temporary protection. With the advent of helicopter warfare in Vietnam, the Army was forced to consider other alternatives.

A one-piece flight suit developed by the Naval Aerospace Medical Research Department was manufactured of Nomex, the new DuPont polyamide fiber, which was permanently fire resistant. Single-layered Nomex was equal in protection to fire-retardant-treated cotton fiber, and the fire protection was permanent, whereas cotton required further treatment after being washed 14 times. The Army modified the Navy Nomex flight suit in 1965, cutting the collar similar to the Army fatigue collar, and placing a double layer of Nomex down the flight suit's back, the area proven most susceptible to burns when an individual ran through flames.[3]

The Army declared the modified Nomex

198

1966 Vietnam-issue flight gear: AFH1 helmet, folded flight suit, flight jacket, sunglasses with case, tropical combat boots (discouraged because of fire hazard), navigation plotting computer, plotter protractor, flyer's glove shells, survival knife, gear tie-down thongs, spare boot laces, knife. *U.S. Army.*

suits as suitable flame-protective Army flight clothing on 22 March 1966, and they were officially designated *crew member's fire resistant flight coveralls.* Approximately 95 suits were sent to Vietnam and tested by the 12th and 17th Aviation Groups from 15 July to 20 September 1966. Although these interim flight coveralls were recommended for Army-wide adoption, this action was blocked by the adverse USARV evaluation of 12 January 1967. The final report noted that the clothing was uncomfortable and hot; the fabric caused itchiness and skin irritation, faded badly and turned a brownish color after continuous sunlight exposure, developed burrs, and generated an offensive odor when exposed to rain.[4]

DuPont improved the fiber and produced a new weave to correct these deficiencies. The

Two Army helicopter warrant officers wearing gray K2B flying coveralls. March 1966. *U.S. Army.*

CWO John Foley, 57th Transportation Company (Light Helicopter), wears K2B flying coveralls as he uses a PRC-10 to call in air support at Phuoc Xuyen, 17 April 1963. *U.S. Army.*

Air crewmember Sp4 Kenneth Miller models K2B flying coveralls, AFH1 helmet, and lightweight flight jacket used in Vietnam. *U.S. Army.*

company sent 500 improved suits to Vietnam for further consideration in March 1967. The outfits were produced in various configurations, such as one-piece and two-piece garments with either single or double layers of Nomex. USARV selected a single-layer Nomex jacket and trouser combination on 13 June 1967, and DA approved the request as an ENSURE priority item ten days later. Funding was approved 31 July 1967, and 34,450 flight suits were ordered at an estimated cost of $56.91 each.

This Army *flight suit,* which the Army considered comparable in appearance to the utility uniform, was composed of a 4.4-ounce single-layer Nomex jacket and trousers. The jacket had a covered front zipper, buttoned breast pockets, and a zippered sleeve pocket. The trousers featured covered slash pockets, buttoned hip pockets, thigh pockets with covered zippers toward the inside of the leg, and lower, adjustable outside pockets with covered zippers along the top side. Velcro fasteners at both wrists and ankles provided adjustable snug fit for protection against aircraft fire. Less

Maj. James Foster, Army advisor to the 215th ARVN Helicopter Squadron, wears black-dyed flight coveralls as he discusses a mission with Capt. Nguyen Van Trang, July 1969. *Harry Mall.*

Capt. Judson Perry of the 2d Bn, 20th Artillery (Aerial Rocket), wears the hot weather fire-resistant flying shirt and trousers beside his AH1G Cobra helicopter, 1970. *Author's collection.*

protection resulted when sleeves were rolled up, trouser legs were bloused in boots, or the jacket tails were not tucked in, and this sometimes resulted in disfiguring burns.[5]

Deliveries of the Army flight suit were projected to reach Vietnam in October 1967, but the first 750 uniforms were not flown out of Dover Air Force Base in Delaware until 18 January 1968. USARV received 24,387 uniforms by April, and the entire ENSURE order was not in country until June 1968. These Nomex flight suits were issued within the 1st Aviation Brigade on a priority basis: (1) one suit per crew member of an observation, utility, or armed helicopter; (2) second suit for first priority personnel; (3) one suit per crew member of a cargo helicopter or Bird-dog or Mohawk aircraft; (4) second suit for third priority person-

nel; (5) one suit per crew member of a utility, fixed-wing aircraft; (6) second suit per fifth priority personnel. Although aviators were not allowed to leave Vietnam with the suits, shortages of them persisted into 1969.[6]

During 1968, the Army became interested in developing a flame-resistant combat uniform that could be worn interchangeably by either air crewmen or combat vehicle crewmen. Enemy mines and rocket-propelled grenades caused dangerous vehicular fires, which caused increasing burn losses among tank and armored personnel carrier crews. The Army Test and Evaluation Command envisioned the uni-

The back designs of the flying shirt and trousers are shown by aviators placing battle-damaged UH1 helicopters aboard the USNS *Corpus Christie Bay*, docked at Da Nang, for repair by the 1st Transportation Battalion, which was based on the ship. 1971. *Author's collection.*

form as providing better comfort, increased safety from flash fires, and design features such as oversized pockets to carry large maps.

The resulting uniform was a loose-fitting shirt and trouser combination, fabricated of 4.4-ounce DuPont Nomex nylon twill that was flame resistant. The fiber, however, did not absorb moisture. The uniform was rejected by the Armor branch, which considered it too hot, heavy, and uncomfortable for wear in buttoned-up vehicles under tropical conditions. It was accepted solely for aviation use and designated as the *shirt and trousers, flying, hot weather fire-resistant,* Olive Green army shade 106.

This new flight clothing was not available to meet all normal replacement demands within the Army until 30 June 1970. About that time it was redesignated as the *flyer's shirt,*

high temperature resistant, and the *flying trousers, high temperature resistant.* The uniform officially replaced the K2B flying coveralls, which were declared obsolete on 1 March 1970.[7]

Throughout the war, flight personnel were constantly warned to avoid wearing nylon clothing because of aircraft fire danger, but nylon apparel was favored because it was light and comfortable, and because the combat troops considered some items stylish. Nylon T-shirts, for example, were popular and readily available at post exchanges, but, if worn in a fire, caused extreme burns because the nylon material melted and adhered to the flesh.

At least one general insisted that his VIP flight section wear only tropical combat uniforms and boots.[8] Tropical combat boots were reinforced across the instep, up the back, and around the top with woven nylon. Such reckless disregard for aviation crew safety produced dire consequences. Many crewmen who were wearing this footwear in burning aircraft suffered fire-induced traumatic amputations or severe ankle and foot deformities.

10.3 Chaplains

Chaplain's attire could be quite varied. Authorized chaplain apparel consisted of 9-foot-long black or white scarves, or tippets, with a gold-colored, schiffli-embroidered U.S. coat of arms on each end. The respective insignia for Christian or Jewish chaplains appeared below the coat of arms. Chaplains could also wear denominational vestments or ritual items when conducting religious services.

The chaplain's field altar kit, designed to be carried in a jeep, was too heavy and bulky for Vietnam conditions where chaplains travelled by helicopter. Development of the *lightweight chaplain's kit,* at $125 each, was approved by DA on 16 December 1966. Natick Laboratories air expressed the first 84 Protestant and 44 Catholic kits to Vietnam on 26 May 1967, and the final 200 kits, ordered under ENSURE priority, were air delivered to Vietnam on 19 July 1967.[9]

An experimental Nomex coverall version of the flame-resistant combat uniform for air/armored crewmen that was never adopted. 17 July 1968. *U.S. Army.*

10.4 Army Contractors and Special Services

During the Vietnam conflict, large numbers of Department of Defense civilian employees and contractor representatives rendered technical assistance to the military in the field. USARV policy permitted these personnel to wear utility uniforms, complete with boots and cap, commencing 21 May 1966. Name tapes were worn over the right shirt pocket. Instead of U.S. Army distinguishing insignia above the

A chaplain of the 1st Cav Div wears black chaplain's scarf with Christian chaplain insignia. The ecclesiastical cross, altar candlesticks, Bible stand, and red altar cloth are part of the protestant chaplain's kit for active combat application. 6 February 1966. *U.S. Army.*

Jewish chaplains wear prayer shawls as they hold Rosh Hashanah services with the Torah to herald the coming of the year 5730 on the Hebrew calendar at Nha Trang, 12 September 1969. *U.S. Army.*

A chaplain of the 101st Abn Div wears camouflaged vestment during Easter services, 1966. *U.S. Army.*

left pocket, identification tapes were abbreviated with the commodity command or center name, such as USAAVCOM (U.S. Army Aviation Command) or AVSCOM (Aviation Support Command.)[10]

After 15 August 1969, USARV's plentiful stocks of tropical combat uniforms and boots allowed the military to use this clothing, three sets per person, for civilian personnel, to replace the utility uniforms. This change gave the civilian workers a more military appearance and was implemented to "give more protection to technicians who provide supply and maintenance assistance or engineering and advisory assistance on commodity items of equipment in support of the Army."[11]

Civilian personnel who worked in an office or headquarters, with no field duty, were not authorized to wear military uniforms. This included all DOD civilian personnel in the Saigon-Cholon-Tan Son Nhut area. As an exception, the MACV Secretary Joint Staff

Chaplain (Capt.) William Clearly wears denominational vestments while conducting a prayer service at FSB Jack, 22 November 1970. *U.S. Army.*

Decca Navigation Company technical representative wears his identity tape on the utility uniform while installing equipment on a helicopter in Vietnam. 20 April 1966. *U.S. Army.*

Equipment specialist Ira Dodd, Jr. teaches the USARV OH6A Cayuse Transition School at Vung Tau wearing AVSCOM (Aviation Support Command) identification tape on his tan uniform. 12 April 1969. *U.S. Army.*

Army special services recreational specialist Rose Mary Underwood wears the standard gray-blue dress and jacket at the Pacesetter Service Club, Long Binh, 1 November 1969. *U.S. Army.*

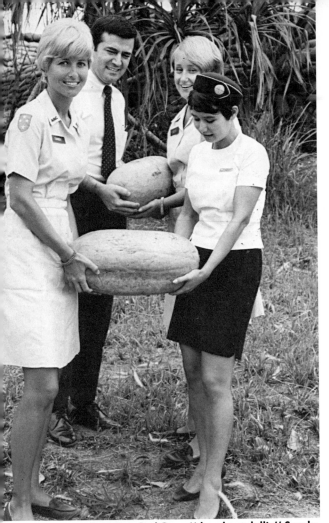

American Red Cross "doughnut dollie" Sandy Lockhart wears the 23d Inf Div shoulder sleeve insignia as she takes a Georgia watermelon from Pan American ground hostess Kathy de Massiac for delivery to a soldier at Chu Lai, 20 August 1969. *Americal Div PIO.*

Master salvage diver Sp6 Richard Dooley of the 497th Engineer Company dons standard scuba gear prior to beginning the raising of the transport *Green Bay,* which was sunk by VC combat swimmers at Cam Ranh Bay, 1971. His gear consists of dual steel 80-cubic-foot air tanks with a single stage, two-hose regulator. All rubber items are black. His swim shorts were made from utility uniform trousers. *Author's collection.*

(SJS) Protocol Office routinely issued gratuitous uniforms to distinguished visitors.[12]

10.5 Divers

Army diving operations in Vietnam centered around light reconnaissance of harbor bottoms and river channels, recovery of equipment and small water craft, underwater repairs, clearance of hazards, and limited submerged tunnel exploration. Army divers usually relied on scuba equipment for their work, although air-dependent, lightweight diving and deep sea gear was used occasionally. Naval personnel were normally called upon if underwater operations involved heavier search, construction, repair, or specialized recovery work requiring mixed-gas operations.

In Vietnam, most Army divers relied on open-circuit scuba equipment. This gear included twin 90-cubic-foot air cylinders with a

Members of the 49th Infantry Platoon (Scout Dog) search the village of Long Truong, 7 May 1967. Note leashes for German shepherd dogs. *199th Inf Bde PIO.*

regulator assembly, pressure gage, mouthpiece, mask and snorkel, swim trunks, fins, and a weight belt. Additional equipment included depth gage, watch, compass, signal flare, slate, life lines and preserver, floats, protective clothing such as wet suits or tropical combat uniforms, nose clip, and knife. The open-circuit scuba gear was designed for maximum depths of 130 feet with a duration limit of 20 minutes, but an hour's work at 60 feet was considered normal operational use of this apparatus. Duration of the dive, however, was contingent on depth, air supply, water temperature, and physical exertion.

The *CCR-1000* closed-circuit scuba system was designed to recycle oxygen so that no exhaust bubbles appeared on the water surface. It was introduced into Vietnam operations late in the war. The assembly consisted of an oxygen bottle and a diluent bottle, a carbon monoxide absorbent canister, a two-hose regulator and mouthpiece, an oxygen pressure gauge, a diluent pressure gauge, and two other instrument displays. Additional equipment included a mask, a snorkel, fins, a depth gauge, a dive watch, a wrist compass, a knife, a signal flare, a slate, a lifeline, floats, protective clothing, and a nose clip.[13]

The most common life vests were modified Navy Underwater Demolitions Team (UDT) swim vests or Mark III swim vests.

10.6 Dog Handlers

The scout dog team consisted of a handler and his German shepherd scout dog, which was trained in early silent detection of enemy infiltrators, booby traps, tunnels, or hidden caches. The scout dog handler used different equipment for scouting and sentry tasks. This gear included a whistle, a chain choke collar for movement control, a leather collar, 5-foot and 25-foot leashes, kennel or "stake out" chains, an equipment holder, and the military construction worker's apron used to carry dog food.[14]

Combat tracker teams were five-man teams that pursued the enemy by following visual or scent tracks. Each team consisted of a visual tracker, a cover man, a team leader, a

4th War Dog Company (Provisional) combat tracker team searches for retreating NVA soldiers west of Pleiku, 20 February 1969. *U.S. Army.*

A scout dog team of the 35th Infantry Platoon (Scout Dog) patrol the perimeter of Bien Hoa, 21 November 1968. *U.S. Army.*

radio telephone operator, and a tracker dog handler. The Labrador retriever was usually preferred for this type of military tracking. Each dog handler was issued a leather muzzle, 5-foot and 25-foot cotton webbing leashes, a leather leash holder for the belt, a leather collar, a steel chain choke collar, a zinc-coated kennel chain to tie dogs in the field, and a cotton webbing harness for dogs engaged in actual combat tracking.

Dog trainers and personnel who handled dangerous dogs in Vietnam used the *dog attack training* ensemble. The *dog attack training coat* was a special 3-ply duck and burlap jacket with two *dog attack training sleeves* laced to it. The *dog attack training cuffs* were special 2-ply outer burlap cuffs that covered the lower arm from fingertips to elbow and fitted over the sleeves. The sleeves and cuffs took the brunt of damage and were detachable for economical replacement purposes. The material of the *dog attack training trousers* was identical to that of the coat. There was padding extending up the leg, from instep to crotch in front and from heel to buttocks in back. The trousers were worn with suspenders.

The dog attack training ensemble is used by a 97th Military Police trainer at Cam Ranh Bay, 1968. *Author's collection.*

Food service personnel wearing white paper caps and a mix of undershirts and coats with full insignia at the 24th Evacuation Hospital during Thanksgiving dinner, at Long Binh, 1967. *Author's collection.*

10.7   Food Service Personnel

Food service personnel in Vietnam usually wore white cotton drill trousers and undershirts. White *baker's and cook's coats* were available in rolled or full collar design, with two pockets and short sleeves. The white full-length *apron,* which extended from the neck to the knee, was usually folded in quarters and worn like a loincloth from waist to mid-thigh only. This allowed for a clean quarter of the apron daily and extended the time between cleanings. White, paper food service caps or utility caps were commonly used as headwear.

10.8   Honor Guards, Color Guards, and Bands

Honor guards and color guards existed primarily for ceremonial purposes. A unit's color guard normally consisted of a hand-

White cotton trousers and white or green undershirts with utility caps constituted typical food service attire, worn here in the 64th Transportation Company Mess at Pleiku, December 1968. *Author's collection.*

A XXIV Corps Artillery battalion Color Guard includes Vietnamese color bearer with white web color sling in center. Flanking him are color bearers for the national colors and organizational colors. Guidon bearer with M1967 individual equipment belt *(left foreground)* holds battery guidon. *U.S. Army.*

picked detachment, which carried the national colors alongside either the unit's organizational colors or its distinguishing flag (and often the colors of the Republic of Vietnam), and escorts to either side, armed with either M14 or M16 rifles. These were distinguished from guidon bearers, who carried the guidon individually without an accompanying escort party. Honor guards represented the command on special occasions, such as tributes to the fallen or in unit award ceremonies. Some

The Color Guard members of the 69th Engineer Battalion (assembled in front of the 13th Avn Bn headquarters) wear helmets with camouflage covers, tropical combat uniforms with individual equipment belts, and black leather combat boots. The escorts are armed with M14 rifles. Color bearer SSgt. Leon Haywood *(front, second from left)* has subdued web color sling with subdued socket, while color bearer SSgt. Francisco Flores *(front, third from left)* has unsubdued socket. Can Tho, September 1968. *Author's collection.*

The Color Guard of the 64th Quartermaster Battalion at Long Binh wears white boot lacings, web color sling and belts, and white helmet liners inscribed with "Petromain," the battalion nickname in Vietnam. *Author's collection.*

honor guards were permanent contingents that guarded selected memorials or provided protective escort for commanders. Division honor guards were usually drawn from the military police company.

The uniforms worn by both honor and color guards varied with command practices, but most wore starched, fitted combat tropical uniforms; individual equipment belts with or without white coverings; helmets or colored helmet liners; and black leather combat boots (sometimes with white lacings or leggings). The uniform was usually decorated by any insignia considered unique to the unit, such as pocket patches or shoulder cords. Decorative splendor rose with each level of command and became increasingly embellished with noncombat trappings. The USARV Color Guard wore khaki uniforms with white ascots and gloves, white pistol belts with large brass buckle-plates, bright metallic-plated helmets, and black low-quarter shoes.

The Army fielded the 266th Army Band for USARV, along with a band with each division in Vietnam. The 266th Army Band was a specially modified 42-piece band commanded by a warrant officer bandmaster. The band instruments consisted of 1 accordion, 4 recording basses, 2 bass viols, 1 bassoon, 1 bell-lyra, chromatic orchestra bells, chromatic chimes, 16 bass clarinets, 10 B-flat cornets, 3 concert band-type cymbals, 4 bass drums, 1 bongo

The adjustable web color sling with socket is clearly visible as the 22d Replacement Battalion Color Guard advances its distinguishing flag at Cam Ranh Bay, 22 July 1969. *Author's collection.*

1st Signal Bde Honor Guard at the Specialist David A. Russell Monument at Long Binh in 1969 wear individual equipment belts with white coverings, decorated orange helmet liners, and ERDL camouflage tropical combat uniforms with all insignia removed in deference to their fallen comrade. This military courtesy was extended to avoid outranking the deceased. *Author's collection.*

drum, 2 snare drums, 6 field snare drums, 1 service band drum set, 3 euphoniums, 2 silver Boehm flutes, 5 French horns, 1 symphony gong, 1 Spanish guitar, 1 oboe, 2 service band pianos, 2 piccolos, 12 alto saxophones, 4 sousaphones, 5 tenor trombones, 3 tympani, 1 chromatic vibes, 1 viola, 4 violins, and 1 violoncello.[15]

Other important parts of the band were the drum major's baton and the drum major's mace, both used to convey signals to the marching band while in formation. The components of the drum major's baton were the ball, staff, ferrule, and cord and tassels. The drum major's mace consisted of a ball, staff, ferrule, and chain.[16]

The 101st Abn Div Band looks to the drum major's baton for signal direction at Camp Eagle, 21 May 1971. Since standard tropical combat uniforms are worn, the instruments are the only indication that the unit is, in fact, a band. *Author's collection.*

The 23d Inf Div Band marches while wearing black helmet liners decorated with white bands and divisional organizational shoulder sleeve insignia decals on either side. **Chu Lai, 1969.** *Author's collection.*

10.9 Medical Personnel

Army field medical corpsmen and specialists in Vietnam carried the *case, medical instrument and supply set, non-rigid, number 3,* commonly known as the "aid bag," which was made of rubberized cotton cloth after 1968. The case contents varied with mission necessity but typically contained dressings, bandages, Vaseline gauze, instrument set, field medical cards, aspirin, antimalarial tablets, antihistamine, salt tablets, water purification tablets, bacitracin and tetracaine ointments, Gelusil, and cough lozenges. A range of blood-volume

Army medical service personnel wearing typical attire over their tropical combat uniforms. The specialist in the center wears the white medical attendant's coat with red U.S. caduceus insignia on the pocket under his black nameplate. Many medical assistants in this group wear light blue pullover smocks that typified medical workers at hospitals and aid stations. Long Binh, February 1969. *Author's collection.*

A medical specialist of the 1st Bn, 501st Inf (101st Abn Div) *(left)*, wears the medical field pack with extra canteens attached to the pack assembly by carabiners. Note ripped trousers *(right)*, a common problem with tropical combat uniforms. 1968. *101st Abn Div PIO.*

expanders and infusion sets was also available. Glass bottles of normal saline, Ringer's lactate solution, and plasmanate were often carried in canteen covers. Triangular bandages made from muslin were commonly used, often doubling as neckerchiefs.

The *coat, medical attendant's* was a double-breasted cotton tunic with side button adopted on 9 May 1967 and worn in a hospital ward environment. Various medical gowns and masks were available in Vietnam, including *physician* and *medical assistant* polyester *smocks* and other specialized apparel.

10.10   Military Police

Military police were authorized additional articles for their uniforms. These included the Military Police leather belt, white service cap, white cotton gloves, black leather policeman's

Pfc. Larry Blanknan of the 5th Bn, 60th Inf (9th Inf Div), carries his medical case, instrument and supply set through mud near Ben Luc, 24 June 1969. He is armed with an automatic .45-caliber pistol. *U.S. Army.*

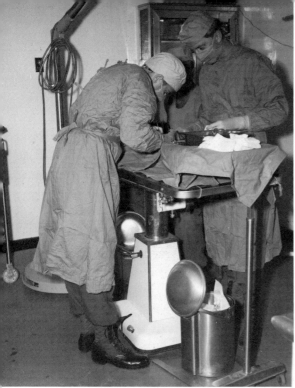

Capt. Michael Paclik *(left)* wears the physician's smock and surgical cap and mask as he performs an ovariohysterectomy on a dog at the 4th Veterinary Hospital in Long Binh, 26 January 1971. *U.S. Army.*

club, carrier, hand irons, first aid dressing case, ammunition magazine pocket, and military sidearm shoulder strap. Many enlisted MPs wore branch of insignia crossed pistols that were officer style because the enlisted disk-version created identification difficulties. On 27 May 1969, however, the 18th Military Police Brigade ordered the practice discontinued.[17]

Army Military Police wore a gloss black–painted helmet liner emblazoned with white 2.25-inch-high "MP" letters on front and a painted band, 1.25 inches wide, around the liner. The band was colored red for divisional and brigade units; divided blue above red for field force and corps units; divided white above red for Army-level units; and white for other MP units. The colored bands were usually interrupted on the sides by unit numerical designation on the left, and either distinctive insignia decals or organizational shoulder sleeve insignia decals on the right.

There were numerous exceptions. The 1st MP Company displayed decals of the 1st Infantry Division organizational shoulder sleeve

716th MP Bn military policeman armed with 12-gauge pump shotgun guards payroll transfer at Tan Son Nhut. He wears the khaki uniform with decorated helmet liner, black leather MP belt with first aid dressing case and ammunition magazine pocket, military sidearm shoulder strap, holster, and MP brassard. 28 July 1965. *U.S. Army.*

The 90th MP Detachment uniform at Saigon consisted of tropical combat uniforms, a mix of 1956 and 1967 individual equipment belts, MP brassards, and painted helmet liners with the numerals 90 or 716—the parent battalion for this detachment. Guidon bearer has rank decal above MP lettering on helmet. *Author's collection.*

Military Police of the 1st Inf Div in typical field service attire. Center MP wears first aid dressing case and ammunition magazine pocket on 1967 individual equipment belt, with no insignia on his tropical combat uniform. 1969. *Author's collection.*

The 218th MP Company arrests a soldier who was armed with a M3A1 submachine gun at Nha Trang. Note black leather policeman's club carrier and MP brassard with subdued 18th MP Bde shoulder sleeve insignia on the MP at right. *Author's collection.*

9th MP Company mounted patrol wears a mix of third-pattern utility and tropical combat uniforms with subdued MP brassards. Their helmet liners are decorated with the 9th MP Company distinctive insignia. Tan An, November 1968. *9th Inf Div PIO.*

insignia on both sides of the helmet. The USARV Commander's Guard, composed of General Abrams' personal body guards, wore dark kelly green helmet liners with yellow bands (MP branch color), a large MACV decal on the right side, crossed MP pistols on the left, and yellow "MP" letters in front. Convoy escort police troops wore M1 helmets with camouflage covers and black "MP" letters centered in front.

10.11 Parachutists

Army parachutists wore a parachute assembly consisting of the T-10 parachute; a T-10 reserve parachute, used in event of main parachute malfunction; and the harness, which strapped the parachutes to the jumper. Combat loads were carried by a combination of H-harnesses and kit bags, or various personnel equipment containers.

The *T-10 parachute* was a troop-type, bag-deployed pack assembly that was static line operated. Its rip-stop nylon MC-1 canopy was

parabolic shaped and had a 35-foot nominal diameter. The T-10 *maneuverable parachute* was identical to the T-10 parachute, except that it contained a 39-square-foot oval-shaped orifice. Approximately 90 percent of all T-10 malfunctions were semi-inversions, occurring when a portion of the skirt was blown through adjacent or opposite gores. This caused the parachute to develop partially inside out in a "Mae West" configuration. In December 1970, the 173d Airborne Brigade at Bong Son used an anti-inversion, 18-inch-wide net on the parachute canopy skirt and apex centering loops.[18]

The *T-10 reserve parachute* was a chest-mounted, manually operated, emergency parachute, which was activated by pulling the rip-cord grip. The reserve parachute consisted of a 3.3-foot-diameter, octagonal nylon pilot chute;

Jumpmaster Sgt. Louther of the 173d Abn Bde gives the ''All Okay'' prior to a parachute jump from a CH47 over An Khe, November 1968. Note parachutist adjustable equipment (''PAE'') bags below the T-10 reserve parachutes. *Author's collection.*

Special Forces Detachment B-55 (5th Mobile Strike Force Command) make a combat jump over Vietnam carrying canvas kit bags below their reserve parachutes. Note static line hookup from the T-10 parachute pack assembly. *Author's collection.*

Staff Sergeant Easton of the 173d Abn Bde exits a CH47 during a training jump over Camp Radcliff in October 1968. The M16 rifle is padded and attached with sling inside the left D-ring of the harness and waistband placed over front handguard. *Author's collection.*

a 24-foot-diameter, circular nylon canopy; and the pack assembly.

The purpose of combat jumps ranged from the insertion into the field of small pathfinder teams to the mass assault of the 173d Airborne Brigade north of Tay Ninh on 22 February 1967. During these jumps, the parachutists descended with their battle gear and weapons. For the jump of the 173d Airborne Brigade, colored tape on each man's helmet identified his unit and sector and assisted the task force on the ground in rapidly assembling the troops.[19]

In Vietnam, most training jumps were also conducted with full equipment. A nylon strap *H-harness* secured individual load-carrying equipment in a canvas *kit bag* beneath the reserve parachute. The *adjustable equipment bag,* with 20-foot lowering strap, could carry up to 95 pounds of radios and other required gear.

Individual rifles were secured at the parachutist's side in combat jumps, but these were well taped and padded because plastic and other fragile M16 components tended to break or become entangled in suspension lines. The M1950 *parachutist's adjustable individual weapon's case,* which could be adjusted up to 50.5 inches long, was used during some proficiency jumps. A quick-release snap attached to the left D-ring on the parachute harness secured the case vertically, and two tie-down tapes around the parachutist prevented swaying. The *container, weapon and individual equipment* was used to carry certain designated combat items and had an 18-foot nylon lowering line.[20]

10.12   Reconnaissance Troops

Army reconnaissance, long range patrol, and ranger troops wore a wide variety of individual gear in Vietnam. These personnel car-

Rangers of Company L, 75th Inf (101st Abn Div), prepare to board helicopters for a recon mission into the A Shau Valley during 1969. Sterile ''counterinsurgency'' rucksacks are worn. Shoulder sleeve insignia has been covered by tape at right. *Author's collection.*

A reconnaissance instructor with Special Forces Detachment B-52 Project Delta wears Stabo extraction harness over fully buttoned ERDL camouflage tropical combat uniform. He stands behind a display of lowering lines and ladders used for extraction. 1969. *Author's collection.*

ried minimal essential equipment in order to reduce weight for combat efficiency. Loads were also modified by special gear needed for particular assignments, for certain weather and geographical conditions, and for varying methods of entry and distances to the target area. These circumstances combined to defy

"typical" categorization, but the following equipment was recommended by the Special Forces MACV Recondo School, which trained most American reconnaissance troops in Vietnam.

The tropical combat uniform, preferably standard ERDL camouflage for infrared pur-

A patrol of Company D (Long Range Patrol), 151st Infantry, returns from a recon mission, 5 May 1969. The men wear a mix of Vietnamese tiger stripe and ERDL camouflage uniforms. *U.S. Army.*

poses, with tropical hat, tropical boots, and triangular bandanna, was worn as the basic uniform. A 10-by-30-inch signal panel, a penlight, an emergency mirror, a notebook and pencil, and a flare gun with 5 red and 5 white rounds were also considered part of the basic uniform. Individual load-carrying equipment included the individual equipment belt and harness, 2 small arms ammunition cases, 8 rifle magazines, 2 water canteens, 1 lensatic compass and case, 3 field dressings, 3 triangular bandages, 2 morphine Syrettes, 1 general-purpose knife of individual preference, weapons-cleaning equipment, and a medical pouch. The latter contained 8 Darvon, 6 codeine, 12

Members of a MACV-SOG team of Command & Control South prepare to launch into Cambodia in 1970. Robert Johnson and interpreter Na-Ku use NVA pith helmets, while Mike Cummings *(right)* wears skull cap and lightweight knitted shirt. *Robert Johnson.*

MACV-SOG Command & Control North members Lt. Ken Bowra (wearing Sino-Viet ammunition pouches) and interpreter Bong, who was later captured and executed by the NVA, prepare to enter Laos on a recon mission in 1971. *Ken Bowra.*

dextro amphetamine, 10 polymagna, 20 tetracycline, 3 chloroquine primaquine, and 20 cold tablets. The indigenous ranger pack was carried with 2 collapsible canteens or bladders, 2 ground sheets, 1 lightweight knitted shirt, 1 blood volume expander and infusion set (usually serum albumin), 1 lightweight poncho, 1 lightweight sleeping bag, 1 indigenous hammock, 1 flashlight, and 2 carabiners. Other special equipment included a 35mm pen EE camera, an emergency radio, a pair of binoculars or hand-held thermal viewers, and personal weapons and ammunition as required.[21]

10.13 Recovery Personnel

Recovery teams were fielded to retrieve bodies when the combat situation or remote area prevented timely removal of American dead. A 9th Infantry Division graves registration recovery team was inserted northwest of Bear Cat following a midair collision between

three helicopters on 28 June 1968. The gear used by the recovery team during the three-day mission included heavy leather gloves, rubber surgical gloves, remains bags, personal-property bags, intrenching tools, axes, slings and ropes, protective masks, potable water containers, sterile drinking cups, and fire extinguishers. The latter were particularly important for cooling off remains inside hot aircraft wreckage in order to prevent body parts from burning through the rubberized canvas body bags.[22]

10.14 Tunnel Teams

The difficulties of tunnel warfare caused special *tunnel exploration kits* to be given priority development under the ENSURE program. USARV requested 6 special kits to be fabricated on 29 April 1966, and these were airlifted to ACTIV on 7 August. Two each were distributed to the 1st and 25th Infantry Divisions, at Di An and Cu Chi, respectively, on 1 September. The two remaining kits were dispatched to the 1st Cavalry Division at An Khe and to the 173d Airborne Brigade at Bien Hoa. ACTIV completed its evaluation on 6 January 1967.

The Vietnam-based testing revealed that the communication components worked well but that the .38-caliber pistol lacked balance and was awkward to handle, and its aiming light was unnecessary within the small confines of most tunnels. The light, mounted on a baseball cap, was obstructed by the cap's visor and was shorted out by occasional bite switch malfunctions. The tunnel kit was not perfect, but the 1st Infantry Division tunnel rats remarked, "It was a vast improvement over previous make-shift equipment used in tunnel exploitation."[23]

The use of the tunnel kit was limited in Vietnam because of its scarcity. USARV requested 250 tunnel exploration kits on 21 March 1967, but DA mistakenly thought the message called for twice that amount. The kits cost $728 each, and fiscal year-end limitations prevented immediate funding. Natick Laboratories was not asked to acquire the sets until 30 September, and the assemblies were further delayed by problems with the communications gear. The 250 requested tunnel exploration kits were delivered to Dover Air Force Base from

Front view of tunnel exploration kit with headlamp and bite switch. The .38-caliber pistol has silencer and spot lamp sighting device. Cu Chi, 25 August 1966. *U.S. Army.*

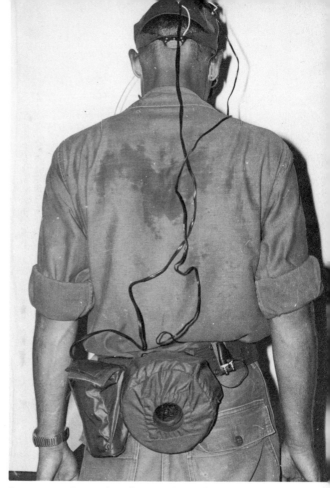

Rear view of tunnel exploration kit with bone conduction microphone at base of skull. Power pack and communications wire reel are on the individual equipment belt. The telephone wire leads to demonstrator's right ear. Cu Chi, 25 August 1966. *U.S. Army.*

22 May to 29 May 1968 and immediately flown to Vietnam. These circumstances forced units to resort to various field expedients in outfitting their tunnel teams.[24]

The crude form of tunnel warfare terminated during late 1968, as the Army employed increasingly sophisticated technology. Beginning in 1969, infantry division and brigade tunnel teams were composed of four Army combat engineer specialists and two Vietnamese Kit Carson scouts, instead of previous on-the-job trained infantry troops. The engineers were equipped with specialized equipment, such as tunnel-destruct, liquid explosive demolitions kits; goggles; flippers; rope; and breathing apparatus composed of chlorate-candle oxygen-generating systems attached to filter respirators. Army divers were also used for tunnels requiring expert underwater exploration. (*See section 10.5,* Divers.)[25]

The *tunnel weapon,* a powerful, .44-caliber modified magnum revolver with special ammunition, was evaluated at Aberdeen Proving Ground from July to September 1968. After ammunition changes were incorporated to eliminate misfires and cylinder binding, the item was field tested in Vietnam during April 1969. The rounds were of trapped piston design, each containing 15 shot pellets, giving tunnel exploitation teams a low-noise, multi-projectile weapon.[26]

Notes

1. MACV Directive 670-1, 2 Jul 65.
2. MACV Directive 670-1, 20 Jun 66.
3. *Aviation Digest,* May 67, 50.
4. Army Concept Team in Vietnam, *Report: Project ACA-11/67,* 12 Jan 67.
5. *Aviation Digest,* Oct 68, 54, and May 70, 50.
6. *Aviation Digest,* Dec 67, 52; Defense Supply Agency Action Off letter from Lt. Col. Stanfield, 30 Jun 68; *1st Aviation Brigade Commander's Notes #19,* 19 Feb 68, 5.
7. *Aviation Digest,* Jul 70, 60.
8. USARV Aviation Pamphlet 95-2, Nov 67, 44.
9. USARV Commander's Notes, 30 Nov 66, 3, and Defense Supply Agency, ACSFOR DS Status Report, 19 Jul 67.
10. USARV Reg 670-2, 21 May 66.
11. USARV Reg 670-2, 15 Aug 69.
12. MACV Directive 670-2, 30 Oct 70.
13. Gordon L. Rottman, *U.S. Army Special Forces, 1952-84,* Osprey Publishing Ltd., London, 1985, 57-58.
14. DA FM 7-40, 1 Mar 73.
15. U.S. Army Pacific letter, MTOE 12-107E, 9 Jun 68.
16. DA FM 12-50, Dec 69.
17. 18th Military Police Brigade Reg 670-5, 27 May 69.
18. 173d Airborne Brigade, *Operational Report,* 31 Jan 71.
19. U.S. Infantry School, *A Distant Challenge,* Battery Press, Nashville, 1983, 6.
20. DA Technical Manual 57-220, Jun 68.
21. MACV Recondo School AVSF-PS letter, Subj: Uniform and Equipment Requirements for Reconnaissance Patrols, 21 Sep 66, with changes.
22. 9th Supply & Transport Battalion, *Recovery Mission Report,* 25 Jul 68, 6.
23. 1st Infantry Division, *Operational Report,* 31 Oct 66, 25.
24. Defense Supply Agency, ACSFOR DS Status Report, 30 Jun 68.
25. 1st Infantry Division Circular 525-20, 10 Jan 70.
26. Army Materiel Test Directorate, *Engineer Design Test of Caliber .44 Tunnel Weapon,* 28 Apr 69.

11

Uniform Insignia

11.1 Subdued Insignia

Vietnam combat quickly manifested the need for insignia that was less visible than standard insignia to enemy marksmen. Forces fighting in Vietnam received early permission to subdue uniform insignia as combat circumstances warranted. The threat of imminent combat throughout Vietnam, even in so-called rear areas, caused DA to authorize subdued insignia and accouterments on all field and work clothing, including flight suits, commencing 9 June 1966.[1]

The *name tape* had consisted of black letters on a white cloth strip, and was worn over the uniform's right chest pocket. The *U.S. ARMY distinguishing insignia,* worn over the left pocket, contained gold lettering on a dark olive drab background. On 10 April 1965, MACV authorized name tapes with black lettering on olive green backgrounds. Over a year later, on 14 July 1966, DA ordered all name tapes and U.S. ARMY distinguishing insignia switched to subdued patterns.[2]

Subdued insignia made by Vietnamese tailors was generally poorly made or hard to obtain. The II Field Force, Vietnam, encouraged soldiers being assigned to Vietnam to secure professionally made name tapes and distinguishing insignia while still in the United States. "Due to the varying quality of subdued tapes on the local market, it is recommended that you obtain them prior to departure from CONUS [Continental United States]."[3]

Some specialized name tapes could only be acquired overseas, especially if foreign lettering was incorporated. For example, the U.S. Military Assistance Command, Thailand, authorized name tapes displaying a combination of English-Thai lettering commencing 3 January 1967. English-Thai name tapes were typically worn by advisors to Royal Thai Army contingents in Vietnam and 46th Special Forces Company personnel operating throughout Southeast Asia.[4]

When USARV ordered name tapes and distinguishing insignia to be subdued in 1966, General Westmoreland wanted all Army cloth insignia on field and work uniforms converted to subdued colors. A mandatory conversion

Capt. John Mills (*right*), 20th Engineer Bn, wears subdued insignia, including his subdued pin-on insignia of branch on the collar, that blend with the tropical combat uniform. The metal Vietnamese rank worn centered and the battalion distinctive insignia on pocket flap contrast sharply. Ben Het, 4 November 1969. *U.S. Army.*

date of 15 January 1967 was set, but persistent shortages forced postponement of this goal until 31 December 1967. Even then, subdued organizational shoulder sleeve insignia was exempted because of continued manufacturing delays. On 26 February 1968, USARV declared that subdued shoulder sleeve insignia would be worn as it became available and was issued. After several further delays, the Army mandated subdued insignia on all field and work uniforms throughout the world on 1 July 1970.[5]

Formations like the 101st Airborne Division—which exhibited intense pride in its fiercely colorful "Screaming Eagle" patch—

Sergeant First Class Jenkins wears an example of a specialized nameplate on the left pocket flap of the tropical coat at the Army Da Nang Depot. The lettering "QA INSP" stands for Quality Assurance Inspector. *Author's collection.*

Col. Thomas Guidera, commanding the 97th MP Bn, wears unsubdued insignia typical of early war uniforms. Note white name tape and gold "U.S. Army" lettering, as well as Vietnamese-made 18th MP Bde shoulder sleeve insignia. *U.S. Army.*

Capt. David Froberg, commanding the 513th Engineer Company at Qui Nhon, wears name tape and U.S. Army distinguishing insignia parallel to pockets. Note fading of letters induced by tropical sunlight. He wears identification tag necklace from upper buttonhole. Senior Parachutist Badge is sewn parallel to ground, while 1969-style Pathfinder Badge is parallel with pocket. *Author's collection.*

blatantly ignored the regulations in Vietnam. Thus, due to shortages of subdued patches and tapes, coupled with a certain degree of subordinate unit contrariness, a mixture of many subdued and unsubdued insignia items appeared on uniforms throughout the war.[6]

In July 1967, USARV concurred with the adoption of subdued pin-on metal insignia of rank for enlisted men, in leiu of sew-on cloth badges. A year later, on 1 July 1968, the Army authorized worldwide wear of the devices on tropical combat uniforms, field jackets, utility uniforms, and white duty uniforms worn by medics and cooks. The insignia was worn on both collars, point up for NCO chevrons, and

Maj. John Frazee, 9th Aviation Bn (9th Inf Div), wears name tape and U.S. Army distinguishing insignia parallel to the ground, battalion distinctive insignia on left pocket flap, suspended unit pocket patch, and a "We Try Harder" button on his tropical coat. Dong Tam, July 1969. *Author's collection.*

Sp4 John Jewel of the 3d Bn, 7th Inf (199th Inf Bde), wears only U.S. Army distinguishing insignia on the tropical coat but has subdued pin-on insignia of rank on his tropical hat. *Author's collection.*

Squad Leader Sgt. Gary Barneau of the 3d Bn, 7th Inf (199th Inf Bde), decorated with the Bronze Star for valor, wears name tape and U.S. Army distinguishing insignia, and subdued pin-on insignia of rank on collars and tropical hat. *Author's collection.*

Pfc. Alan Hornack of the 3d Bn, 7th Inf (199th Inf Bde), decorated with Army Commendation Medal for valor, wears no name tape on his tropical coat but has Combat Infantryman's Badge and U.S. Army distinguishing insignia sewn parallel to the ground. *Author's collection.*

Pfc. Dale Thompson of the 3d Bn, 7th Inf (199th Inf Bde), recipient of the Army Commendation Medal for valor, wears no insignia on his tropical coat. *Author's collection.*

TYPICAL SQUAD INSIGNIA VARIANCES

Lt. John Bowles, 92d Engineer Bn, wears name tape and U.S. Army distinguishing insignia parallel to the pockets. Note how the tropical sun faded name tape lettering. Long Binh, 1971. *Author's collection.*

arc up for the specialists. Three pairs of pin-on insignia were issued to each enlisted man, but their wear by Vietnam-based flight crew members was prohibited because of safety concerns.[7]

11.2   Insignia Variance on Tropical Coats

The proper placement of the name tape and U.S. ARMY distinguishing insignia on the tropical coat presented a dilemma because of the chest pockets' slanted design. Regulations positioned this insignia one-quarter to three-eighths inch above the top point of the upper left pocket. Where tunic pockets were sewn straight across the chest, the insignia was "parallel to the ground." On tropical coats, however, the regulation could be interpreted to mean that insignia should either appear straight across, which left a considerable gap above the inner pocket corners, or follow the slanted line of the pockets.

Soldiers initially interpreted the regulations according to personal preference or local unit dictates. Slanted tapes permitted full visibility of the name tape but appeared awkward,

especially if combat or skill badges were worn straight. Tapes sewn straight across the uniform followed normal Army practice but became partially hidden by the open lapel of the coat if worn normally. In its first ruling on the matter, USARV ordered name tapes to be worn parallel to the ground on all field and work uniforms, effective 26 February 1968.

This ruling was reversed by a DA message of 5 September 1969 that directed the name tape and U.S. ARMY distinguishing insignia on the tropical combat uniform to be worn parallel to the tops of the slanted pockets. The purpose of this ruling was to insure their visibility. USARV implemented the DA directive on 6 October 1969 when it published Change 5 to USARV Regulation 670-5, covering the wear of uniforms in Vietnam. This revision, which mandated the sewing of name tapes and distinguishing insignia parallel along the top of the slanted pockets, remained in effect for the rest of the conflict.[8]

Maintenance of uniform insignia in Vietnam eroded quickly. The 9th Infantry Division resolved the problem by regulating on 12 October 1968, "Military personnel dependent on direct exchange laundry facilities for field uniforms need not wear the standard name tape."[9] After the bitter November 1967 battle of Dak To, the 4th Infantry Division relented on field insignia altogether. "Due to DX [direct exchange] of individual clothing after contact, loss of clothing through laundry services, and medical evacuation, many personnel did not have fatigues with name, rank, etc. sewn on. The requirements to sew on these items is to be eliminated from clothing in the field."[10]

Because of the difficulties of exchanging laundry under field conditions, laundered clothing was rarely returned to its proper owner. Also, replacement uniforms were often needed because the uniform attrition rate in the jungle environment was high. These facts brought about the elimination of most personalized insignia. Unit logisticians, then, were able to dump bundles of clean clothing at fire support bases, and since the tropical coats contained only U.S. ARMY distinguishing insignia and appropriate shoulder sleeve insignia sewn on by Vietnamese workers in base camps, the front-line troops could fit themselves to any uniform of the correct size.

Captain Nyfeler of the 1st Special Forces Group observes Vietnam training conducted in 1963. He wears the pre-1964 solid gold group flash on his beret. *U.S. Army.*

Wounded officer *(right)* wears the post-1963 1st Special Forces Group flash (gold with black inner border) during change of command on Okinawa, 11 July 1972. Note trooper *(left)* wearing beret with recognition bar instead of flash, which signified non-qualified Special Forces status. *U.S. Army.*

Distinctive insignia (DI) were metallic emblems or "crests" approved for battalions and larger units within the Army. DIs made locally in Vietnam were painted rather than enamelled on thin sheet brass and came to be known as "beercans" by the soldiers. Distinctive insignia was worn either in conjunction with the combat leader's identification (*See section 11.4,* Combat Leader's Identification) or, more commonly, on the upper pocket flaps of the tropical coat when worn in a "duty uniform" configuration. All approved or authorized distinctive insignia are illustrated in color in the author's *Vietnam Order of Battle.*[11]

11.3 Beret Flashes

The Special Forces *flash* was a shield-shaped felt or embroidered flash with a semi-circular bottom centered upon the beret stiffener and authorized for Special Forces-qualified members. Initially, the style of the flash worn in Vietnam depended on group origin of the teams serving there temporarily: black for 5th Special Forces Group, red for 7th Special Forces Group, or gold for 1st Special

Members of 5th Special Forces Group Detachment A-502 wear the group flash on their berets in this last picture taken before team disbandment at Nha Trang, 1 February 1970. *Author's collection.*

Forces Group. These colors were randomly selected by the Army and published in DA Message 578636 of 27 October 1961.

The gold flash of the 1st Special Forces Group had an inner black border that was proposed in memory of President Kennedy after his assassination. On 28 February 1964, Major General Yarborough authorized "the 1st Special Forces Group to add a black border to its Asian gold flash." The black border symbolized, in 1st Special Forces Group commander Col. Robert W. Garrett's words, "our perpetual mourning for the loss of President Kennedy." Group Sergeant Major O'Donovan designed the new flash, and it was first worn on Okinawa on 5 March 1964. The Institute of Heraldry, however, did not officially recognize the new design until 5 November 1973.[12]

U.S. Army Special Forces, Vietnam (Provisional), was formally established in Vietnam by MACV on 8 November 1962. Col. George C. Morton, the provisional group commander, adopted a flash for this unit that represented the 1st, 5th, and 7th Group operational teams serving in Vietnam on a temporary duty basis:

The black background with white border indicated the 5th Special Forces Group which provided the U.S. Army Special Forces Vietnam headquarters and some of the TDY [temporary duty] teams, while the yellow and red stripes emblazoned diagonally across the black field were taken from the beret flashes of the 1st and 7th Special Forces Groups, which also sent teams to Vietnam. These latter two colors are also the national colors of the Republic of Vietnam as displayed on the country's flag.[13]

Lt. Larry Lincoln of the 46th Special Forces Company wears the company flash while testing crossbows at Ban Kam Perm, Thailand, 18 November 1967. *U.S. Army.*

1. The flash currently worn in Vietnam has acquired a degree of tradition as that worn by all personnel participating in the first large-scale commitment of Special Forces units into an active theatre of operations, and this tradition should be retained.

2. The addition of the Vietnamese colors to the current black and white flash of the 5th Group is a traditional method of recognizing a unit's service in a particular country or theatre and would permanently identify the group's tour of duty in Vietnam.

3. The change to the black and white flash could be misinterpreted by the Vietnamese as the eradication of their colors from the flash rather than a simple change of uniform to conform with a unit redesignation.[14]

The Institute of Heraldry approved this new flash for the 5th Special Forces Group on 21 December 1964.

Lt. Col. Kenneth Mertel, deputy commander of 1st Bde, 1st Cav Div, wears distinctive insignia pinned through the combat leader's identification "green tab," which is worn on the shoulder loops of the second pattern tropical coat. An Khe, 17 June 1966. *Author's collection.*

The 5th Special Forces Group was formally established in Vietnam on 1 October 1964 and absorbed the men and materiel of the provisional group. On 14 October, the 5th Special Forces Group requested that their black flash be redesigned to duplicate the authorized flash used by U.S. Army Special Forces, Vietnam (Provisional). The reasons given in this request were:

Lt. Col. John Whisler, Sr., 54th Signal Bn commander, March 1965–July 1966, wears unsubdued insignia and combat leader's identification, with battalion distinctive insignia, on his first-pattern tropical coat at Nha Trang. *Author's collection.*

The flash of 46th Special Forces Company, which deployed to Thailand on 15 October 1966, was approved on 14 June 1967. The symbolism of this flash was explained in a letter to the Institute of Heraldry requesting the design.

> The black field was a reflection of the suffering and strife caused by the communist insurgency and the traditional wearing of the color by Thai Special Forces soldiers as evidence of their defiance of death. The border of yellow signifies our heritage in the 1st Special Forces Group in Okinawa. Use of the Thai national colors as the stripes in the flash symbolize the origin of the 46th Special Forces Company in and for service in Thailand to help stem this insurgency. The use of the bar sinister indicates the first formation of a Special Forces company without a parent Special Forces Group.[15]

11.4 Combat Leader's Identification

The *combat leader's identification,* or "green tab," consisted of a green felt piece, wrapped around and centered on the shoulder loops of any uniform with loops (including

early-style tropical coats) worn in a garrison situation. Unit distinctive insignia was usually pinned through the "tab," fixing it in place. The combat leader's identification was worn only by personnel having leadership positions in units with direct combat missions, or in units controlling or supporting such units. Many organizations in the Army were not eligible, but virtually every Army unit serving in Vietnam met the criterion.

In Vietnam, this privilege extended to most unit commanders, platoon leaders, flight leaders, sergeants major, first sergeants, platoon sergeants, section (flight) sergeants, squad leaders, and tank commanders. On 20 May 1970, however, DA announced that the combat leader's identification devices could no longer be worn by command sergeants major, who were considered key staff members rather than combat leaders.[16]

11.5 Special Authorized Insignia and Badges

Combat and special skill badges were awarded to signify excellence in duty performed under hazardous conditions and in circumstances of extraordinary hardship. They were also awarded in recognition of attaining a high standard of proficiency in certain military skills after successful completion of training. Prior to the Vietnam conflict, the following badges had been approved: (1) Combat Infantryman Badge, (2) Medical Badge or Combat Medical Badge, (3) Pathfinder Badge in cloth, (4) Ranger Tab, (5) Parachutist Badges, (6) Army Aviator Badges and Army Aviation Medical Officer Badges, (7) Diver Badges, and (8) Explosive Ordnance Disposal Specialist and Supervisor Badges. Color plates of Vietnam-era badges, organizational shoulder sleeve insignia, and distinctive insignia can be referenced in the author's previous work, *Vietnam Order of Battle.*

Several changes transpired during the Vietnam conflict. On 15 June 1969, DA announced that a *Master Explosive Ordnance Disposal Badge* was authorized. This new award redesignated the 1957-era Explosive Ordnance Disposal Supervisor Badge as the *Senior Explosive Ordnance Disposal Badge,* since both Master and Senior EOD personnel

An officer of the 4th Inf Div wearing the President's Hundred Tab receives a field decoration. Pleiku. *Author's collection.*

Brig. Gen. Harry Hiestand wears the *Thiết Giáp Binh* (Armor Corps) Service Badge uppermost over the right pocket on his army green service uniform, 1970. *U.S. Army.*

Brig. Gen. Kenneth Cooper, commanding the 20th Engineer Bde at Bien Hoa, wears the *Công-Binh* (Engineering) Service Badge over his embroidered name on the tropical coat. *Author's collection.*

permitted until 1 July 1969. Finally, the Army approved a *Scuba Badge* in addition to the Diver Badges on 23 May 1969.[17]

The *Ranger Tab* and the *President's Hundred Tab* were initially the only DA-approved individual awards worn over the shoulder sleeve insignia. The latter tab was awarded to each person who qualified among the top 100 successful competitors in the annual President's Rifle or Pistol Match of the National Matches at Camp Perry, Ohio. The *Line Haul Tab* was approved by USARV on 25 November 1968 in recognition of the combat skills exhibited by drivers required to truck essential cargo across hundreds of miles of hostile territory in Vietnam. The "LINE HAUL-RVN" tab was worn above the 1st Logistical Command shoulder sleeve insignia. DA authorized this tab for "the field clothing of assigned drivers of long-distance convoys" on 15 March 1969 but prohibited its wear outside Vietnam. Over 15,000 soldiers earned this award during the war.[18]

For security reasons, special DA authority had been granted to military police detectives and investigators, as well as to military intelli-

A captain of the 709th Maintenance Bn (9th Inf Div) wears the *Quân-Cụ* (Ordnance) Service Badge on his right pocket flap at Dong Tam, 1969. *Author's collection.*

were technically supervisors. The metallic *Pathfinder Badge* was approved by DA on 24 January 1968 and replaced the larger cloth badge worn on the lower sleeve or shirt pocket. The new Pathfinder Badges, however, did not become available in post exchanges until January 1969, and wear of the older badges was

Lieutenant Colonel Whiteside (left), commanding the 55th Military Intelligence Detachment with two agents at Nha Trang. Staff Sergeant Barrientes (center) wears no insignia on his tropical coat, while Specialist 4th Class Woo (right) wears the "U.S." block-letters. *Author's collection.*

gence agent handlers and counter-intelligence specialists, to wear civilian clothes on active duty. In Vietnam, however, uniforms were mandated in conformity with rules of engagement and personal protection. Army regulation 670-5 permitted personnel who normally wore civilian clothing on duty to wear tropical combat uniforms with the block letters "U.S." as their only collar insignia. These devices were usually blackened metal U.S. officer insignia, but cutouts from Army distinguishing insignia tapes were also used.[19]

11.6 Vietnam-Era Shoulder Sleeve Insignia

The Military Assistance Group, Vietnam, was established on 1 November 1955 and used standard blue-starred MAAG shoulder sleeve insignia with a "country tab." Its successor, Military Assistance Command, Vietnam, was created on 8 February 1962 and used organizational shoulder sleeve insignia designed to reflect United States concerns about the region. The yellow-bordered red shield contained a white sword with yellow hilt breaking through an arched "embattled fess" (a heraldic fortified wall). The symbolism, according to MACV Staff Memorandum 670-1, was:

Yellow and red are the Republic of Vietnam colors. The red ground alludes to the infiltration and oppression from beyond the embattled wall (i.e., The Great Wall of China). The opening in the wall through which this infiltration and oppression flow is blocked by the sword representing U.S. military aid and support. The wall is arched and the sword pointed upward in reference to the offensive action pushing the aggressor back.[20]

The increased roles of Army combat units in field operations spurred creation of a provisional field force headquarters in II CTZ on 1 August 1965. This element, initially known as Task Force Alpha, was expanded and redesignated I Field Force, Vietnam (I FFV), on 15 March 1966. On the same day, II Field Force, Vietnam (II FFV), arrived to control Army elements in III CTZ. The Army's lineage for the I FFV and II FFV units stemmed from the XXX and XXII Corps of World War II, respectively.

Capt. Paul Bloomquist, a pilot of the 57th Medical Detachment (Helicopter Ambulance), receives the Distinguished Flying Cross and Oak Leaf Clusters to the Air Medal and Purple Heart at Tan Son Nhut, 28 November 1964. Note unsubdued MACV organizational shoulder sleeve insignia. *U.S. Army.*

The field force concept was adopted instead of a normal corps headquarters for three reasons. First, since the headquarters was to operate within an existing South Vietnamese corps zone, it would be confusing to introduce another corps designation within the same zone. Second, unlike a corps having only tactical functions, the field force was to have additional responsibilities, such as supply pacification, and an advisory role to the South Vietnamese. Third, the field force organization was more flexible, making it possible to add additional subordinate units if required, even including one or more subordinate corps headquarters.

The adoption of shoulder sleeve insignia for both units proved to be extremely difficult. On 19 January 1966, the Institute of Heraldry declared that field forces, which were not technically corps, did not fall in the category of those units authorized shoulder sleeve insignia. The wearing of the lineage-approved corps insignia for each field force was rendered impossible because of heraldic problems, as relayed by the Chief of Military History Brig. Gen. Hal C. Pattison in a letter to Maj. Gen. Jonathan O. Seaman, II FFV commander, on 1 April 1966:

You mentioned the subject of insignia, etc. for the command. I am not in a position to give any authorization or to state anything officially, but this is the situation as I know it. Several actions taken since World War II have resulted in an unfortunate situation with respect to the availability of corps designations. For some reason, which I have not been able to ascertain, and by some agency, which I have not yet been able to identify, many of the corps artillery designations were allocated to the National Guard or the Reserve organization after World War II. Additionally, a number of the corps headquarters are still being utilized in the Reserve training organization; although the reorganization of the Reserve and National Guard was expected to free these, they are not available because the reorganization planned by Defense has not come about because of Congressional action, at least in part. In any case, very few designations have been available for use up to now, and in only one case has a corps headquarters and a matching artillery corps been available, that is the XXX Corps which was recommended early last year for use by Field Force I, Vietnam [sic].[21]

The "battle-ax" shape of the subdued I Field Force, Vietnam, organizational shoulder sleeve insignia is worn by soldier of the 8th Bn, 26th Artillery, at An Khe, November 1968. *Author's collection.*

Later that month, on 21 April, the Institute of Heraldry authorized II FFV to use the XXII Corps insignia, but the field force commanders felt that using older corps insignia had no significance for their commands. On 5 May 1966, MACV suggested that both I and II FFV be authorized an insignia consisting of a Roman numeral superimposed upon the

Cannoneers of the "Jungle Battery," 2d Bn, 13th Artillery, wear unsubdued II Field Force, Vietnam, organizational shoulder sleeve insignia in 1969. *Author's collection.*

MACV insignia. On 3 June, USARV recommended that its shoulder sleeve insignia be used, with I FFV or II FFV tabs worn over the insignia to distinguish them.

A solution was finally reached when the Institute of Heraldry approved new designs for each field force. On 5 October 1966, the shoulder sleeve insignia for II FFV was authorized. It consisted of a MACV-type sword on a blue stylized arrow within a white-bordered shield. The shield portions on each side of the tapered shaft were yellow and the areas on each side of the arrowhead, red. The symbolism was explained in a letter from the Institute of Heraldry to the II FFV.

> The shape of the shield and the unsheathed crusader's sword (the Sword of Freedom) were suggested by the shoulder sleeve insignia previously authorized for U.S. Military Assistance Command, Vietnam, and the U.S. Army, Vietnam. The stylized blue arrow and sword are

used to represent the purpose and military might of the II Field Force pressing against, sweeping back, and breaking through enemy forces symbolized by the red areas. The dividing of the red and yellow areas of the shield into two parts allude to the numerical designation of II Field Force, the colors red and yellow also being those of Vietnam. The colors red, white [*sic*], and blue are the national colors of the United States and further allude to the three major combat arms: Infantry, Artillery, and Armor.[22]

On 5 October 1966, I FFV was also authorized its "battle-ax"-shaped shield with an arrow pointing up through three bands of red, yellow, and blue, having the following symbolism:

> The crusader's sword (the Sword of Freedom) was suggested by the shoulder sleeve insignia previously authorized for the U.S. Military Assistance Command, Vietnam and the U.S.

Army, Vietnam. The one diagonal refers to the numerical designation of the I Field Force. The sword in "piercing" the red area alludes to the constant probing of enemy territory and positions and the driving back and crushing of enemy forces. The colors red, white, and blue are the national colors of the United States, and the colors yellow and red are those of Vietnam. The colors blue, red, and yellow, are also those of the three major combat arms: Infantry, Artillery, and Armor. The silhouette of the shield is shaped like a battle-ax to symbolize the smashing power of the I Field Force and the constant combat readiness of its personnel to engage the enemy. The battle-ax shape, in itself, is also an additional I Field Force identification.[23]

During the Vietnam conflict, shoulder sleeve insignia was also developed for USARV; Capital Military Assistance Command; U.S. Army Engineer Command, Vietnam; the 4th, 5th, 124th, and 125th Transportation Commands; and the following brigades: 11th, 196th, 198th, and 199th Infantry; 1st Aviation; 18th and 20th Engineer; 16th Military Police; 1st Signal; and 44th Medical. These insignia are illustrated in color in the author's *Vietnam Order of Battle*.

11.7 Detachable Pocket Patch

The *detachable pocket patch* was designed to provide unit identification in Vietnam on uniforms on which sewn insignia was prohibited, such as the Army khaki. The patches were suspended from the right pocket flap buttons and came in two styles: metallic replica shoulder sleeve insignia mounted on a leather or plastic strap, or cloth/paper shoulder sleeve insignia encased in transparent plastic. MACV detachable pocket patches became mandatory for khaki and tan uniforms of headquarters personnel commencing 2 July 1964.[24]

The practice was later extended to all Army personnel assigned to Vietnam-based units. The detachable pocket patch was worn most commonly by uniformed Army personnel travelling to and from Vietnam, while undergoing processing in Vietnam, and while at R & R and leave locations outside the United States. The 5th Special Forces Group required all members to wear the LLDB organizational shoulder sleeve insignia as a pocket patch commencing 1 August 1967.[25]

Parachutist leaving Vietnam (top right) wears khaki uniform and holds field coat while boarding aircraft. He wears 101st Abn Div distinctive insignia on pocket. Sergeant behind him wears USARV detachable pocket patch. Soldier at left wears 18th Engineer Bde detachable pocket patch suspended from right pocket button. Cam Ranh Bay, January 1968. *Author's collection.*

On 18 November 1966, as part of General Westmoreland's desire to present the image of a "Free World" alliance supporting South Vietnam, Army soldiers were encouraged to wear the Free World Military Assistance Forces detachable pocket patch on the left pocket. Although considerable command emphasis attended this new directive, most troops did not wear this patch.[26]

When the 23d Infantry Division (Americal) at Chu Lai was formed from three separate infantry brigades, each with its own shoulder sleeve insignia, on 25 September 1967, the question quickly arose as to which shoulder sleeve insignia, divisional or brigade, should properly be worn by members of its 11th, 196th, and 198th Infantry Brigades. On 19 October, USARV regulated, "The Americal

Sp4 Thomas Montez wears the 4th Transportation Command brassard with 1st Logistical Command shoulder sleeve insignia as he inventories 750-pound bombs being unloaded at Cat Lai, March 1969. *Author's collection.*

Patch will be worn on the left sleeve and the brigade patch will be worn on the upper right breast pocket of all duty uniforms. Pocket patches will be worn so that the horizontal axis is parallel to the ground. The pocket patch may be sewn on the uniform or worn in a detachable transparent plastic holder which fastens onto the pocket under the flap." These brigade pocket patches were rarely worn in actual practice.[27]

11.8 Brassards and Armbands

The *military police brassard* was an official symbol of authority worn by Army on-

The explosive ordnance disposal brassard is worn during a memorial service in Vietnam for a fallen EOD specialist. *Author's collection.*

Cam Ranh Bay area identification passes are worn on tropical coat right pockets during an inspection of the 278th Supply & Service Bn Cam Ranh Bay, 22 March 1968. *Author's collection.*

duty military policemen. The brassard, dark blue cloth with white "MP" letters, was pinned to the upper left shoulder. Variant black oilcloth and even plastic brassards with olive drab or other colored letters were locally produced. Organizational shoulder sleeve insignia was usually pinned or sewed to the larger brassards, which extended to the shoulder seam.

The *security guard brassard* was dark blue with white "SG" letters, and was worn by the separate infantry companies assigned to military police battalions as security forces. Unlike the MP brassard, the SG brassard was merely a means of identification.

The *explosive ordnance disposal brassard* was worn primarily by metropolitan Army explosive ordnance disposal detachments, since field tactical detachments rarely wore them except for formal occasions in Vietnam. The brassard was dark blue or black with either a red or yellow conventionalized drop bomb

pointing downward. The letters "EOD," in the same color as the bomb, appeared below it.

The *explosive personnel hazardous purpose armband* was worn by soldiers as a control device when planting explosives or destroying munitions. Unlike the explosive ordnance disposal brassard, which was authorized only for wear by EOD specialists, this armband could be worn by all soldiers while engaged in such work. This was not an issue item; any white piece of cloth could be worn around the arm. Soldiers in Vietnam often used white engineer tape wrapped around the upper arm for this purpose because it was easy to remove and discard once the work was accomplished. USARV encouraged use of the armband after several unit accidents occurred in noncontrolled circumstances, but the actual wear of the armband depended on individual command preference.

Soldiers of the 3d Bn, 7th Inf (199th Inf Bde) wear explosive personnel hazardous purpose arm-bands as they prepare charges to destroy captured VC bunkers near Binh Chanh, 2 February 1967. *U.S. Army.*

Notes

1. DA Circular 670-2, 9 Jun 66.
2. MACV Directive 670-1, Change 1, 10 Apr 65; DA Message 773785, 14 Jul 66.
3. II Field Force Vietnam Adjutant General, *Welcome to Vietnam Pamphlet,* 1967 edition, 7.
4. U.S. Military Assistance Command Thailand Reg 670-1, 3 Jan 67.
5. DA Message 042112Z Mar 70.
6. *Army Reporter,* Vol. 2, No. 36, 17 Dec 66, 13; USARV Circ 670-2, 28 Aug 66; USARV Reg 670-5, 26 Feb 68.
7. MACV *Observer,* Vol. 7, No. 18, 4 Sep 68, 2, and MACV Directive 670-1, Suppl 1, 23 Sep 72.
8. DA Message 051718Z Sep 69, as quoted in *Army Personnel Letter #18-69,* 1 Oct 69; USARV Reg 670-5, Change 5, 6 Oct 69.
9. 9th Infantry Division Reg 670-5, 12 Oct 68.
10. 1st Brigade, 4th Infantry Division, *After Action Report: Battle of Dak To,* 9 Dec 67, 39.
11. Shelby L. Stanton, *Vietnam Order of Battle,* Kraus Reprints, Millwood, New York, 30–46.
12. 1st Special Forces Group, *Historical Report, 1964,* 13.
13. 5th Special Forces Group letter, Subj: Proposed Change of Beret Flash, 14 Oct 64, paragraph 2. Researched by Danny M. Johnson.
14. 5th Special Forces Group letter, Subj: Proposed Change of Beret Flash, 14 Oct 64, paragraph 3a-c. Researched by Danny M. Johnson.
15. Company D (Augmented), 1st Special Forces Group letter to DA Institute of Heraldry, 7 Mar 67.
16. USARV Reg 670-5, 26 Feb 68, 5; DA Message 201407Z, May 70.
17. *Army Personnel Letter,* 1 Nov 68 and 15 Jun 69; information researched by Danny M. Johnson.
18. *Army Personnel Letter #6-69,* 15 Mar 69; USARV Reg 670-5, 24 Aug 69, 4.
19. Author's conversation with John C. Andrews, 21 Dec 87.
20. MACV Staff Memorandum 670-1, 31 Jan 71.
21. DA Office of the Chief of Military History letter, 1 Apr 66.
22. DA Institute of Heraldry letter, Subj: Shoulder Sleeve Insignia for the II Field Force, Vietnam, 5 Oct 66.
23. DA Institute of Heraldry letter, Subj: Shoulder Sleeve Insignia for the I Field Force, Vietnam, 5 Oct 66.
24. MACV Directive 670-1, 2 Jul 64, 2.
25. 5th Special Forces Group Reg 670-2, Change 1, 6 Jul 67.
26. MACV Directive 670-1, Change 1, 18 Nov 66.
27. USARV Reg 670-5, Change 3, 19 Oct 67.

STATUS REPORT

EXPEDITED NON-STANDARD, URGENT REQUIREMENTS FOR EQUIPMENT

(E N S U R E)

(Non-Standard or Developmental Items)

DA ENSURE ITEM #95

DESCRIPTION OF ITEM		ACTION	DATES OF ACTION
DA ENSURE # 95		Validated	21 Jun 66
		Cancelled	
RAINSUITS			
A lightweight rainsuit consisting of jacket and trousers.			

REMARKS			
REQUESTOR	DESIRED DELIVERY DATE	ISSUE PRIORITY DESIGNATOR (IPD)	
CGUSARV	1 Aug 66	Unknown	

REMARKS:

21 Jun 66 - DA approved requirement and requested AMC to fabricate and ship 300 suits to ACTIV.

20 Jan 67 - AMC (NLABS) shipped 300 rainsuits to Dover AFB for shipment to ACTIV.

Estimated Cost $53,000 RDTE.

26 Aug 67 - USARV reports that preliminary results indicate combat service support units like them and combat units dislike them.

22 Sep 67 - ACTIV evaluation report recommended ENSURE be cancelled because item not appropriate for RVN. (Ltr AVIBLED, ACTIV, 22 Sep 67, subject: Letter Report of Evaluation - Lightweight Two-Piece Rainsuits (ACL-19/67M).

ACTION AGENCY	
DCSLOG	
DCSOPS	
ACSI	
AMC	X
ASA	
CCE	
CDC	
CRD	
TSG	
Other (NLABS)	30 Jan 67

AVAILABILITY	
Estimated	Feb 67
Adjusted	
Actual	30 Jan 67

DELIVERY OF EQUIP	
Recd by User/ Evaluator	

EVALUATION ACTIV ACL 19/67	
Eval Plan Apprvd	
Eval Started	
Eval Terminated	
Eval Rpt Recd	Sep 67
Eval Review Recd	

ACTION COMPLETED	30 Sep 67
POSTED AS OF:	31 JAN 68

TYPE OF EQUIPMENT	DEVELOPER/PRODUCER
Developmental	X
Commercial Design	
Other Service/Agency	

USER - QUANTITY - PURPOSE - DATES			
USER QUANTITY & PURPOSE	User	Operations	Evaluation
	U.S.	( )	(300)
	Indig	( )	( )
	Total	( )	(300)

DATES OF INPUT & REFERRAL		
Date of Req	DTG	15 Jun 66
Recd by FORACTIV	DTG	17 Jun 66
Referred	DTG	17 Jun 66
Div/Branch ACSFOR PROPONENT	Action Officer	
FOR DS SSS	LTC VULEY	
Info Copies to:		

FOR FORM 84
8 Dec 66

DOWNGRADED AT 3 YEAR INTERVALS;
DECLASSIFIED AFTER 12 YEARS.
DOD DIR 5200.10

CONFIDENTIAL

The ENSURE Status Report was used by Department of the Army and U.S. Army, Vietnam, for control of critical items during the Vietnam conflict. This official record provides vital data on the procurement, cost, shipment, and project history of many military items used during the Vietnam conflict. This sample document is a typical example of the references used in the preparation of this book.

Army Uniform Compositions in Vietnam

Item	Uniforms, Male Personnel — Army Green	Army Blue	Army Tan	Army Khaki	Army White	Army Utility	"Field" Tropical Combat	"Duty" Tropical Combat	Uniforms, Female Personnel — Green Cord	Hot Weather Field	Hospital Duty
Aiquillette, dress	X	X							X		
Aiguillette, service	X	X			X				X		
Armor, body, frag. protective						X	X	X		X	
Badges	C	X	S	S	X	S	S	S		S	
Band, helmet, camouflage			R	R		R	X	X		P	
Belt, individual equipment	X		R	R		R	X	X		R	
Belt, waist w/buckle	X	X	X	X	X	X	X	X		R	
Beret, rifle green	A		A	A		A	X	A			
Boot, combat, black						A	X	A			
Boot, combat, tropical							X	X	X	X	
Boot, service, women											
Box, match, waterproof			R	R		R	S	R		R	
Canteen, w/cover						R	X	R		R	
Cap, blue		X							X		
Cap, garrison, green cord	X		X	X							
Cap, garrison, green						X	X	X		X	
Cap, hospital, white											X
Cap, utility					X						
Cap, white					X						
Cape, blue		X									
Carrier, sleeping bag			R	R		R	S	R		R	
Case, field, first aid			R	R		R	X	R		R	
Case, lensatic compass			S	S			S	R		S	
Case, small arms ammunition (2)			X	X		X	X	X		X	
Coat, matching	X	X	S	S	X	S	S	X	X	S	
Coat, field	X	X	X	X	X	X	S	S			
Cord, shoulder, infantry	X	X	P	P		P	X	P		P	
Cover, helmet, camouflage			C	C	X	X	X		X		
Cuff links, gold	X	X	C	C	X				X		
Decorations/Ribbons	X	X	X	X	X		X	X	X		
Distinctive Insignia	X	X						X			X
Dress, white											
Field pack, combat							X				
Fourragère	X	X	X	X	X		X		C	X	
Gloves	C	C	C	C	C	P	X	P	X	X	X
Handbag, black, service									C	X	
Hat, tropical w/insect headnet			P	P		P	X	X		X	X
Helmet, M1 steel						P	X	P		X	
Insect bar							S			P	

Item							
Intrenching tool w/carrier	X				X	P		
Liner, helmet, ballistic	X				X		
Liner, poncho			P	P	S		
Mask, CBR protective w/carrier					S		
Mattress, pneumatic	X				X		
Mess kit, field				X	X		
Necktie, black							C
Net, multi-purpose					S		
Packboard, plywood w/pad	C	C	C		S		
Pocket, ammunition, 2-clip	C	C	C		S	C	
Poncho	X	X	X	X	X	X	X
Raincoat	X	X	X		X	X	X
Rucksack		C	C				C
Scarf, distinctive branch					S		
Shelter half, tent	X	X	X	X	S	X	
Shirt, as appropriate	X	X	X	X	S	S	X
Shirt, lightweight knitted	X	X	X	A	X		
Shoes, low quarter, black	X	X	X			X	
Shoes, oxford, white						X	X
Shoes, pumps, black							X
Skirt, green cord						X	
Slacks, cotton, poplin					S		
Sling, universal load-carrying	X	X	X	A	X		
Socks, black	X	X	X	X	X	X	X
Socks, cushion sole					S		
Stockings					S	X	
Survival kit, individual	X	X	X	X	X	X	X
Suspenders, field pack	X	X	X	X	X	X	X
Tag, identification w/necklace	X	X	X	X	X	X	X
Trousers, matching	X	X	X	X	S	X	X
Vest, carrier, grenade M79					S		

Uniform Composition Chart Key

Note: This chart displays compositions after the tropical combat uniform replaced the utility uniform in the field combat role. For situations prior to this transition, troops wearing utility uniforms on combat operations would have individual load-carrying equipment identical to that displayed in this chart under the "Field" Combat Tropical Uniform category.

A As prescribed by local regulations or guidelines. For example, black leather combat boots were worn in lieu of tropical combat boots where fire hazards existed.
C Ceremonial occasions as locally authorized
P Permitted under combat circumstances
R Required outside secure area (as defined by MACV or USARV)
S Special Issue, contingent upon availability and circumstances
X Part of normal composition

Glossary

ABC: *Atomic Biological Chemical*
Abn: *Airborne*
ACTIV: *Army Concept Team in Vietnam*
ARPA: *Advanced Research Projects Agency*
ARVN: *Army of the Republic of Vietnam*
BAR: *Browning Automatic Rifle*
Bde: *Brigade*
Bn: *Battalion*
Cav: *Cavalry*
CCN: *Command & Control North*
CIDG: *Civilian Irregular Defense Group*
CONUS: *Continental United States*
CORDS: *Civil Operations and Rural Development Support*
CTZ: *Corps Tactical Zone*
DA: *Department of the Army*
Div: *Division*
DMS: *Direct Molded Sole*
DOD: *Department of Defense*
DSU: *Direct Supply Unit*
ENSURE: *Expedited Non-Standard Urgent Requirements for Equipment*
EOD: *Explosive Ordnance Disposal*
ERDL: *Engineer Research and Development Laboratory. ERDL developed the four-color camouflage pattern in 1948.*
FFV: *Field Force, Vietnam*
FSB: *Fire Support Base*
GP: *General Purpose*
Inf: *Infantry*
LCM: *Landing Craft, Medium*

LINCLOE: *Lightweight Individual Clothing and Equipment project*
LLDB: Lực-Lúóng Dặc-Biệt *(Special Purpose Forces)*
LRP: *Long Range Patrol*
LZ: *Landing Zone*
M: *Model*
MAAG: *Military Assistance Advisory Group*
MACV: *Military Assistance Command, Vietnam*
MACV-SOG: *Military Assistance Command Vietnam – Studies & Observation Group (Special Operations)*
MAT: *Mobile Advisory Team*
MOD: *Model*
MP: *Military Police*
NVA: *North Vietnamese Army*
R & R: *Rest and Recreation*
RON: *Remain Overnight*
Rqn: *Requisition*
RVN: *Republic of Vietnam*
T: *Test*
TAP: *Toxicological Agents Protective*
TDY: *Temporary Duty*
TRECOM: *Transportation Research and Engineering Command*
USARV: *U.S. Army, Vietnam*
VC: *Viet Cong*
WAC: *Women's Army Corps*
XM: *Experimental Model*